RINGING IN THE WILDERNESS

Selections from the

NORTH COUNTRY
ANVIL

RINGING IN THE WILDERNESS

Selections from the

NORTH COUNTRY ANVIL

edited by Rhoda R. Gilman

The voice of one crying in the wilderness,
Prepare ye the way of the Lord,
Make his paths straight.

—Mark I :3

Lay me on an anvil, O God,
Beat me and hammer me into a crowbar.
Let me pry loose old walls;
Let me lift and loosen old foundations.

—Carl Sandburg

Cover photograph of *North Country Anvil* staff (left to right: Kathy Herron, Dick Herron, Barton Sutter and Jack Miller) handcolored by Marian Lansky (Clarity, Duluth, Minnesota).

Sandra Gue's article, "Mississippi River Revival," includes a verse from "She'll be Clean Once More," words and music by Larry Long. Copyright © by Larry Long Publishing, 1982/BMI and used by his permission.

ISBN 0-930100-63-8

PUBLISHER'S ADDRESS:
Holy Cow! Press
Post Office Box 3170
Mount Royal Station
Duluth, Minnesota 55803

This project was supported, in part, by a grant from the National Endowment for the Arts in Washington, D.C., and by generous individuals.

Contents

Preface

THE IDEA FOR AN ANTHOLOGY of "the best of the *Anvil*" took root in the fall of 1989, almost as soon as Jack Miller let it be known that he was laying the magazine down. Many readers and contributors were enthusiastic, but the same pressures that had proved too much for the *Anvil* itself bore heavily on the effort. New jobs and new causes quickly absorbed the slender margin of energy that people had given to the magazine for so long. Some moved away; some had babies; some went on to new careers; one died. In the end there were only a handful of us to carry on.

Those who gave significant time and work to this book were Barton Sutter, who helped with the selection of poetry; Emilio De Grazia and Evelyn Roehl, who read through and evaluated the fiction; and Paul Gruchow, who contributed the introduction. Others whose critiques and faith in the project supported me through the years are Joe Paddock, Ken Meter, Paul Gilk, Todd Orjala, Mary Dwyer, Betsy Raasch-Gilman, and, of course, Pauline Redmond and Jack Miller. The book also owes a debt to the Minnesota Historical Society, which has added the records of the *Anvil* to its manuscript collections and provided help and cooperation in many informal ways during the years I worked on the project. No one got paid. As I've often observed, "If you ever did anything for the *Anvil*, you did it for love."

The editorial decisions were ultimately mine, and a few words need to be said about them. I decided at the outset to use only pieces that had first appeared in the *Anvil*. I also decided to exclude news notes, book reviews, and letters to the editor (except when published as articles or in connection with articles). These sections bulked large in the magazine and were not unimportant, but for the most part they did not stand the test of lasting interest. Graphics and pictorial material were also important in the *Anvil*, but the photographs and art work that remained available were far from a complete collection. Moreover, cost of reproduction limited their use — just as it had done with the magazine itself.

A guiding principle among those who published the magazine — one often voiced by Jack Miller — was the indivisibility of social change. Reform in one area was impossible without fundamental transformation in all aspects of the industrial world. Theirs was an organic vision, encompassing not only politics, government, and social institutions, but, some might say, human nature itself. They advocated a revolution in human society, and human society is a seamless web. This commitment to wholeness extended also to modes of expression, whether fiction, poetry, or visual art. All of these carried the message, along with the personal conversations and annual gatherings that were a part of the *Anvil's* life.

Thus organizing the anthology by themes proved a difficult task, involving many hard choices and much overlapping material. Nevertheless, discussion congealed around certain topics, and new issues emerged with the passage of years. From the perspective of today's readers, the *Anvil* is history (even though they may find some startlingly contemporary observations). It is the function of history to give structure to the memory of times past. Since this book is, above all else, a record of the alternative movement of the 1970s and '80s in the upper Midwest, the structure seemed necessary, and, in a way, inevitable.

—Rhoda R. Gilman

Introduction

By Paul Gruchow

ALTHOUGH THE *NORTH COUNTRY ANVIL* was deeply rooted in agrarian Minnesota and so might be described as a regional publication, and although it was explicitly anchored in the sensibilities of the generation that came of political age in 1968, it belongs in the largest sense to a literary tradition stretching back to Hesiod and to an historical movement dating to the beginnings of the Industrial Revolution.

The literary tradition is of the Golden Age. Virgil, that urbane celebrant of pastoral virtue, would have been quite at home in the pages of the *Anvil*. Listen:

> *The farmer has no idea (why should he)*
> *how endlessles lucky he is, how blessed by the gods.*
> *Far enough away from the noise of war,*
> *justice lights like the shy dove on an earth*
> *that rewards with more than justice all his toil*
> *and plays fond patroness with her abundance.*
> *No villa, maybe, with ornamental gates*
> *inlaid with tortoise shell, but then no toadies,*
> *no hangers-on to loiter at those gates,*
> *to come on through them first thing in the morning*
> *and spoil his breakfast, buttering him up*
> *before they put the bite on him.*
> *He butters*
> *bread which is all one wants first thing in the morning.*[1]

It was not that Virgil wanted, or was equipped, to lead a pastoral life himself — he got his information about farming not from farmers but from books — but that he hungered for something that seemed missing in his citified life. About farmers, he said:

---

[1]David R. Slavitt, *Eclogues & Georgics of Virgil.* Baltimore, 1990, p. 84.

I speak with the special expertise of the starving
who better than all the chefs understand food.
Silvanus, Pan, the nymphs become important
in city streets.[2]

So, too, the *Anvil* writers were, for the most part, people who came out from the cities to the countryside, often ill-equipped as a practical matter to be agrarians, prepared not so much with answers as with questions, convinced that the culture they knew was lacking in some essential nutrient, which they sought to identify, the source of which they hoped to find. That the communes they established eventually broke up, that the nourishment they sought proved in the end elusive, that their journal of inquiry ultimately folded, is less significant than that they kept alive in the late 20th century an idea that, although always denigrated, has endured for some thousands of years. One would be reckless to suppose that an idea of such durability is utterly groundless.

Lewis Mumford provocatively suggested that this idea had its origins in mining: "Apart from the lure of prospecting, no one entered the mine in civilized states until relatively modern times except as a prisoner of war, a criminal, a slave. Mining was not regarded as a humane art; it was a form of punishment; it combined the terrors of the dungeon with the physical exacerbation of the galley. . . . Possibly the myth of the Golden Age was an expression of mankind's sense of what it had lost when it acquired the harder metals."[3]

Whatever the accuracy of this speculation, the myth has persisted at least since the beginnings of written literature; humans have had, for as many years as can be remembered, the conviction that once, in a happier time, we lived in greater harmony with nature. It is now conventional wisdom to believe that this myth is a hoax, the product of a nostalgic or romantic longing to stop the clock. There may be something to this if Mumford is correct in arguing that the conceptualization of the clock set the stage not only for the marvelous technological advances of the last several centuries, but also for the most disagreeable regimentations of modern life. The idea of the Golden Age does

[2] *Ibid*, p. 86.

[3] Lewis Mumford, *Technics and Civilization*. San Diego, 1934, p. 67.

imagine other, and arguably more humane, ways of apportioning time; according to the Circadian rhythms of the body, for example, which do not coincide with the 24-hour day; or according to the natural rhythms of sunlight and darkness; or according to the seasons.

These older conceptualizations of time do literally stop the clock. This does not mean that they are less rational than the clock, or imply any resistance to natural change. The difference is not in orders of rationality but in organizing principles. Which pattern, nature or the machine, is more likely to produce a satisfying human society? Since the eighteenth century in Western culture, the preference has been for the pattern of the machine. Even this preference, however, keeps alive the myth of the Golden Age; it has not been dispelled, but merely relocated, transported from the past into the future. The faith of the moment is not in some long-vanished Eden, but in the day just around the bend, perhaps somewhere along the information superhighway, when the perfect technology will deliver us, at last, into eternal bliss. We have substituted futurism for nostalgia, but not, in the process, reason for emotion.

There have been since the very beginnings of the Industrial Revolution those who doubted the efficacy of the machine as a model for human affairs. Industrialism has endured these doubters, but it has not been able to shake them off. In fact, the most distinctive intellectual movements of the Industrial Age have all been built upon some kind of opposition to it, including Romanticism, Transcendentalism, Marxism, Existentialism, some forms of feminism, and environmentalism. Even ancient agrarianism has managed, by fits and starts, to survive into the twentieth century, where it has found reinvigorated expression. As the classical writers survived, mostly unread and often forgotten, into the Middle Ages, when their ideas gained new utility, so the notion that an advanced society might be constructed with nature as a model has persisted, despite the prevailing intellectual currents, bobbing into view from time to time in such unlikely places as Millville, Minnesota.

That the *Anvil* was published where it was, and that its vision for a better Minnesota was so explicitly rural (if sometimes hilariously, naively so — "One woman stood calling out directions from Robert Rodale's *Organic Gardening* while the rest of us struggled with the seeds. How deep do they go? How far apart? Few of us had ever done anything like it before.") almost goes without saying. Technological innovations in farming have lagged behind those in other industries because there has been no imaginable way, until very recently, to divorce the enterprise from its essentially biological character. No matter how mechanized farming became, or how much it was scaled up — bigness being one of the central goals of the mechanistic vision — still a cow could be bred only once a year, and you had to plant seeds in soil, and the vagaries of the weather could not be entirely avoided.

The *Anvil* writers were among the first to see what is now common knowledge: that colonialism has survived imperialism, that the same tendency to exploit human and natural resources — to mine them — for the good of the empire still persists, although it is not now alien cultures or landscapes that we devour, but our own land and our own people. It is a colonialism mentality that justifies the ghettoes of both the inner cities and the countryside as the necessary price to be paid for economic progress. Only a colonialist frame of mind could propose technological innovation as a serious alternative to maintaining the biological integrity of the land.

It is also unsurprising that the little flowering of anti-industrialism that the *North Country Anvil* represented should have arisen out of the anguish of the Vietnam War. Again as Mumford has argued, industrialism has found its highest expression in the arts of war, where its most distinctive attribute, the subjugation of human interests to technological ones, is afforded its fullest rein. The aims of the United States in entering the Vietnam War had not been persuasively articulated, the circumstances there were such that technological superiority did not necessarily spell victory, and the war dragged on long enough so that its human costs, made plainly visible on television, could be appreciated. Young Americans saw with great clarity that they were to be enlisted not as human beings in defense of a great moral cause, but as entirely dispensable cogs in a vast machine being wielded toward the ends of an abstract geopolitical stratagem.

What was so shocking about Vietnam was not that it was a war, or that it was so bloody — this century, after all, has been characterized by an epidemic of war-making — but the revelation that the people who were to fight it did not matter to the strategists as human beings. (This indifference may have reached its nadir in the Gulf War, perhaps the first in which the victors did not bother to count the enemy dead.) But for one shining moment in the 1960s, a generation of Americans found the willpower to refuse to cooperate in their own dehumanization.

When they thought about it, this generation saw parallels to their dehumanization: of Africans to the interests of plantation owners, of native Americans to the expansionist impulses of the American empire, of farmers to the industrialization of food production, of every citizen to a materialist economic system in which they were merely consumers — people, that is, valued not for who they were but for what they owned or aspired to own.

Although it was denounced at the time as hedonistic and naive — as it in some ways was — and dismissed later as ineffectual and irrelevant — as it proved at least for the moment to be — the countercultural movement of the late 1960s and 1970s was actually based upon stoutly old-fashioned ideas: the democratization of labor, self-reliance, social equality, antimaterialism, and the power of nature to inform culture. There was little about the movement that Emerson would not have endorsed in a sermon or that Whitman might not have praised in a song. The counterculturalists were the proponents of what, in American society, really are the traditional values. That their movement seemed so radical is one measure of how far we have advanced toward what Neil Postman calls technopoly, the ceding of cultural authority to technology, allowing our machines to run us rather than we them.

The counterculture was also, it must be said, although with populist undertones, essentially a white, middle-class movement. The black civil rights struggle had moved, by the 1970s, from the agrarian south to the urban north; it does not much figure here. The American Indian Movement's dramatic action at Wounded Knee is here, but in the voices of its white attorneys; Indian culture was also, by this time, large-ly an urban phenomenon. In rural Minnesota, the sugar beet industry was bringing robust profits to a few farmers and drawing Mexican migrants to the countryside; the story of the exploitation of migrant labor is conspicuous by its absence. So is the story of the "restructur-ing" of the meat processing industry, which led ultimately to the bat-tle at Albert Lea of Hormel workers against both their employers and their trade union leadership, and to the creation of rural ghettoes in packing towns like Worthington and Willmar with all of the racial and social tensions of their big-city counterparts. The farm crisis of the 1980s — a crisis to a significant extent organized by the Nixon ad-ministration — is here, but not its underlying pathology: the impov-erishment not so much of farmers as of their small-town cousins.

The counterculture represented less a social movement, for all its rhetoric of The People, than a quest for personal redemption. Its fol-lowers were those — mainly young, mainly unattached, mainly well-educated — who had, or felt they had, the freedom to disavow con-vention. This is not a criticism. Who might better lead the way toward change than those individuals least encumbered by the status quo? and, as Thoreau argued in *On Civil Disobedience*, when one does not have the power to change a system one thinks evil, there remains the indi-vidual power — indeed the moral imperative — of refusing to partic-ipate in it. The argument that social reforms must first be practical is an argument against any kind of change at all. Changes with *a priori* practicality manage to be so precisely because they do not threaten the status quo. Real reforms are, in the beginning, impractical by defini-tion.

One lasting appeal of the *North Country Anvil* writers, long after the currency of the particulars of their work has dissipated — these are, for the most part, pieces of journalism — is how undogmatic they are, how frankly they search for alternatives that are not apparent, how freely they admit and describe their fumbling attempts at living lives for which they have been ill-prepared by experience or training, how receptive they are to ideas from everywhere. This is especially true of Jack Miller's meditative columns, which have the unguarded and confessional charm of a diary. There is an honesty at work in these pieces, a lack of certainty and finish, that models, on the page, real intellectual work.

One could not imagine a comparable anthology of articles from a mainstream newspaper. The *Anvil* reminded us, in case we had forgotten, how staid mainstream journalism is, how narrowly tied to convention, how hostile it is to anything resembling thought, especially political thought, encouraging us to believe, as we do with profound cynicism, that politics is not about ideas and ideals as they are expressed in policy, but merely about the rawest kind of power. In the pages of the *Anvil* one found politics, for once, treated as if the subject mattered, as if it could be practiced generously, as if it were something more than another kind of athletic contest.

As a result, the *Anvil* anticipated, long before conventional newspapers did, many of the ideas that now preoccupy us: multiculturalism, feminism, environmentalism, communitarianism, sustainability. It anticipated the sense, as we approach a new century, that greater material wealth is not necessarily the highest or best of our aspirations. If the *North Country Anvil* failed to spark a revolution, it nevertheless helped in its own quiet and modest way to keep the hope for one alive. And it surely never did anyone any harm, a judgment one can make about precious few institutions in this rapacious century.

Jack Miller and press

Anvil production staff,
early 1970s

Anvil workers in Winona, Minnesota, 1981

The Story of the ANVIL

By Rhoda R. Gilman

THE FIRST ISSUE OF THE *NORTH COUNTRY ANVIL* appeared in June, 1972. That same month the Watergate break-in hit the news like a bizarre scene out of some third-rate spy thriller. A few weeks later the Democrats nominated George McGovern for president. War still raged in Southeast Asia; the black power movement of the '60s had been effectively repressed; the new feminism was gaining momentum. In Minneapolis, Charles Stenvig was mayor. In South Dakota, American Indian Movement leaders were planning the march on Washington that would end with occupation of BIA offices on election day. Hope struggled with disillusion in the hearts of those who had seen the vision of a new world coming in the '60s. Yet it seemed clear, for better or worse, that something had shifted fundamentally at the foundations of American society.

Jack Miller, the 33-year-old publisher and editor of the *Anvil*, had abandoned a career in mainstream journalism that had taken him to Duluth, Washington, and back to Minneapolis. With his wife, Karen, and their young son, Erik, he had left the cities for what he saw as the self-sufficiency and wholeness of life in a small community. In returning to live on the land or close to it, the Millers were part of a widespread movement that testified to a profound alienation from urban America.

Millville, the place they chose, was the home of Jack's grandparents. It was a community of about 130 people, tucked into a deep fold of the hills where the prairies of southeastern Minnesota break down into bluff and coulee country along the Mississippi. The gristmill two miles up the Zumbro River had vanished generations before; the school would soon be closed, the rural mail route was being eliminated, and the businesses along the main street seemed to shrink each year. Yet Millville was tenacious.

In the fall of 1971 the Millers met with a group of friends, mostly from Minneapolis, to discuss starting an alternative publication. At first conceived as a statewide newspaper, the idea soon evolved into a general interest regional magazine. It would carry articles, fiction, poetry, and art. The name they picked resonated in Jack's mind with the popular song "If I Had a Hammer." It also deliberately recalled *The Anvil*, a flaming red literary journal published by John W. (Jack) Conroy in Chicago between 1933 and 1941. In a congratulatory note Conroy himself saluted the project from his retirement in rural Missouri. "Skoal to the *North Country Anvil!*" he wrote. Then in the course of some rambling reminiscences, he observed shrewdly, "It used to be a hell of a lot easier and cheaper to get out a magazine."

There were many friends who helped, but no financially blessed angels, and Jack then and always scorned the compromises that went along with foundation grants. While Karen Miller taught English and journalism in the high school at nearby Elgin, Jack did part-time work as a mail carrier and janitor. But the *Anvil* became the real work of both.

Six issues and one year later, energy and enthusiasm were still high. Although paid subscriptions remained below 500, interest and circulation were far greater. After a first ambitious print run of 6,000, the number of copies was reduced to 3,000, most of which were given away. In his report to readers on the *Anvil's* financial status, Jack concluded: "We haven't paid anybody much of anything for the long hours of work that go into this mag. It's all been volunteer labor." Among the volunteers were Harlan Olafson of Colfax, Wisconsin, who worked with Jack as political editor, Syd Fossum, noted Minnesota artist and radical, who served as art editor, and Ellery Foster, a retired forester and government worker, who moved to Millville and helped with production. Clay Oglesbee received nominal pay to handle distribution in the Twin Cities and recruit advertisers.

In the summer of 1973 they celebrated with a fund-raising festival at Walker Church in Minneapolis. It was highlighted by familiar faces from the past — old left-wing Farmer-Laborites, who had found in the *Anvil* a new voice after the long silence enforced by McCarthy-ism and red-baiting. Those present included Madge Hawkins, James Shields, and Meridel Le Sueur, who gave a reading from her work.

Although from the start the magazine was more libertarian than Marxist, it also gained credibility as a militant voice for younger radicals. In the first two years it delivered regular broadsides at the mining companies, big oil, the grain trade, and the food monopolies. With the siege of Wounded Knee in the spring of 1973, it began long-sustained and steamy coverage of the new Indian wars waged by the FBI and BIA in South Dakota.

By the time of the next festival, held in July, 1974, at Powderhorn Park, confidence was sagging, and the need for more funds and volunteers was evident. The speaker that year was David Dellinger, who urged a smaller-than-hoped-for crowd "to keep the faith through a period when all of the commentators are declaring the movement dead, but when, in fact, it is deepening and broadening." Later, in the October-November issue, Jack announced that Karen would take a year's maternity leave from teaching and that he would soon be looking for full-time work. It sounded ominously like the end of the *Anvil*.

The next issue (number 14) did not appear until mid-spring of 1975. It had ragged edges and uneven type, but there was a keen note of triumph in Jack's editorial column. In what he described as "the wildest couple of months of our lives" he had bought a well-used Davidson 233 press, had converted his grandfather's old barn into a print shop, and had managed painfully to print the magazine himself. It had cost him hours of despair and a part of one finger. "No press," he admitted, "should be called the names I called ours." Nevertheless, a printer friend in Wabasha, who had sworn it couldn't be done, looked over the result and admitted, "Well, it's a cold day in hell!" Meanwhile Karen had given birth to nine-and-a-half-pound Karl Miller.

With a print shop of his own and steadily improving skills, Jack now had not only the means to produce the *Anvil*, but a livelihood as well. During the next three years a new shop was built, more equipment was added, and the printing business began to pay. Although the magazine was often pushed aside by more urgent jobs, its appearance and size improved, and it attracted fresh talent. The work of artist Becky

LaMothe continued to add movement and whimsy to the pages. Barton Sutter, Eric Steinmetz, and Emilio De Grazia helped with editing and contributed material. Roberta Hodges, Matt Hoffman of Rochester, and Evelyn Roehl and Kevin Pomeroy of Winona also became part of the informal collective that grew around the Anvil Press. Karen Miller, meanwhile, was drawing away from the enterprise, and in 1978 Jack announced her departure from Millville and the breakup of their marriage.

Other changes, too, had come, in both the *Anvil* and the world. The war in Vietnam had ended; Richard Nixon had resigned to escape trial and been pardoned by his successor. In 1976 Democrat Jimmy Carter moved into the White House after twelve years of Republican rule, taking along Minnesotan Walter Mondale as vice president. The country's attention, meanwhile, was riveted on the economy and the oil shortage.

In the northern mines the taconite boom of the '60s had ended and once again the Iron Range faced grim times, not now from depletion but from foreign competition. In 1976-77 a 138-day steelworkers' strike became the longest on record but won few concessions. Even closer to *Anvil* country were the growing militancy of desperate farmers and struggles over energy. Across the Mississippi in Wisconsin, five years of protest ended only when Northern States Power Company abandoned plans for building a nuclear plant in Pepin County. At the same time in western Minnesota a 410-mile high tension line, bringing power to the Twin Cities from coal-fired plants in North Dakota, was completed in 1978 over the passionate but futile opposition of farmers and local communities in its path.

In the alternative movement, the deepening and broadening referred to by Dellinger was tagged by others as a retreat into self-absorption and facile "New Age" answers. The traditional politics of the left were steadily losing ground to environmentalism, feminism, and the demand for decentralized, grass roots decision-making. This was dramatized in 1975-76 during a fierce struggle for control of the Minneapolis natural food co-operatives. In the *Anvil* it was reflected by Jack Miller's vigorous espousal of anarchism, along with a new interest in thinkers like Ralph Borsodi, Murray Bookchin, and E. F. Schumacher. Some supporters were alienated. "I am beginning to feel that the *Anvil* is ceasing to function as a force for progressive social change," wrote long-time activist friend John de Graaf in 1977.

In a reminiscent editorial for issue number 30, Jack admitted that "In the early days the *Anvil* was more clearly a political publication than it is today. I began with a hazy sense of socialism as some kind of structural thing. I now see more clearly that the essence of *social* action is not political; it is personal. It is not mere collective ownership. Socialism is people working together." Those words, written in the summer of 1979, were the last for a long time. Without a direct announcement of it, Jack had decided to put the magazine to rest, although he continued to operate the Anvil Press. In 1980 he married Pauline Redmond of Detroit, who brought to Millville a background in urban activism and the printing trade.

When *Anvil* number 31 finally came out in late summer of 1980, the place of publication was Winona and the editor was Reggie McLeod, a reporter and free-lance writer. "I had turned it over in my mind many times and felt pretty strongly about it," recalled the new editor, "so I hitched to Millville to meet Jack Miller and talk it over with him. He politely told me that I should consider doing something else; the *Anvil* was finished. A few of my closest friends encouraged me. Just about everyone who knew anything about publishing a small magazine — except Evelyn Roehl — told me I was crazy."

Joined by Roehl and by Kevin Pomeroy, who ran a printshop in Winona, McLeod persisted. At a meeting with *Anvil* stalwarts held in April on the bank of the Mississippi, they discussed ideas, hopes, and plans, while twilight deepened and a full moon rose above the Wisconsin bluffs. At last they received "a vote of confidence to continue the *Anvil*."

The next 11 issues of the magazine were edited and published in Winona. A fresh crew of workers included Roger Lacher as poetry editor and Leanne Law on production. Roehl continued as typesetter, kept the accounts, and eventually took responsibility as managing editor. Actual printing was still done in Millville under Pomeroy's oversight. For assembly and mailing, the magazine returned to Winona, where laborious and time-consuming hand collating was eventually replaced by an old collating machine so simple that even McLeod's six-year-old son Ben could operate it.

The Winona team gave the *Anvil's* design a bolder, more eye-catching look; articles tended to be shorter, illustrations and fiction more plentiful. The trend away from traditional politics was accentuated, and environmental emphasis increased. Women's issues were slower to appear. As subscriber and contributor Neala Schleuning noted in a caustic letter: "The gender revolution occurring in our culture over the past fifteen years has been strangely overlooked. Even so 'safe' an issue as the ERA has not come in for a minimention." In response, issue number 41, edited by Evelyn Roehl and Patricia Wolff, was devoted to women's topics and women authors.

Contributions had never really stopped coming during the changeover in management, and the subscription list remained substantially the same. A survey of readers in the summer of 1981 revealed that 90 percent were college educated and more than half lived in small towns or rural communities. Income figures clustered at two poles — those under $8,000 and those over $20,000.

Also unchanged by the move to Winona were financial worries and the problems of personal burnout. A divisive element was added when some staff members were paid with federal job grants received under the CETA program. Others remained volunteers. At the end of two years, tension between Roehl and McLeod had grown to the point where one or the other had to leave. McLeod resigned. In issue number 40 Roehl wrote: "Out of this conflict — a very painful and angry one for both Reggie and me — is a revitalization of interest in the *Anvil* by Jack Miller, Pauline Redmond, and others who have been affiliated with the magazine. A goals and visions day is planned for August 14 [1982] in Millville to reaffirm and clarify the direction of the *Anvil*."

The gathering in Millville, coinciding with the magazine's tenth anniversary, was an emotional one. Out of it came a new commitment on the part of many people. The *Anvil* would move back to Millville, with Jack Miller as editor and printer. Pauline Redmond and Paul

Schaefer of Hager City, Wisconsin, would serve as associate editors. Jim Mullen of Wabasha began a long stint as literary editor. Another significant addition was Joan Stradinger of Whitewater, Wisconsin, whose art work was to give striking character to *Anvil* covers for several years.

The last 17 issues of the magazine appeared on an irregular schedule from 1983 to 1989. Two were entire books. Number 44, *Handful of Thunder: A Prairie Cycle*, was a volume of poetry by Joe Paddock (summer, 1983); number 53 was *Nature's Unruly Mob: Farming and the Crisis in Rural Culture*, by Paul Gilk (fall, 1986). Some issues were focused loosely around particular themes. These included farming, technology, community, and the emerging Green movement.

The tradition of a summer meeting or festival, started in the early years, had been carried on irregularly. The most memorable had been a two-day "Folk School" held at Millville in 1978. It was led by Danish-American minister Erling Duus and by Meridel Le Sueur, who spoke eloquently out of her own life's experience and the way it had reflected the Native American concept of the Circle of Life. Later Jack Miller commented: "If there is one person who has best embodied the spirit of the *Anvil*, that person would have to be Meridel Le Sueur. In her search for an organic wholeness, Meridel insists continuously on uniting functions which the culture separates."

During the 1980s, such summer gatherings became an annual event at which readers and contributors came for a day or two of family camping, socializing, and discussion in the Millville town park. It was highlighted by poetry readings, lectures, singing, and a potluck picnic. Le Sueur continued to be a regular participant, and others who contributed over the years were community organizer Harry Boyte, socialist-pacifist Mulford Sibley, and urban activists James and Grace Lee Boggs from Detroit. A notable presence in 1985 was Gerd Shaefers, a traveling member of *Die Gruenen*, who discussed with eager questioners the growing Green movement in Europe. A series of smaller gatherings, held around Jack and Pauline's kitchen table in the winter, devoted hours to more searching talk about themes like technology, community, feminism, and religion.

Reagan's America held few promises for those who gathered at Millville. With the opening of the '80s the farm crisis deepened into disaster — what Jack Miller aptly described as Secretary of Agriculture Earl Butz's "final solution" to the problem of the small farmer. Depression elsewhere in the economy was quickly countered by a massive increase in military spending, and the warlike stance was further bolstered with a new draft registration law.

In response to fears raised by a fresh generation of hair-trigger automated weaponry, the Nuclear Freeze movement swept the country, but its limited goals only discouraged those who sought more fundamental change. The new women's peace movement held greater hope. At Greenham Common in England and at the Seneca Army Depot in upstate New York hundreds of women camped and demonstrated against the apparent buildup toward nuclear war. On a smaller scale, a similar group established a women's peace encampment outside the Sperry Univac plant in St. Paul, where they lived and protested for several months before being cleared away by police.

Meanwhile environmental news was moving steadily out of the "nature" columns and toward the front pages. Science reported troubling evidence that earth's ozone layer was being eroded and its atmosphere altered by human industrial activity. Less commented on was the long-predicted snowballing of population in the so-called Third World. Responding to a passionate "pro-life" movement, the Reagan administration withdrew all U.S. support for population control. The issue was a difficult and thorny one even for alternative activists. Like most of them, the *Anvil* avoided it.

Also in the early '80s a less threatening but more ubiquitous force was affecting the lives of all Americans. The swift spread of small but powerful personal computers to homes, stores, and offices everywhere seemed likely to affect not only how people worked and played, but even how they thought. Some welcomed the "Information Age" with high hope; others viewed it with misgivings; but there was little choice about embracing it.

Jack Miller's convictions on technology were firm, and he cheerfully accepted being called a "neo-Luddite." In theory, at least, he was drawn to the position of French theologian Jacques Ellul, who argued that "technic" had become an end in itself, shaping human activity toward the nonhumane objectives of maximum efficiency, speed, and power. Stubbornly, Jack wrote letters by hand and often cut wood for cooking and heating without using a chain saw. Running a printing business required technology, of course, but the scale of operations was small, and growth was not a prime objective. Expensive new machines were out of the question, so the equipment used by the Press was generally antiquated — although not necessarily uncomplicated. The skill of local mechanic Harvey Melcher was constantly needed (and generously given) to keep it going.

As before, members of the *Anvil* team came and went through the '80s. In the winter of 1983-84, Paul Schaefer was joined by Luther Askeland of Red Wing to edit issue number 46. Jack and Pauline, meanwhile, turned their attention to the birth of Daniel Miller, which took place "in the midst of family, friends, a couple of toddlers and a dog" in the home they occupied and where Jack's grandparents had once lived. Again the next winter Schaefer and Askeland were called on when a siege of flu and a rush of business at the press threatened to postpone the magazine indefinitely. That spring, surveying the exhausted woodpiles beside both their house and the print shop, Jack admitted ruefully: "There is no 'margin' in our lives — no room for anything to go wrong."

Temporary relief came the next year when journalist-poet Paul Gilk and artist Jo Wood volunteered to help and moved to Millville for the winter. One result was a special issue devoted to "Green Visions," which appeared early in 1986, and another was the publication of Gilk's book the following fall. But the collaboration ended when Paul and Jo returned to Wisconsin to start an intentional community.

Ongoing assistance with editing during the *Anvil's* final years was given by John Grobner of Ellendale, Minnesota, while neighbors Bob Stuber and Cherie Lozier were regularly on hand to help with production and the many other chores that turned up. Jack's parents, John and Emily Miller, who had moved to Millville in retirement, also gave crucial support, but the burden on Jack and Pauline grew still heavier with the birth of a second son, Peter Miller, in March, 1987. The decisive blow to the magazine's tight little band of friends and supporters came in the spring of 1989 with the suicide of long-time literary editor Jim Mullen. Their distress and bewilderment were intensified by the prelude to the tragedy — Mullen's conviction on charges of sexually abusing a young family member.

Meanwhile the movement for which the *Anvil* had tried to speak was undergoing such fragmentation that the magazine's purpose and audience were becoming unclear. Environmental organizations had multiplied; so had feminist groups, both following a wide diversity of paths. New immigration from Asia, Latin America, and the Caribbean was bringing more varied racial and ethnic minorities, each struggling to establish its own place in American society. Deep ecologists, animal rights groups, and nature-oriented spiritual movements were challenging the most fundamental tenets of the Western Judeo-Christian tradition. Only a few voices for change still tried, like the infant Green movement, to address the whole country in broadly political terms. On city streets the very fabric of civil society itself seemed about to unravel.

Jack Miller had always insisted that social change must be spiritually based. His father had been a minister, and his own convictions about simple living, community, and mutual help were rooted in his upbringing. Contact with the Catholic Workers through Bob Stuber and others influenced him deeply and drew him at last to reassert the need for a religious community and an ethic of self-sacrifice. In the fall of 1989 he made the decision to discontinue the *Anvil*, lock up his printing shop, and study for the Lutheran ministry.

Pauline Redmond   Jo Wood

Madge Hawkins and friend,
Anvil gathering, 1974

Meridel Le Sueur and friend, 1973

David Dellinger, 1974

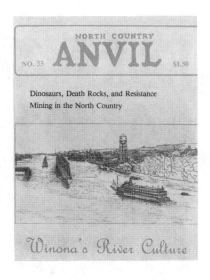

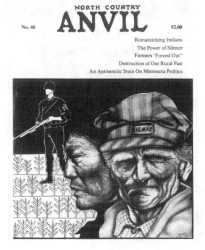

Hammering it Out—
The First Thirty Issues

In his editorial column, "Hammering it Out," Jack Miller pounded on many issues and subjects over the years, but it was at all times an intensely personal statement of his quest for answers — and therefore of the Anvil's direction. Sometimes he addressed a single topic; sometimes he rambled and reflected; often he came back again with new arguments and insights, but always he took readers with him, revealing his own uncertainties. "Hammering" was a favorite with those readers, and they often followed it up with lively dialogue in the Letters to the Editor section. The excerpts here form a collage of impressions and ideas from the first 30 issues of the Anvil, 1972-1979.

June, 1972—

Well, here we are with a pilot issue of this magazine. It surprises us about as much as anyone else. The whole idea was pretty unlikely: starting a new, regional magazine with no money and practically no experience in such things. . . . Up to this point we have followed the advice of back-to-the-land leader Scott Nearing, "Pay your own way. Don't spend a dollar until you have it. Don't go into debt. Don't accept interest slavery any more than any other form of slavery."

I want to tell you a little of what this magazine is about. To do that, I need first to tell you something of our developing view of ourselves and of the world. . . . We need, most importantly, to free ourselves. We need to free ourselves from a whole way of living and looking at the world. The values, the assumptions, the systems that we have been given simply do not make us the kind of people we want to be, do not give us the kind of a world we want to live in.

For many of us, the first great disillusionment came with the Vietnam War. We saw our forces killing innocent people and destroying a beautiful and quiet land in order, we were told, "to give these people the right to choose their own form of government without outside coercion." Our killing, apparently didn't count as "outside coercion."

For others, it was the cold-blooded killings at Kent State, at Orangeburg, at the homes of Black Panthers.

For others, it was seeing the way our nation gobbles up precious resources and despoils the land, all in the name of a grosser Gross National Product.

For still others, it was seeing the emptiness and the sterility of the American Way of Life: a mindless, fleshless consumerism. And on and on.

What we need to do, clearly, is to begin taking charge ourselves — of our personal lives, of our work, of our government.

We need to start close to home. To be better citizens of the world, we need to understand our families, our communities, our regions, and our various cultural heritages. We need a sense of where we came from to know where we need to go. This is why this first issue of the *Anvil* may seem quite backward-looking. . . . We wanted to share with you what we have found to be some exciting trail-blazing that's been done in years past by some courageous and daring leaders from Minnesota and this region.

Where are we headed?

I don't think any of the doctrinaire solutions are sufficient to the problems. I think we are going to have to go beyond traditional answers of the Western religions, of free-enterprise capitalism, of Marxism, of individualism, of nationalism, of Americanism. We are going to have to move beyond the top-down systems and dogmas that try to apply standards and regulations to all human endeavor.

If there is a name for what we are driving at, I don't know it. Populism, progressivism, personalism, communitarianism, these all have a nice ring for us. But they express only a part of what we are seeking. We'll kind of have to find out the rest as we go along.

❖ ❖ ❖

October, 1972—

I become increasingly convinced that the countryside is crucial to the alternative movement, to the search for better ways to live.

One reason is that many of us need the therapeutic change in perception that comes from living close to nature, in a quieter, simpler, more direct existence. It is no accident that some of this nation's most radical movements (sometimes radically conservative) have come from the rural areas.

Another reason is that any movement advocating profound change in the society needs protection from the massive forces of the *status quo*. The countryside offers sanctuary. When urban activists have lost their jobs and their means of subsistence, country-based radicals can always raise a big garden, burn wood in the winter and survive.

In a broader sense, this entire region, cities and all, is countryside: Even the cities take their character from the great farmland, lakeland and woodland that stretches from Illinois to Canada, from the Dakotas to Lake Michigan. Partly because of this country character, the region is a place specially blessed. It has grown up healthy and strong, with some sense of its locale, with some feeling of community and, most importantly with a closeness to the land and the seasons. If there is a place where new ideas can grow and reach fruition, this North Country is it.

❖ ❖ ❖

February, 1973—

There should be joy, but there is no joy. For even the relief that we feel in the seeming end of the [Vietnam] war is so overwhelmed by the shame, the remorse, the revulsion at what we have done. The war has exposed a brutality and an ugliness in us that will haunt us for generations. . . . It shows us not merely as a brutal society, but as a sick society.

❖ ❖ ❖

April, 1973—

I'd like to begin this column with some thoughts that are profoundly optimistic and confident and joyous. . . . They are at one with the warming faith of the spring sun. Of Erik playing peacefully in our back yard, letting the sun envelop him as he looks out over the Zumbro River and its bluff-guarded valley. Of Karen's excitement about putting in a big garden, to grow much of our food. Of our growing contacts with other change-minded folk. . . . There is something good and exciting that is happening among us, brethren. There is a new spirit of determination.

❖ ❖ ❖

June, 1973—

In the spring of the year, when there is garden work and yard work and dozens of winter-delayed jobs to be done . . . this is when I realize how far I am from my goal of becoming an accomplished manual worker.

What I want to do is learn to work with tools; with my hands. I love to read about it. All winter, I plan the things I will build and repair and grow, come spring. Then comes spring. And I find myself doing my usual stuff— my clerical work— and saying to myself, "Now as soon as I get a few days of this (paper) work done, I'll roll up my sleeves and get at some real work."

There are three main reasons why I want to become a manual worker: 1) personal satisfaction; 2) the capability of living at a lower level of consumption — to live more cheaply and independently; and 3) to become a classless person.

Middle-class people, which most of us are or would like to be, have generally been taught to look down on those who work with their hands. It is time that all of us learn to honor such labor for what it is: the most important work there is to be done. We can do without space scientists, but we can't do without garbage collectors. We can do without publicity agents, but we can't do without road builders and road repairers. We can do without most of the advertising people, but we've got to have someone to do housework.

We need at the same time to achieve a higher standard of living and a lower one. In our homes, we need to rely less on elaborate machines and gadgets, and to do more for ourselves. We need to stop playing the manufacturers' game, which is to convince every family that they need every piece of equipment. Instead, we need community centers that are equipped with tools and appliances that can be shared by many people. In order that every family doesn't have to own a car (or two or three), we need public transportation and group-owned vehicles. We also need communities planned so that to get a half-gallon of milk, you don't need to drive a couple of miles in a car.

But to achieve any of this, we've got to shuck off the money-makers' value system, which says that our personal worth can be measured by the total of our accumulated property and by how much we spend for our leisure. . . . Moderate poverty, or voluntary poverty, is not to be confused with real poverty, which is a hellish existence that plagues millions of people. To achieve moderate poverty, and to help the poor live decently, we are going to have to first renounce privilege and all that it stands for; we are going to have to become, again, just people. If we can achieve this, we will be more free, more independent, more powerful in constructive ways. We will spend less time working at meaningless, boring jobs to pay for superfluous "goodies" that merely make us passive.

❖ ❖ ❖

August, 1973—

The fundamental problem of our age is a lack of belief. . . . There is, in fact, a spiritual vacuum in our society. We are living in a period of profound and rapid change, in which old truths and established values are disintegrating — and nothing has taken their place.

The search for meaning has led people in many new spiritual directions — Zen Buddhism, transcendental meditation, astrology and many forms of the occult. While these approaches may help some people find new paths to better lives, they could also become dead-end diversions of energies away from changes that need to be made.

There are, I think, some examples of powerful new affirmation that may begin filling some of the need. I think it has shown up in the spirit and commitment of groups like the Quakers, among radical Catholics like the Berrigan brothers, among radical Protestants like Martin Luther King, Jr.; among Christians who have broken away from the established churches; among people in the civil rights movement, the anti-war movement and the cooperative movement, among many others.

Being in the forefront of this new affirmation, this new search, is one hell of a struggle. The old structures that told everyone how to live here have been torn down, and the people searching for something new are like a band of pioneers trying to put up some shelter in a fierce prairie storm. Some of them cannot cope with the absence of structure, and like the pioneer woman in Ole Rolvaag's *Giants in the Earth*, they come apart.

Albert Camus has grappled in a profound way with the central realization of our age — absurdity — and come out on the other side. If any person has understood the problem, he did. He stared the beast in the eye and he found the courage to go on.

When I first explored Camus in some depth, around 1965, I remember thinking that, while he expressed the dilemma perfectly, his transition from hopelessness (absurdity) to affirmation involved a terrific leap of faith. I wasn't prepared, at that time, to make the leap. Looking back and examining where I am now, I think I have made the leap. At least I am living as if I had — and that is, I think, what existentialism is about: You live as if you have faith, and in the process of living, in the act, you do have faith.

❖ ❖ ❖

October, 1973—

Fall is a time when things change fast. It makes a perfect metaphor for the present period in history. We are in an autumn (perhaps the autumn of Western Civilization) of violent, variegated change.... The fall is a time of reckoning with the past, too; it is a time when we know that some things are gone forever, that we are getting older.

Granny Utigard, my last grandparent, died late this summer.... For me, Granny's passing is the end of the Millville I knew as a boy. The buildings are still here, and many of the people are still around, and the high, ancient hills are the same; but without Granny, the Old Millville is gone.

As a town, Millville probably reached its peak around 1920. Then there was a railroad, two grain elevators, a water-wheel stone mill at nearby Jarretts, a newspaper, a bank and a lot more.... It was during this period that Gramp Utigard started his garage, which he operated until his death in 1950. It was a good time for Millville.

Since then, it's been steadily downhill. The railroad went out in the mid-30s, and, with improved roads, people started doing business in bigger towns. Bit by bit, the centralization of the economy and of people drew away the life blood of Millville. A lot of the young people grew up, went away and didn't come back. With the shift from people-power to machinery, the farms couldn't support them.

In truth, Old Millville has been dead for a long time. By the time I was a kid, during the Depression, it was in its old age. The oldtimers used to hang around Gramp's garage, playing cards and telling the stories that carry the burden of what little culture we have. Now, the average age in Millville is very high, and already the village has passed into a new time. It is a quaint remnant of an age past. It is a relic.

The future? If present trends continue, Millville is going to waste away into little more than a bedroom community. It will undoubtedly have some nice homes for the indefinite future, because the valley at Millville is a beautiful place to live. If that happens, I won't want to live here. I don't like suburbs, or exurbs, as Millville would be, even if they're pretty. Houses grouped together don't make a community, and to me, community is a big part of what makes living enjoyable.

Autumn is the time to think about passings. It is a time to use the strong awareness of our mortality to focus our lives on what is most important to us, and to dig in and do what we are "called" to.

❖ ❖ ❖

February, 1974—

There are times when, walking back from the Millville Post office in the silent white brilliance of a winter day, I think we must be mad to publish a magazine from this isolated hamlet. There are times, in fact, when I think we are mad to be producing the *Anvil* anywhere, given the size of the task and the little money and resources we have.

❖ ❖ ❖

July, 1974—

Writing and editing a magazine in this back-country part of America has given me access to all kinds of ideas about how our society might be changed for the better. And it has given me the time and space to think about these things. I'd like to share some information and thoughts that recently have come to me as a clanging surprise — and inspiration. The information is contained in a just-published book called *The Anarchist Collectives* . . . a compilation of writings and reports about various aspects of the peasant-worker movement in Spain.

What I have learned simply by being part of a country village has helped me understand the full meaning of the Spanish movement and to see how many of the same principles could be applied in our society. For example, the movement's base of strength was in the country. The "collective" movement, which used a technique that amounts to an extension of the co-op, drew upon the ancient traditions of community mutual-aid in the Spanish villages. . . . In the late 19th century — around the 1870s and thereafter — the already established Spanish "movement" received an important infusion of ideas from the anarchist theorists in Europe, including Kropotkin and Bakunin.

A critically important characteristic of the Spanish movement — and one that makes it so exciting for movement people of today — is its libertarianism. So concerned were the Spanish anarchists of the development of a new tyranny that they would allow no "bosses" in their movement. Everyone who was elected to a position was a worker who did a regular job during the day and conducted his "official" duties in the evenings and on weekends. They wanted no bureaucrats and they had none.

Another principle that prevented any centralized authority from taking control of the movement was its total decentralization. Each local group or unit was independent and autonomous, linked with the other units by voluntary consent. So the largest federations. . . did not control the smallest local unit — they were simple expressions of the will of the people and workers who comprised them.

This created democracy in a more pure form than America has ever seen, in all probability. For it was not mere political democracy — it was direct democratic operation of the whole society, including the crucial economic functions that determine much of the shape of everything else. In America, by contrast, the lack of democratic decision-making in the economic (industrial) sphere makes our political democracy a sham. Most of our crucial decisions are made not by voters or their elected representatives but by the heads of the largest corporations. And even if we were suddenly able to elect the president of General Motors, Pillsbury and the rest, we would probably have no more true "people" control of the economy than we have people control of the government.

❖ ❖ ❖

March, 1976—

The most elementary facts about violence in our era are almost beyond human comprehension. So far in this century, more people have met violent death at the hands of their fellow humans than in any other comparable period in history. . . . But there is an even more difficult fact for us to grasp, which is that the violence that has touched off these wars and massacres and slaughters is not limited to the dirty souls of madmen like Hitler. No, *the source of this violence is within us.* It is like a leukemia in the blood of us all. And it is not merely the capacity for anger, which is one of the basic feelings of any healthy human. It is the capacity to kill, either directly or by giving assent (or by failing to act against) those who kill in our behalf.

An explosive violence is within us, waiting for an excuse to go off. It is born of frustrations of a thousand kinds that come from living lives that are out of touch with our essential natures — lives that are perverted by the needs not of people, but of machines and systems and governments. We have been enslaved by an economic and social and political system that serves its own mad ends, not ours. This is a system that for the last hundred years, especially, has led us through a series of suicidal wars, through an unending series of recessions and depressions and through a mad process of unchecked industrial overdevelopment that is now threatening to devour the very necessities of life on earth — the air and the water and the land — as the price of continuing what it calls "the good life."

This frustration is quick to emerge in hatred, and hatred prepares the way for violence. I have felt this in myself, in rages I have expressed to my loved ones and to people in my community. And who among us has not heard, if not felt, the vicious hatreds of our times: "They ought to line up those hippie protesters (niggers, Indians, radicals) and shoot 'em."

❖ ❖ ❖

July, 1976—

For several years I had been wanting to make a trip up to northern Minnesota to visit Lee Clausen, the founder-editor-publisher of a rowdy backwoods paper called *Common Sense*. Lee's paper, which is named after the Thomas Paine pamphlet that helped spark the American Revolution, is essentially a radical-conservative-libertarian publication. Lee is a sackful of contradictions: He looks and lives like a hippie (long hair, beard, old jeans and boots; old homestead with no running water and an outhouse; wood heat). On personal and social issues such as the rights of young people, minorities, and everyone else, he is a radical libertarian. But on issues like gun control and The Communists, he sometimes sounds like a reactionary. On issues of economics he is a free-enterpriser.

Resisting The Monster has been one of the main themes of *Common Sense*, which has a readership of 5,000 spread over the great stretches of woods and water and farmland in northern Minnesota. *Common Sense* has helped people fight a plan to drain and mine a vast peat bog (to make natural gas for the cities to the south), to fight the gun control moves (in part by organizing township militias!), to restrict or halt construction on big power plants (nuclear and otherwise), to fight the construction of huge power lines through the region, to resist massive copper-nickel mining, and perhaps smelting, in the region. The list is long.

The *Anvil* is mainly a libertarian Left publication. While we've given a lot of space to socialist and Left-pacifist perspectives, we have also presented the ideas of people who are back-country conservatives, even reactionaries. And in the last year or two we have published a considerable amount of material presenting the (Left) anarchist perspective. So while we have some basic differences with folks like Lee and his *Common Sense* constituency, we share many ideas and goals. We both believe, for example, that getting the government off the backs of the people is essential. We both believe that the corporate-government combine has made a mockery of our supposedly guaranteed freedoms and of our capacity to live free, creative lives. But I wondered. Can the Left and Right really get together? And *should* they?

To Lee's way of thinking, the way to a good society is to restore the Constitution, strictly interpreted. And he believes that an integral part of such restoration is to re-value money, to again base it strictly on silver and gold, redeemable by anyone who walks into a government banking facility. He also believes that the basis of any good society is small individual property holdings — freeholds — especially country property.

To me the problem is not with the Constitution — the problem is with the massive forces concentrated within places like the Pentagon, the offices of ITT, and the universities, which have overwhelmed not only the Constitution but the entire society (not to mention a lot of other societies around the world). I personally believe that the basis of any better society here must be some form of communitarianism — that is, the use of limited, local forms of common ownership and use of some of the basic means for making a living, such as agricultural land and forests, major factories and shops and large buildings and businesses. Homes, too, could be owned by the community, if occupants were guaranteed leases for as long as they wanted them. The need for such common ownership, as I see it, is just this: The people who control the major means for making a living in any society control the society. So if you want a democratic society, you've got to have common (democratic) ownership. At the same time, anybody who wants to own and run his or her own business or farm should be able to.

❖ ❖ ❖

March, 1977—

The powerline protests seem to fit into a pattern of citizen resistance to too much development — to too much of everything. One of the laws of life is that nothing can expand indefinitely. And we are coming to a point at which further development, unchecked, will cost us an awful price, perhaps the price of our civilization itself. If we do as our leaders have planned and go ahead with massive strip-mining of coal on the Great Plains (as the Minnesota power companies would do at the terminus of their powerline in North Dakota), we risk the destruction of an especially fragile part of our land. After this destruction has occurred — and enormous amounts of scarce water have been used — the land will be restored to its original condition, we are assured by the energy company spokesmen. And will they do it, as God did, in seven days?

❖ ❖ ❖

March, 1978—

It is in the nature of living and learning to continually have to back up to more basic things before you can go on. It is like setting out to insulate an old house and finding that you need a new foundation or a new floor or even a new basement, if the place is to heat properly and be snug. So it has been in my experience of editing the *Anvil* over the last six years. As I try to understand what is wrong in our individual lives and in the society, I find myself going backward to ever more elementary matters.

To some socialists and collectivists (as well as to the media), the personal search seems to be a rejection of the organized movements of the antiwar and civil rights era. It is a widely accepted notion that society can be transformed only by the traditional means of organizing to apply political pressure. A corollary of this, accepted by most advocates as well as opponents of social reform, is that the new interest in self is a form of egotism and self-indulgence that effectively removes the participants from involvement in charting the society's course. While this is true with some people, it appears to me that others are finding the path to ways of living that are not selfish, but self-fulfilling.

The highest duty of the self is to become all that one can, to become, in Erich Fromm's phrase, a productive person. This is the essence of what it is to be human. It is what the philosopher Spinoza described as the first principle of all ethics. . . . The best Christian teacher I have encountered, Nicolas Berdyaev, asserts not merely the freedom of the self but its sovereignty. That which is the essence of the person cannot be the means to any end whatever. . . . A person who tries to live toward the fulfillment of this essence is, in our society, a dissenter, a radical.

❖ ❖ ❖

Fall, 1978—

The people in power and their spokesmen in the media have tried to indicate that the powerline battle is over; that there remains only the matter of bringing a few hard-core "vandals" and "terrorists" under control. But they know better. . . . The powerline is but one part in a series of struggles that are going on between the little people and the forces in control of the society. Politically, there has been an alliance of new populists who span the spectrum from traditional left to traditional right. . . . To people who are sitting in positions of authority, who are used to working their will with little or no resistance from solid middle class citizens like the farmers, the new coalitions are a frightening development. It is the kind of thing that led the staff of the Trilateral Commission to conclude that America is now suffering from "an excess of democracy."

What people are learning, on the contrary, is that the democracy we have in America is almost meaningless. As Gloria Woida puts it, "I have no respect left for the court system. The only place where there is a little justice is in the jury trial. The state agencies are just a farce. And as for the political system, it just doesn't work for the people. I don't care who's in, Republicans or Democrats, nothing changes."

The significance of the powerline struggle lies not only in its example as a way people can stand up for themselves but in its appeal to all the rest of us. For the problems uncovered by the farmer/protesters are going to have to be faced by the entire society. The people planning our national energy system now are interested only in money and power; they are, therefore, incredibly stupid about the broader implications that affect us all. If there is no money left to develop energy technologies that are renewable, that we can afford, that we can control and that do not do damage to ourselves and our land, we and our descendants will be the losers. And it won't do any good to call a legislative hearing to determine who was to blame.

❖ ❖ ❖

Winter, 1979—

Science today seems everywhere triumphant, and yet people everywhere are struggling against the inevitable hopelessness and despair that flows from its mechanistic dogma. There is that within us that will not accept the idea that life is a cosmic accident. We experience in ourselves that which is infinite, eternal and part of something absolutely good.

In time, people will reassert the ancient wisdoms and declare again the transcendent meaning of life. In the meantime, we will see a transition — already begun — in which scientists themselves will debunk the false dogmas of Science and depose it as a pseudo-religious phenomenon and a philosophical falsity. To a great extent, the discoveries of 20th century physics have already done this, though the news has yet to penetrate even to most of our informed minds. New theories, which evolved from studies into the structure of space and time, matter and energy, have completely shattered classical views of the nature of reality and of the cosmos, and of the relationship of humans to both. This revolution has toppled all of the pillars of the mechanistic temple — objectivity, solidity, determinacy. It amounts to a shattering discovery of the limits of science in describing reality.

In the upheavals of the 1960s and early '70s there is a strain of authentic spiritual search that goes on in a multitude of forms, deepening, growing, spreading. And as it becomes ever more apparent that "the party is over" — that the brief era of unprecedented affluence and its accompanying orgy of production, consumption and pollution is ending — we may be entering upon a period in which the collective consciousness of mankind will take a sharp turn toward the great traditions of community, based on the truths of brotherhood and sisterhood, awe before the mystery and beauty of creation, respect and love for the land that nurtures us, responsibility for the tasks of individual and communal life, including the protection and care of those in need, and veneration for that in all things and all people which is part of the sacred and ultimately unknowable.

❖ ❖ ❖

Summer, 1979—

In the years since *Anvil* No. 1, I have lost a good deal of innocence; I have realized how difficult things are; I have had to face all kinds of illusions and pay the sometimes high cost of learning how to make vision into reality. I have suffered, and I have sustained losses. I have gone through the pain of having to discard unreal ideas. I have felt isolated and alone. I have gone through despair. But I have developed new strengths. I have learned to print and to work with machinery. I have studied and tested ideas and learned more of what I am about. And I have found good work, good friends and the love of family and community in the midst of an extraordinarily beautiful place. I have rediscovered my home.

There is much for which our highly dispersed and varied movement can be criticized. . . . And yet, as I look back I am impressed by the extent to which its essential vision has been correct. My own sense from early on has been that people were going to have to find ways to free themselves, both psychologically and physically, from depending on the traditional values of getting and spending, of a narrowly defined goal of career success and of our society's definitions of the good life. Without this, we would have no serious resistance movement and no significant force for the creation of a new set of values and priorities.

To maintain our spirit, and to cope creatively with moments of despair, seems to me to be one of the most important tasks. I know that many other people have undergone despair much greater than mine; and I am continually humbled by fresh awareness of how narrow is my understanding of the human condition. The natural forces of life are cruel enough, and the added savagery of man-made brutality is unspeakably horrible. Yet if we cannot control our thirst for retaliation and vengeance we will only bring down more violence upon ourselves and upon those we love. . . . The lessons of history are clear about that. Our movement will be crushed unless it acts with Gandhian power and gentleness. Only in this way will we succeed.

NORTH COUNTRY
ANVIL
No.30 $1

The ANVIL at Thirty
Jud Jerome on Cults and Communes

Looking to the Radical Past

A distinctive feature of the Anvil *was its consistent attention to the long background of farm protest and radicalism in the north country. Several authors looked back at 19th-century populism and at its eloquent midwestern spokesman, Ignatius Donnelly. Rhoda Gilman wrote about this "Wayward Prophet" in connection with an exhibition on Donnelly that opened at the Minnesota Historical Society in 1981. The piece first appeared the same year in* Anvil *number 36 and was reprinted as part of the brochure that accompanied the exhibit.*

Jim Shields produced numerous historical sketches for early issues of the Anvil. *"No!", published in number 2 (1972), was based on an interview with single-term Minnesota Congressman Johnny Bernard. Also recalling the 1930s was noted artist and longtime radical Syd Fossum, who served as art director of the magazine during its first two years. In addition to a periodic column, he contributed to number 10 (1974) his recollections of the WPA art program and his own troubles with federal authority. Looking at more recent times, Tom O'Connell described the travail of independent trade unionists during the witch hunts of the 1940s and '50s. His article appeared in* Anvil *number 9 (1973-74).*

Ignatius Donnelly
MINNESOTA HISTORICAL SOCIETY

Minnesota's Wayward Prophet

By Rhoda R. Gilman

OLD RADICALS AND THOSE WHO have roots deep in Minnesota's agrarian past will remember the name of Ignatius Donnelly. They will know him as the relentless gadfly of the state's early political bosses and railroad barons. For nearly 40 years, with untiring energy, he marshaled angry, exploited farmers — first behind the Grange, then the Greenback Party, then the Farmers Alliance, and at last the People's Party. Probably the best orator the state has ever had, he framed the ringing words of the 1892 platform that became the rallying cry of populism across the nation. The highest office he ever reached was Congress, where he served three terms as a young man in the 1860s. Thereafter he championed lost causes, but in defeat he shaped the political life of Minnesota far more than the long line of party hacks who beat him. He was still fighting when he died on January 1, 1901 — the first day of the 20th century.

But that was 80 years ago, and though Donnelly was easily the best-known Minnesotan of his time, both in the state and throughout the world, he is nearly forgotten now. His contemporaries — Henry H. Sibley, Alexander Ramsey, John S. Pillsbury, Knute Nelson — all have their durable monuments. Like establishment pioneers everywhere, they have counties, towns, schools, and highways named for them. For Donnelly there is only the town of Donnelly in Stevens County, and that carries his name simply because he started a money-losing wheat farm there. — Why, then, a museum exhibit on Ignatius Donnelly in the decade of the 1980s?

Those who go through the gallery will find an answer. Behind the extended hand and genial Irish smile of Minnesota's "Great Commoner," there was another Donnelly. Like an onion, he had many layers. The perennial protest politician was the outer skin; inside were levels of speculative scholarship, of brooding Celtic mysticism, and of doom-saying prophecy. Sitting in the pine-paneled library of his house at

Nininger, just north of Hastings, he delved into science, history, and literature, and he wrote a number of strangely disquieting books. This was the Donnelly that a St. Paul editor referred to as "the Sage of Nininger," half in derision and half in awe. The name stuck. This is the Ignatius Donnelly that speaks to the late 20th century.

His interests ranged from geology and archaeology to the authorship of Shakespeare's plays, from spiritualism to monetary policy. He questioned accepted dogma wherever he found it, probing for meanings and mysteries beneath the surface appearance of things. With a keen eye for unexplained anomalies he confounded the experts and then battered at them with the wit and polemics of a political orator. Like his contemporaries, historians have puzzled over just how seriously to take his arguments, and most of them have written him off as a clever crackpot.

Still read today are two works of popular science, *Atlantis: The Antediluvian World* (1882) and *Ragnarok: The Age of Fire and Gravel* (1882). In the first book Donnelly created a milestone in the long history of the Atlantis myth. The legend started with a story told by Plato of an island kingdom in the ocean westward from the Strait of Gibraltar. According to the Greek philosopher, this kingdom for many years controlled the western parts of Europe and northern Africa. But the people of Atlantis angered the gods, and their island sank beneath the sea in a mighty cataclysm.

Over the centuries many writers — including Francis Bacon — used the story as a parable. Sometimes Atlantis was a vanished Eden, sometimes it was a symbol of the good society yet to come, and sometimes it was a lesson in the retribution that follows pride and corruption. Its actual existence was never seriously discussed until the 19th century, when a few authors began to speculate along the lines of geology and history. It was Donnelly who developed the evidence into a plausible theory.

Fascinated by the then little-known subject of American antiquities, he cited examples from Peru to Canada that suggested similarity to the art, architecture, and traditions of the Old World. Atlantis, he maintained, had to be the common source. It was a powerful argument, and he buttressed it with scraps of linguistic and geological evidence and with tales of primordial flood and disaster drawn from both sides of the Atlantic. Although a century of archaeological study has discredited most of Donnelly's examples, a few still provide fuel for controversy between diffusionist and evolutionist theories of human culture.

Donnelly's *Atlantis* was translated into several languages and went through uncounted editions, two of which are still in print in the United States. It became the Bible of believers in Atlantis. Those believers over the past century have included Theosophists and other occult theorists, clairvoyants like Edgar Cayce, one master hoaxer claiming to be the grandson of the great archaeologist Heinrich Schliemann, undersea explorers, extraterrestrialists, and in the 1970s and 1980s classicists who think the tale originated with a volcanic explosion that wiped out the island of Thera in the Aegean Sea. Well over a thousand books have been written, and they continue to pour out. Nearly all refer to Donnelly, and many still rehash his arguments.

Donnelly carried the theme of disaster one step further in *Ragnarok*, referring in the title to a Norse legend of the world's destruction. He rejected the then-new idea of geologists that glaciers had shaped the face of Minnesota and other northern states over a period of a million years. Instead, he claimed, the great drift of soil and gravel that covers the land was laid down in a few days by a visitor from outer space. A comet grazing the earth in a past age had brought untold destruction, especially to the northern hemisphere. Again he used the testimony of myth and legend throughout the world to bolster his argument.

In such freewheeling speculation Donnelly challenged the established science of the 1880s. He was also out of step with the whole world view of his time. The expanding industrial society of the late 19th century was rooted deeply in the mechanistic view of nature propounded by the 18th-century Enlightenment. By the 1880s, 19th-century thinkers were being drawn irresistibly to the concept of evolution through random mutation and natural selection. Darwin's evolutionary scenario implied gradual and orderly change over eons without the intervention of the irrational, the arbitrary, or the unknowable. It argued for inevitable progress through selection of the species best adapted to natural conditions.

For all its grim lining of competition for survival, the doctrine of evolution was fundamentally optimistic. It precisely fitted the needs of an expansive and self-confident age. Banished were the fearful edicts of a just or vengeful God, and with them were banished moral and spiritual restraints on the exploitation of nature. As social theorists like Herbert Spencer pointed out, natural selection also implied that the pursuit of individual self-interest would result in the most rapid development for humanity as a whole. Thus the doctrine of evolution served — and was freely used — as a rationale for the controlling classes of a free-enterprise society.

Donnelly was not an anti-evolutionist. Nevertheless, readers for whom he painted pictures of a world twisted by sudden, unpredictable catastrophe felt a cold shadow pass across their orderly landscape of evolution and progress. In *Ragnarok*, even more than in *Atlantis*, there is a sense that catastrophe carries overtones of retribution. "Do not count too much," he warns his readers, "on your lands and houses and parchments; your guns and cannon and laws; your insurance companies and your governments. There may be even now a comet coming with glowing countenance and horrid hair to overwhelm you and your possessions, and your corporations, and all the ant-like devices of man in one common ruin."

Ten years later in 1890, Donnelly extended the theme of retribution to the sphere of economics and politics. In a futuristic novel called *Caesar's Column*, set in the year 1988, he portrayed the collapse of American society. The turbulent decade between the completion of *Ragnarok* and the writing of *Caesar's Column* had seen the Haymarket riot and the suppression of the Knights of Labor; in Minnesota it had seen an explosion of industry and urban growth that more than tripled the population of the Twin Cities. As this happened, the state's wealth was rapidly being consolidated into a few large fortunes. Agricultural depression, meanwhile, had spawned the Farmers Alliance, and at the end of the decade desperate workers and farmers were uniting in the People's Party.

Looking down the next hundred years of American history, Donnelly foresaw the squeezing out of small farmers and the crushing of democracy beneath a pyramid of industrial wealth and power. By the late 1980s, he predicted, injustice and suffering would produce an inevitable reaction. The downtrodden masses would rebel blindly and the great experiment of Washington and Jefferson would end in a nightmarish bloodbath.

Today Donnelly's visions of catastrophe find far more echoes than they did in his own time. Compared to Hiroshima or the Holocaust, the tower of corpses walled around with cement from which *Caesar's Column* takes its title is only mildly shocking. And far from being unthinkable, the concept of an asteroid striking the earth is now seriously proposed by scientists in explanation of the climatic changes that killed off dinosaurs and other life-forms some 65 million years ago.

Late 19th-century science saw the earth as a slowly cooling lump of rock. Shrinkage and cracking of the crust produced mountain ranges and an occasional volcano or earth tremor, but the main features were assumed to be permanently stable. Today's picture is far different. Now we know earth as a constantly changing and vastly mysterious entity. Its restless crustal plates are moved by inner forces whose laws have yet to be discovered; its magnetic poles reverse from time to time, but the mechanism through which this happens and its effects upon life are unknown; here and there the planet carries scars inflicted by meteorites, but wind, water, and the forces of organic life heal them quickly and they disappear; and we are beginning to suspect that the gaseous blanket of atmosphere is deeply sensitive to changes from both within and without. Even the amount of energy our "constant sun" pours upon us is being shown to vary greatly over time.

Thus we are forced to question the stability of our planetary environment along with our bland certainty of progress, growth and social evolution. At the same time we are recognizing that Donnelly was only one manifestation of an undercurrent that appears like a dark thread through the fabric of 19th- and 20th-century thought. It has surfaced as various brands of romanticism and nativism, as political or religious messianic movements, and — most respectably — as transcendentalism. Persistently it challenged the extension of scientific materialism to all areas of life and thought and insisted that the collective human memory embodied in ancient tales and symbols be used in studying the past and present. Thus Donnelly's reliance on myth and legend as evidence in *Atlantis* and *Ragnarok* was far from coincidental.

Donnelly's flights of fancy were not meant as literal prediction. The antiquated assumptions on which he built many of his arguments have long been superseded. Halley's Comet will probably not strike the earth in 1986, and it is not likely that America's poor will rise in bloody revolt by 1988. Nevertheless, it will never again be quite so easy to relegate the Sage of Nininger or others like him to the far edges of the lunatic fringe. They may have something to tell us.

No!

By James M. Shields

THERE HAVE BEEN SO FEW public men in American history, especially Congressmen, of whom it truly can be said, "Here was an honest man who never compromised his principles." But back in 1937, out of the northern iron mines of Minnesota, there appeared in Congress a man who not only believed in, but actually VOTED his deep-set principles regardless of consequences.

John T. Bernard, born in the proud little island of Corsica in 1893, came to this country in 1907, settled in Eveleth, Minnesota, and worked in the iron mines. Later, after service in World War I, when no work in the mines was available, he became a city fireman. He was also chairman of the first Mine, Mill & Smelter Workers Union local. Finally, in 1936, after a militant history of political activity in the Farmer-Labor Party, he was elected by the miners of the Eighth Congressional District as their first — their very own U.S. Congressman. And so it was that John T. Bernard, militant working stiff with deep convictions about democracy and the rights of man, a 5-foot-2 fighter for what he believed in, "went to Washington."

This was that ominous period before World War II when the powerful forces of Nazi Germany and Fascist Italy were exercising their muscles and feeling their way toward an attempt to take over the world. The newly formed democratic Republic of Spain, just having shaken off centuries of servitude under Catholic monarchs, suddenly was invaded by General Franco's hordes from Africa, openly aided by Hitler's bombers and Mussolini's Fascisti. And our own Democratic New Deal government made its one great mistake, thanks to the powerful influence of Catholic prelate bosses such as Cardinal Spellman. It determined to cut off aid of any kind — even medical — to "either side," a decision in the form of an embargo which sounded the death knell to the legitimate Spanish democracy. That embargo was to be the first business of Congress in January, 1937, and while it awaited passage in both houses of Congress, Spanish government ships were being hastily loaded in New York harbor with much needed arms and medical supplies. But let's read Bernard's account of what happened in his own unforgettable words:

"Shortly before the opening of Congress, my secretary and I left for Washington by car. We rented a room near the old House Office Building. On the first day, January 5, after the roll call they had election of the Speaker of the House, an overwhelming victory for William B. Bankhead, Democrat from Alabama. But the Farmer-Laborites of Minnesota and the Progressives from Wisconsin got together and decided to meet the following morning and discuss this Spanish Embargo Resolution to see if we could agree to act as a unit — vote the same way.

"I must frankly confess that that night I hardly slept at all. My secretary was very worried. He said, 'John, you didn't sleep at all last night. I heard you tossing all night. Aren't you feeling well?' I said, 'I'm all right.'

"So I went directly to the office of Congressman Withrow of Wisconsin, where the ten of us, six Progressives from Wisconsin and four Farmer-Laborites from Minnesota, met. The Farmer-Laborites were Henry Teigen and Dewey Johnson of Minneapolis, Richard Buckler of the North District, and myself. The Wisconsin Progressives were Tom Amlie (whose brother Hans Amlie was in Spain as one of the commanders of the International Brigade fighting with the Spanish government against Hitler and Mussolini), Jim Boileau, Withrow, Sauthoff, Marlin Hull and Bernard Gehrmann.

"We discussed the Spanish Arms Embargo Resolution for about an hour and a half. Then we took an unofficial vote to see how we felt. Seven of the ten agreed that the resolution was unfriendly, undemocratic, un-American and pro-Fascist. Why, I thought to myself, John, you're not alone. At least there will be seven of us who will vote against this thing here. 'Well,' I said, 'This is not bad. There are seven of us who feel the same way.' Three of them would not commit themselves. They were Buckler of Minnesota, Hull and Gehrmann of Wisconsin.

"Amlie said, 'John, who will vote against this thing here?' 'Well,' I said, 'as I stated before, there will be seven of us at least.' 'John,' he said, 'any man who votes against this thing here will commit political suicide.' I thought he was kidding. I just smiled. Then Jerry Boileau came to me and said, 'John, we know how you feel, but please try and understand this. Everyone wants this resolution to be passed. The President of the United States, the Senate, the House, the Secretary of State, everybody wants this to be passed, and it is a fact that anyone who would vote against this would commit political suicide.'

"Then I realized that my colleagues, even though they were admitting that this thing was damnably wrong, were serious about not voting against it. I want to try to tell you how I felt, but I can't do it. I — that was, I believe, the saddest moment of my life. To see men whom I considered the cream of the House, those who had become the rebels of America. They were neither Republicans nor Democrats. They had rebelled. The people in their states had rebelled against the dishonesty and corruption in the two main political parties and had formed another party in their states. And to hear them speak that way, I was hurt. I was cut to the core. And I said, 'Look, when you were campaigning for office in the last campaign, when you went to the people, did you tell them that if you were confronted with a situation like this, where you had to make a definite decision, a real choice between going along with what you promised your people — fight for their well-being, fight for that which is right, or do the opposite — fight and work mainly in order to promote your own political ambitions? Did you tell them that you will bend, you will fail the people, you will put convictions aside and work mainly for yourselves, for your own political ambitions? Did you tell them that?'

"Well, they just laughed. 'Of course we didn't tell them that.' Then I said, 'You folks speak a language that is mighty strange to me, and I hope to God I will never learn to speak it.' With these words I walked out. Tom Amlie, whose brother, as I said, was fighting in Spain with the International Brigade, followed me and kept saying to me, 'Johnny, I wish I could go along with you, but I have a funny district. I cannot vote against this thing here.'

"I said, 'Tom, you do whatever you please, but please leave me alone.'

"I went to the floor of the House. I sat down. I was hurt. I felt terrible. I sat on the Republican side. In fact, all the Farmer-Laborites and Progressives sat on the Republican side because there was more room there. The Democrat side was filled. Tom Amlie sat next to me on my left, talking to me. He felt very bad. I could tell his conscience was bothering him.

"I noticed on the Democratic side Maury Maverick of Texas talking to some of his associates. Previously I had gone to Maury Maverick, a well known liberal, and introduced myself by saying I was from the mining district in Minnesota and had heard he was a decent guy, so I came to him for help, as I was very new here. From that moment we had become friends. Now he came over to me and asked, 'Bernard, what do you think of this resolution?' I told him I thought it was very, very bad. When he took his seat I said to Amlie, 'Tom, I don't know, but I believe that Maverick is not going to object to this resolution. If he would, it would have more weight than mine, since he is an old Democrat and I'm just a newcomer. But if he doesn't object, by golly, I will.'

"And Amlie said to me, 'Why do you say that? I've been in the House with Maury Maverick several years and if he says he will do something he will do it.' 'Well,' I said, 'I don't know. But when he came over here and asked me how I feel about this, I had the feeling that he needs encouragement, that's all. I hope I'm wrong.'

"Well, pretty soon the Speaker of the House came in. The House was called to order. And I said to Tom, 'Wait a minute. What am I supposed to do here? I want to object to this, but what is the procedure? I don't know — this is my first day — I don't know how they do things here.'

"'Well,' he says, 'the Clerk will read the resolution. When the resolution is read, then Speaker Bankhead will say, 'Do I hear any objection to the unanimous passage of this resolution?' Then you stand up and you say, 'Mr. Speaker, I object.' I said, 'Is that all there is to it?' He said, 'That's all.' "Well,' I said, 'that's easy to remember.'

"So the Clerk read the resolution. And as Amlie had said to me, Bankhead said, 'Do I hear any objection to the unanimous passage of this resolution?' I looked over at Maury Maverick and he was sitting there quietly. Suddenly very nervous, I stood up and shouted as loud as I could, 'MR. SPEAKER, I OBJECT!' Bankhead looked at me with murder in his eyes. I presume, he thought, why, the temerity of this newcomer! And he wouldn't recognize me. Again and again I shouted, 'I OBJECT!'

"Finally Jerry Boileau of Wisconsin, who we had picked the day before as our floor leader, stood up. He was sitting right behind me. And as soon as he stood up, Bankhead said, 'Why does the gentleman from Wisconsin rise?' Boileau said, 'Mr. Speaker, my colleague from Minnesota has been on his feet objecting to the passage of this resolution and in fairness to yourself and also to him he should be recognized.'

"So Bankhead, still looking at me, said 'Does the gentleman from Minnesota mean to say that he has been on his feet objecting to passage of this resolution?' I said 'Mr. Speaker, I objected four times!' I felt like calling him names which would have been unprintable. After all, what right did he have in trying to refuse to recognize me?

"The House adjourned for fifteen minutes. The committee went into a back room to draft a resolution for a roll call vote. When they came back the resolution was read again and just then a messenger from the Senate came in and said 'Mr. Speaker, a message from the United States Senate. The United States Senate passed the Spanish Arms Embargo Resolution eighty-one to none and asks concurrence of the House.'

"Well, if you can try to put yourself in my shoes! I thought to myself, what happened to George Norris of Nebraska, Bob Wagner of New York, Borah of Idaho, Nye of North Dakota, Thomas of Utah? What happened to Murray of Montana, Claude Pepper of Florida, Schwellenbach of the State of Washington? What happened to our own President, the Secretary of State? Why do they do these things?

"Just then Alex Green, a congressman from Florida, came and sat by me. As he sat down I could see John Rankin of Mississippi stand up and say, 'Mr. Speaker, I demand a roll call. I want to see if there is a single member of this House who has the nerve to vote against such an American patriotic resolution.' Well, I thought to myself, I will show you one who will vote against this damnable thing. But now Alex Green, whom I had met in northern Minnesota during the campaign, started talking to me. 'Bernard, I'm glad you made it. What committee would you like to get on? I know a lot of people and I can help you.' 'Well,' I said, 'I would like to get on the Committee on Labor, Mines and Mining, if I can.' He said, 'Take these names down. You write to them, then I'll contact them.'

"Just then the roll was being called. I said, 'Wait a minute, Green. They're going to call my name now. It starts with a B.' So they called my name and I voted 'NO.' Without a word, Green got up and went to his seat. He never sat by me again during the two years I was there. He was simply trying to distract my attention from the roll call so that I would fail to vote.

"I went back to my office a beaten man. I laid down on the couch — every congressman has a couch in his inner office. My secretary came in and asked, 'What happened in the House?' I said, 'It passed the Spanish Arms Embargo Resolution.' He asked, 'How did you vote?' 'I voted against it.'

"'Well, how many votes were against?' I said, 'I was the only one.'

"'The only one! What about the Senate?' I said, 'In the Senate they voted unanimously for it eighty-one to none.'

"He said, 'My God, what have you done?'

"Well, at that time I was not in a mood to accept any preaching. So I said, 'Tony, you go back to your office. If I need you I will call for you. Now go and leave me alone.'

"And that is the story of my 'NO' vote against the Spanish Arms Embargo Resolution."

No, not quite the whole story. Thanks to the delay of two days caused by Bernard's refusal to make the resolution unanimous, two ships loaded with essential arms and supplies for the Spanish government were allowed to leave New York harbor that same day and duly arrived in Spain.

However, it is significant to note historically that Bernard's career in Congress was abruptly terminated two years later by tremendous opposition from the highly organized and powerful pro-Franco Catholic hierarchy, plus betrayal by leading American Federation of Labor officials who were embittered by Congressman Bernard's help in the young CIO's campaign to organize the miners of the Iron Range.

❖ ❖ ❖

The publication of this article drew a letter from Bernard himself, which supplied the sequel to the story. It was printed in the next issue of the Anvil:

In 1938, the forces of reaction made a strong comeback, and 68 New Deal Congressmen were defeated. I was naturally one of them. That was followed by four years of intense and futile search for employment. I was determined not to let the exploiters of the people force me out of that territory where I had spent the most exciting years of my life; where my father, mother, my son and my oldest brother, whom I worshipped, were buried.

I covered a radius of over 60 miles. I tried the Iron Range mines, the Duluth steel mills and lumber yards, etc. etc. looking for common labor, or anything. It was not to be. I was hurt, but not surprised. They were determined to get me out, to get rid of me.

They only succeeded in giving me more strength, more determination in remaining true to myself, to my brothers (all workers).

On the day that Pearl Harbor was attacked by Japan, and after listening to President Roosevelt speak to the nation over the radio, I immediately sent him a letter offering my services. . . . A few days after, I received a telegram . . . which read, "Will you accept commission in Army Specialist Corps for immediate active field duty."

I answered in the affirmative. Another telegram directed me to Major Harry C. Piper of the Army Intelligence in Minneapolis. . . . I passed all tests with colors flying. . . . Many days passed. Major Piper phoned me from Minneapolis several times. He could not understand what was holding it up.

I suspected and understood what it was — I was a premature anti-

Fascist, and the Establishment simply didn't trust me. That is mutual. . . .

In October 1942 I received a letter from the U.E. (United Electrical, Radio & Machine Workers of America) District 11 in Chicago, offering me a job in their organization. I remained with them 11 years.

During those 11 years I was asked many times to address other labor union memberships. . . . Instead of separating me from the workers, the Establishment actually made it possible for me to be continuously in contact with much greater numbers of my brothers. I must confess that I relished it.

After 11 years with the U.E., I had what I considered the distinct honor of serving as chairman of the Civil Rights Congress in Chicago for five years. After that, a few little odd jobs, then to Long Beach, California, to be close to our daughter and her family. . . .

Good luck with the ANVIL. Fraternally yours,

John T. Bernard

But that was not the conclusion. Four years later, in 1977, a celebration in honor of Bernard was held at Mesaba Park on the Iron Range. The gathering became in retrospect a historic event in its own right. Jack Miller attended and published a report of it in issue number 23:

The kid at the gas station in Hibbing doesn't even know where Mesaba Co-op Park is, and no wonder. The park was the summer gathering place for Finnish and other radicals on the northern Minnesota Iron Range; and it still is, for what few folks are still in touch with their ethnic-political origins. The park is a place in the tall pines, encompassing a small, clear lake and focused on a worker-built wooden building with a big kitchen/dining room and an upstairs auditorium and dance hall. In the old days, most recently in the 30s, there were thousands of people on hand for the highlight of the season, the mid-summer festival. Recently, a few hundred have come.

But this year was special. The old radicals, and a small but growing group of younger activists, were putting on a tribute to one of their number they consider great — John T. Bernard.

The event was an extraordinary re-creation of the past in this country where we are taught to believe that history is something that other people make. Here were perhaps 500 people giving honor to an 84-year-old trade unionist who, 40 years ago, had served one two-year term in Congress representing the Iron Range. Not only was Johnny on hand (he had come from California, where he has lived for some years), but here also were such Farmer-Labor Party venerables as former Governor Elmer Benson and party secretary Viena Johnson Hendrickson.

The reason Johnny Bernard is a hero to these people is that he was a radical and he — unlike many of the politicians, who make their compromises with the system — acted on his principles. He was put to the test on his second day on the floor of the U.S. Congress, January 6, 1937, when President Roosevelt asked for an embargo against sending supplies to either side in the Spanish Civil War. The newly elected (Republican) government of Spain was facing an attempted military takeover by the fascist Francisco Franco. And while Franco was being supplied lavishly by Hitler and Mussolini, the people's forces had almost nothing to fight with. Johnny realized immediately that unless the working people of Spain got help, Franco would slaughter them.

All of his colleagues told Johnny that it would be political suicide to vote against the resolution. But Johnny stayed by his conviction. "I lived before without being a Congressman," he told a colleague at the time, "and I guess I can do it again."

When the vote came, John T. Bernard was *the only member in either house of Congress* to vote against the resolution. The vote in the House was 406 to 1. The people's forces were badly beaten in Spain, and Johnny Bernard was attacked by reactionary forces and defeated in the next election.

It is difficult for younger people, who may hardly have heard of the Spanish Civil War, to realize how it stirred a generation of radical young people all over the world. From everywhere, including America, they went as volunteers to fight Franco. And on this day at Mesaba Park, four of the volunteers, members of the "Abraham Lincoln Brigade," were present to lead Johnny Bernard to the platform. They and

Johnny raised their fists in the revolutionary salute (usually accompanied by the greeting, "Salud!") that was widely used in Spain.

Johnny was introduced too by Governor Benson, now advanced in age and in ill health, who left his retirement home in Appleton, Minnesota, to make what he said was "my first public speech in 30 years." Benson, who with Bernard had addressed 10,000 cheering people at this Mesaba Park in 1936, was perhaps the most radical governor Minnesota ever had. Now, the Norwegian banker from western Minnesota, who used to call out the National Guard to *help* strikers, took the occasion to denounce Carter and Mondale, "who led the American people to believe they were populists" who would make major cuts in military spending, pass national health insurance and provide decent price policies for farmers.

A good case can be made to suggest that the politics of these old leftists were drastically in error; that they thought they could use the machinery of government, the state, to solve problems, when *the state itself* (the national power structure) was the problem; and that the politics of Carter-Mondale are different only in emphasis and in degree. It is obvious at very least that the old leftists, most of whom venerated the Soviet Union and some of whom were members of the Communist Party, have been unable to understand what has happened in Russia, how the real revolution of the people was taken over in the early years by a bureaucratic elite and destroyed — turned into an ugly new tyranny.

But in spite of that glaring deficiency, these indigenous American radicals are to be respected for their contributions and for their authenticity. They are rooted, as later political movements are not, in real places and in people's whole lives. By contrast with people like Walter Mondale, who is one dimensional, the oldtimers are fully developed members of real communities; they are human.

When Johnny Bernard spoke, he didn't dwell only on politics, though he said some tough things ("We have here in our beloved country, the worst enemy of democracy on the face of the earth — the military-industrial complex."). He spoke about how, in his homeland of Corsica, which he left at 14, he was already a liberationist. He sang, unaccompanied, the Corsican anthem. His older brother, who is 86, also sang, in an accomplished and amazingly strong and beautiful voice. Johnny talked, too, about life in his high-rise apartment building for older people in Long Beach, California. He told how, on a visit to the Soviet Union, he wept when he stood between the trenches at Leningrad where half a million war dead were buried.

The rest of the festival also expressed a cultural and personal richness that could hardly contrast more with the unrooted, one-dimensional machine politics of today. Among the older folks at the festival, the predominant language was Finnish. And the dancing, which went on til midnight, was hard-core Iron Range folk: you drink and dance and sweat until you give out. Then, everyone goes out for the traditional bonfire, and afterward, as most people head for their cabins or tents or homes, a few of the hardier young go swimming in the nude. Throughout the weekend, the informal talk between friends and comrades is more vital than the speeches. In one group we found Gus Hall, the chairman of the U.S. Communist Party, telling about his family farm, a few miles away, and how his father had helped acquire the Mesaba Park land and started it as a logging camp for World War I draft resisters.

Whatever the contradictions, this is an essential part of our cultural and political heritage. We do well not merely to venerate it, but to learn from its weaknesses, and to build on its strengths.

John Bernard at Mesaba Park, 1977

"The Meeting" by Syd Fossum, 1937
MINNESOTA HISTORICAL SOCIETY

Militant Minnesota Artists

By Syd Fossum

IN A RECENT *ANVIL* (NUMBER 8), I made a passing reference to my two grand jury indictments, federal trial and four days behind bars — all a part of my involvement with the government art projects of 1933 to 1943. Little seems to be known about this period of American art. It was during the Great Depression, with its theme song, "Brother, Can You Spare a Dime?" In 1933, there were over 12 million unemployed — an awful lot in those grim days. I emerged from art school in that year and joined them.

Nobody was buying art. There were few teaching jobs. There were practically no jobs. Lawyers were digging ditches. Doctors were laying bricks.

For me, the government art projects began in December, 1933. They were set up to help unemployed artists. I had been unemployed since art school in June. I was chosen for this first project (PWOAP) because Russell Plimpton, the director of the Minneapolis Institute of Arts, was the local selector and he was looking after his own. So there began eight years of government art projects for me — PWOAP, SERA and WPA.

There were about 30 or more artists on PWOAP — mostly from the Twin Cities. We lined up on provided chairs in a Minneapolis Institute of Arts basement corridor each week. Each artist had a quota of works to turn in. Mine was three watercolors a week. Another artist, who worked faster, brought in four gouaches. Bob Brown, an established artist, came with a watercolor every other week. The oil painters produced a painting about every three weeks. The printmakers and sculptors had varying quotas. I think mine was established when I turned in three the first time. Once, I came with two and the Technical Committee, with whom we met, asked if I weren't feeling well.

The Technical Committee, composed of outstanding local artists (not eligible for PWOAP — not jobless, in other words) appraised our

submissions and invariably accepted them. The works were then allo-
cated to government institutions — schools, colleges, libraries, government offices, etc. When I was being inducted into the army in 1943,
I saw two of my art project oils in recreation rooms at Fort Snelling. It
was the only time that the army and I were in rapport.

Each week, we were paid. There were two categories — $28 and
$42. Fortunately, I was in the latter. At that time, to me, just out of art
school, the sum seemed immense.

PWOAP lasted four months and wound up with a big national
exhibition in the Corcoran Gallery in Washington, D.C. of selected
works from throughout the country. I was lucky to have two watercolors included.

The organizers of PWOAP apparently thought that this four
months would put artists on their feet and they would be absorbed by
private industry. But we weren't, and the government projects continued. The next one I was on was under SERA (State Emergency Relief
Act). It was an art center in the Sexton Building in Minneapolis. It
was under the auspices of the adult education program. Classes in drawing, painting, fashion illustration and sculpture were held. Tuition fees
were minimal. There were art centers in St. Paul and Duluth too.

The most important government art project began the fall of 1935
under WPA (Works Progress Administration). It was part of President
Franklin Delano Roosevelt's New Deal Program. It was better organized than the others, but even so, every year, there was a battle in
Congress over fiscal allotments. The reactionaries considered WPA to
be boondoggling and there was bitter opposition. And the cultural
projects — art, writing, music and theatre — were the most vulnerable.

Here, the Minnesota Artists Union played an important part in
representing project artists. We were a local in a national organization
of about 22 locals. There was a broad program, focusing on a federal
bureau of fine arts. The Minnesota Artists Union at one time had over
100 members. We were a militant organization. We boycotted a Minneapolis Institute of Arts exhibition, packed the state WPA headquarters in St. Paul, staged a work stoppage at the WPA art project, etc.

I dwell upon this, instead of pointing out the many good works which were produced by the Minnesota WPA art project, because it was my activities with the union that brought about my two grand jury indictments — four days behind bars and a federal trial. I held every office in the union, as well as being chairman of countless committees.

My first indictment was in the summer of 1939. It all began July 1, the start of the fiscal year. When the yearly appropriations were to be voted, a bill was introduced in Congress by a reactionary to limit yearly wages to $1,000, which would have meant the end of the WPA cultural projects.

On project after project, workers walked out in protest. At that time, Bunny and I were living on a farm near Taylors Falls. I painted rural landscapes and brought them to project headquarters once a month. Shortly after the walkouts began, I received a phone call from an artist union friend, saying the union was having an important meeting that evening about whether the art project workers should walk out. Practically all the project people were in the union. So I caught a ride with the postman into Minneapolis. The meeting was jammed and the vote to walk out was 100 per cent. I stayed in Minneapolis a couple of days (a visiting woman friend kept Bunny company) and helped with picketing, addressing post cards, etc. Then I returned to the farm.

The walkouts and demonstrations were nationwide, with the Minnesota projects leading in the percentage of workers out. And the protests paid off — the offending bill was withdrawn and the yearly appropriations voted. But then there were reprisals, led by the WPA timekeeping department, which hated worker organizations. There were also accusations by disgruntled malcontents and a few who crossed the picket lines and felt they had been jostled. It resulted in 167 grand jury indictments!

In the rustic seclusion of our farm, Bunny and I listened to the daily reports on radio (no TV then) of new indictments and workers being picked up. Many we knew — some were good friends. Then one day, a couple of U.S. marshals appeared and served me a subpoena. I was indicted too!

The marshals took me back to Minneapolis to the courthouse. I spent four days in jail, until Bunny bailed me out. My bail was $2,000;

some were as high as $10,000. Bunny raised some of the $125 for the bail bondsman, through the sale of a painting. I was kicked off the project, of course, and blacklisted.

The reason I was indicted was because I was supposed to have prevented a clerk from crossing the picket line. This was a lie. Administrative personnel were allowed to cross. Another project artist shared the indictment for the same reason. When the clerk learned about this, she was furious and signed an affidavit that the indictment was completely false. This was filed with our lawyer and we could hardly wait for our case to come up. Three trials were held and 33 of 37 were sent to prison. My cell-mate served 10 months in Sandstone. But President Roosevelt "pardoned" the rest of the 167. We were terribly disappointed. We would have made fools of the timekeepers.

So I was released from the indictment but was still blacklisted from the art project. Bunny and I returned to the farm, where we stayed until late October. And a little after the first of the year (1940), I got back on the project, which was then located at the Walker Art Center. It was under an arrangement with the Walkers, who provided the building; the project staffed it and used it for headquarters. There were classes, exhibitions, lectures and symposia. WPA workers were gallery guards. The galleries were repainted under art project supervision. Some of the color schemes were rather startling. I remember one gallery with a midnight black ceiling and walls of canary yellow, dusty rose, powder blue and egg shell white!

In January, 1941, Bunny and I decided to take a bus trip to New York City, where we'd never been. I went to Clem Haupers, the state art project director, who gave me permission to go. I said I would turn in work to cover the three-week period and would arrange for someone to take my classes in exchange. The only problem was the daily time cards (foisted upon us by the stupid timekeeping department). But they were always arbitrarily filled out by us anyway, so I simply made out the required number and got a project friend to turn them in at the proper times.

Bunny and I had a marvelous time. We saw foreign movies, went to plays and many art museums and galleries and I even had my picture taken at a meeting of the New York Artists Union local.

But somehow the timekeeping people got wind of the trip and put a former FBI agent on my tail. He was in the WPA equivalent of the FBI. I was called in and questioned and knew I was in trouble. And sure enough, I was fired with two pink dismissal slips. One was for violating timekeeping procedures and the real one was for falsely swearing that I wasn't a member of an organization advocating the violent overthrow of the government. For that, just being an officer in the artists union was enough.

This firing happened on the eve of Thanksgiving of 1941 and not only was I fired, but my last pay check of $70 was withheld, though it had already been mailed! I don't know how they did it. So, there was another grand jury indictment, but this time no bail. Nor jail.

On December 2, a story about this appeared on the top of the front page of the Minneapolis *Tribune*, along with a photo of a recent self-portrait painting. The story was quite sympathetic to me and quoted my lawyer, Doug Hall, who denounced the indictment and firing.

The federal trial began in mid-March, and I appeared in a grey sharkskin double-breasted suit I'd bought for $3 at a left-wing fund raising rally. One of the Minneapolis papers said they would print any courtroom sketches I did, so I brought my sketchbook and a couple were printed. One was of the prosecutor and the other was a caricature of the WPA snooper, whom I called Tomato Face (to his tomato face). The trial went fast and the time keepers thought they had it wrapped up. But after the concluding speeches by the prosecutor (Earl Larson, now a judge), Judge Nordbye summed up. He said, and I quote, "The only thing at issue in this case is whether Fossum had the right, under WPA regulations, to claim 49 hours credit when he returned from New York, for a watercolor entitled 'Winter, 1941,' which he did on his own time two months previously. Whether he had a laudable purpose in making the trip, is immaterial. He could have gone to San Francisco or swimming in the river or fishing in Tahiti and it would have made no difference."

The trial was recessed and scheduled to reopen on Monday morning (this was Friday). During the weekend, I got busy. I keep exhibition catalogs. So I picked up a few for recent local shows and went to WPA headquarters at the Walker Art Center, where I matched prize-winners (dating back months and even years) that had later been turned in to the project — and not at the times indicated on the time cards. While at the Walker, I came face to tomato face with the snooper. He was scouting too. As I left, I heard him over the partition, "Boy, that Fossum is certainly a slippery character."

When the trial renewed Monday morning, I had all this evidence, plus a number of project artists as witnesses, who testified that this was project procedure. No one put down the exact hours on the time cards, which they all considered ridiculous. At one point, Doug got the chief timekeeper to admit that it didn't make any difference whether I painted a stroke during a work day — just so he made the time card out properly!

The jury was out 25 minutes and came back with an acquittal!

Bunny, friends, Doug, I and Earl Larson — the prosecutor! — went to the nearby Casanova Bar to celebrate. (Earl had agreed to drop the charge before the trial, after Doug and I had met with him. Earl thought the charge was ridiculous. But when Earl was out of town, Tomato Face had gone into Earl's office, picked up the papers and presented them to the grand jury.)

Doug put in a claim for my withheld $70 pay. Four years later, when I was with the army near Saarbrucken, Germany, I received an overly stapled check to endorse. I finally found a space amid all the holes. The amount was not $70, but about $25. The government deducted $49 (which they claimed I owed because of my absence from the job. They never recognized the results of the trial!) plus interest.

That was the end of my years on government projects. And soon, the projects themselves ended. World War II solved the unemployment problem. The projects had been set up as temporary expedients. But a surprising amount of good work was turned out, in spite of all the hazards and harassments.

The Union That Kept the Faith

By Tom O'Connell

JOE MILLER, ORGANIZER FOR LOCAL 1139, United Electrical, Radio, and Machine Workers (UE) was riding down the elevator from the WCCO news studio in Minneapolis with Danny Gustafson, czar of the Minneapolis Building and Trades. Danny and Joe had just appeared on a WCCO special on the Domed Stadium controversy, and had taken different sides on the issue. To Joe, the Stadium was a real lemon — a project opposed by the majority of Minneapolis citizens, a proposal that would essentially benefit a few downtown businessmen at the expense of the general taxpayer. To Danny, the Stadium meant jobs. No matter that Building and Trades muscle could better be used rehabilitating inner-city neighborhoods or constructing mass transit facilities. The Stadium was the plan the boys downtown and their friendly politicians (Democrats and Republicans) had come up with to get some jobs for Danny, to "improve the city's tax base," etc. etc. The Stadium, thought Danny, was it.

There was a reporter on the elevator with Danny and Joe. He expressed surprise that two labor guys could be disagreeing on such a basic issue. Joe smiled at him, and let him know that he and Danny disagreed on most things — and have for years. In fact, the United Electrical Workers, for years labor's most progressive union, maintained a tradition of hard organizing, progressive politics and democratic unionism through a period of history when the bulk of organized labor took its place as part of the reactionary fabric of Cold War politics and corporate expansionism. And the price UE paid for its integrity was nearly death.

The UE was born in the heyday of industrial unionism, the 1930s. Alongside militant unions like the steelworkers and auto workers and mine workers, the UE became an early leader in the movement that resulted in the creation of the CIO — and a social revolution. National contracts were won in major chain shops like General Electric and

Westinghouse — contracts that gained working conditions the likes of which workers had never known before: decent wages, seniority rights, effective steward systems, pensions, and paid vacations. Stated the preamble of the UE constitution:

"We, the United Electrical, Radio and Machine Workers, realize that the struggle to better our working conditions is in vain unless we are united to protect ourselves collectively against the organized forces of the employers . . . form an industrial organization which unites all workers in our industry on an industrial basis, and rank and file control, regardless of craft, age, sex, nationality, creed or political beliefs, and pursue at all times a policy of aggressive struggle to improve our conditions."

And they meant it.

The Great Depression ended with World War II, and the UE, like all unions of the period, gave its best to the war effort. Better wages, improved working conditions, were secondary to producing the implements and goods necessary to supply our boys overseas and keep the country going over here. Meanwhile, the corporations got fat, as corporations often do during wars.

In 1946, the UE moved fast to achieve a better distribution of the big wartime profits. The militant solidarity of the CIO was still intact. Joining with steel and auto workers, the UE sparked the "Big Three Unity" and won an 18.5 per cent pay increase, across the board.

But, the victory was short lived. Corporate leadership, unable to break the power of the CIO on the picket line, turned to political attack (Taft-Hartley) and propaganda attack (red baiting). The result was the death of militant unionism on a large scale, and the near death of the UE itself. The CIO, which had managed to fight off charges of communism in the '30s, not only succumbed to the attack in the late '40s and early '50s, but often led it. In 1949 the CIO formed a new union for the electrical industries, the IUE, and began a devastating campaign of red baiting and union raiding against the UE — managing in a few short years to reduce a union of 700,000 workers to a mere shadow of itself.

In Minneapolis-St. Paul, the survival struggle of the UE was especially heroic; the attack upon it particularly devastating. On January 1, 1949, the UE was the area's largest union. UE had organized 30,000 workers in plants like Honeywell, Minneapolis Moline (with its big branch in Hopkins) in smaller shops like Butler Manufacture and Paper Calmenson, in garages, scrapyards, little metal working operations. There were five locals then. The UE owned the main union hall of Minneapolis (sharing space with the United Auto Workers, Grain Millers and others). The hall is now Friars Restaurant, at 4th Avenue and 8th Street.

By the end of 1949, the UE was on the ropes in the Twin Cities. Under the leadership of former UE organizers like Roy Wishart (the man who ran things at Honeywell's local) and politicians like Minneapolis' newly elected mayor Hubert Humphrey (who used to send telegrams of congratulation every time another "communist dominated" shop was successfully raided), UE shops went down like dominoes. First Honeywell, later Moline out at Hopkins, then the smaller shops and garages. The Moline plant at Lake Street, Local 1136, held out against the red baiting but later left UE to join the more powerful UAW. By the early '50s, the UE was down to two locals. After Moline left, there was only one, Local 1139, with a membership of 1,000.

How could this happen? How could a powerful union like UE — a union that had fought so hard and so successfully for its workers — be brought to the very edge of ruin so thoroughly, in so short a time? Was anti-communist hysteria so great that the men and women of UE could be stampeded so easily? Did the leadership of the UE stand up against the red baiting, cave in, lead it themselves?

According to Ken Enkel, the UE's battling lawyer, the anti-communist hysteria even before Joe McCarthy worked up his full head of malicious steam, was more than anything we experienced in our campaign against the war in Indochina. But anti-communism was as much a method to the accomplishment of UE destruction as a cause. Certain UE leaders (George MacDonald at the Lake Street Moline plant; Al Anderson out in Hopkins; Clem Hathaway, a former editor of the *Daily Worker*; Ken Enkel himself) had views that were too far left to make them dependable DFLers, and the UE's split from the CIO on a national level divided the union locally as well. These facts, combined with some legitimate differences of opinion, some tactical blunders by leftists within the union, the usual array of personal and political ambitions, all were factors in the crisis that followed. In the end, as many UE leaders supported, or were persuaded to support, the secession movement as opposed it.

The actual pattern of raid, switchover, secession, differed from plant to plant. Honeywell, controlled by Wishart, went over with barely a cry of protest. Other shops changed after long debate, struggle, court challenge. In some of the more recalcitrant shops, red baiting was used generously. To stand against it meant serious repercussions for oneself and one's family. Most workers weren't in a position to risk that. Some did. George MacDonald, for example, was banned from the UAW, and a job at Moline, when that union took over the Lake Street operation. Ken Enkel says there wasn't a single lawyer in town to discuss his court cases with, when he was handling UE's legal defense.

But today, UE still survives, both locally and nationally, its commitment to progressive unionism still intact. Local 1139 has organized 700 new workers in the last few years, and following the national policy of "organizing the unorganized," will continue to grow in the future. The local now has 25 shops. Litton Microwave is the largest, with 350 workers. Then there's Northwest Automatic Products, and Butler Manufacture. Butler makes steel and aluminum tanks for gas transport. There are smaller shops, and UE still has its scrapyards — seven in all. They employ a total of 135 workers.

Like all the UE locals, 1139 is organized along democratic lines. Officers are elected by the rank and file. So are the paid business agents. All paid staff of the UE must actually have worked in UE shops to be eligible for their posts. And no UE staff person can make more than a shop worker at maximum wage. UE international president Albert Fitzgerald makes $14,000. Compare that with teamster president Frank Fitzsimmons, who makes $125,000 and has a fleet of Cadillacs at his disposal.

The UE has also maintained its commitment to progressive politics, a politics that goes beyond the business unionism that dominates the AFL-CIO, to a view of the labor movement as a custodian of people's justice. On a national level, UE was the first union to oppose the war, has fought for nationalized health care, tax reform (no tax for anyone under $12,000, high taxes for the wealthy) women's rights, and racial solidarity. And it has taken advanced positions on specific worker's issues: pension reform, a shorter workweek, occupational health and safety. But unlike most unions, the UE's commitment to progressive political action doesn't stop with high-sounding resolutions, or fancy position papers. UE makes a real commitment to the political education of its members. It conducts political education through a national newspaper and local newsletter, through occasional (and usually brief) political discussion in shops at monthly grievance sessions. And while efforts in this area hardly add up to the left's wistful images of old time Wobblies with a first-grade education huddled in mining shacks poring over volumes of Karl Marx by candlelight, the political work of the UE is a step in the right direction, and it is a commitment so rare in the ideological no-man's land of the American labor movement as to deserve commendation.

Of course the main business of any self-respecting union is organizing (though George Meany may have forgotten it). Only 25 per cent of the work force in this country is organized — a fact that no doubt surprises people who have the notion that unions have brought most everybody into the secure and irrevocable regions of the Great American Middle Class. But the business of organizing is much the same as it was in the good old days (though perhaps a bit safer). As Joe Miller explains, "The companies use the same anti-union propaganda whether they have 10 or 10,000 workers. The job is to get people to see that they can accomplish more by working collectively than as individuals on their own."

What are the anti-union tactics? Well, there is red baiting, though employers are about ready to give up on that one for a while. It hasn't been working lately. There's the threat of workers losing their jobs ("Our company is in bad financial straits. We'll have to close down if you organize.") Occasionally an employer will attempt to downgrade a union's usefulness. In fatherly tones, "Hell, why do you want to join them. All it will get you is a lot of dues to pay." And firing workers for organizing activities is not uncommon. The burden of proof is on the unions to prove that the worker was fired for organizing, as opposed to something else.

Labor organizers, like Joe Miller overcome these obstacles by patient support, clear explanation to workers of their rights, and what to expect from their employer. Though UE sets particular shops as potential targets for organizing, Joe never begins an effort if there is not a core group of workers in the shop who are really willing to accept responsibility for organizing. After putting together an organizing committee, Joe will accompany two or three workers to other workers homes. If interest is generated, if enough people are ready to go union, a vote will be taken, and another shop will have been organized as United Electrical Workers.

Nationally, by 1969, UE had revived sufficiently to spearhead an alliance with UAW and IUE against General Electric — an alliance that resulted in a 102-day strike against GE and major concessions from that corporation. In 1970, it concluded a no-raid agreement with its old arch-enemy, the IUE, formally ending the battle with that union. In 1972, it followed Westinghouse to Atlanta and organized successfully there. This year, UE sent nine additional organizers South — good companions for the corporate executives who move their plants down to take advantage of that good, cheap, southern labor.

UE is growing at a time when there are some little signs that we may be seeing a rebirth of militant and progressive unionism in this country. There are some encouraging examples: Caesar Chavez's Farm Workers; the successful insurgency of Arnold Miller's forces in the United Mine Workers; The Hospital Workers, Local 1199 — Black and Puerto Rican women who have organized in Boston, New York, and Philadelphia; the young insurgents in the UAW. But as yet, these examples are isolated, and the prospects on a national level are far from bright — at least for the near future.

For the challenges that face unionism in 1973 are enormous. The growth of the multinational corporation has resulted in an institution that is something between a nation-state and a business — an entity that has power to create an international monetary crisis, set up shop in countries all over the world, tyrannize "host" governments. And there's inflation, eating up workers' gains as fast as they are made. There's the fact of automation, resulting in an unemployment rate of 5 per cent and a lessening of leverage for the industrial worker. There's speedup, as employers drive to get the maximum productivity per man hour to "stay competitive" in capitalism's international rat race.

Most basically, there's the steady encroachment of a growth economy on our neighborhoods, communities, natural environment. In identifying its own interests with those of big business, organized labor has simply added to the schizophrenia of political choice-making in this country today. The American worker is also the American consumer, neighborhood resident, nature lover, world citizen. By failing to challenge the very nature of business expansionism, by identifying itself with the aims of corporate America, by making itself dependent on industry's growing profits in order to get its own cut of the pie, the unions have allowed us Americans to be caught in political pickles like:

— Having to choose between domed stadiums and jobs for construction workers.

— Having to decide whether drinking taconite tailings is worth the economic advantages gained by having the taconite plants in the first place.

— Having to choose between decent salaries for our public employees and high unfair taxes.

— Having to choose between a more modest "defense posture" and unemployment at Lockheed, Boeing, Honeywell.

There was a time when the CIO, militant and independent, might have moved to challenge that dichotomy. It didn't. The United Electrical, Radio, and Machine Workers are the direct descendants of that time. They have kept the faith. Theirs is the legacy.

Today, as the point of conflict between business and the people moves to new areas . . . as consumers challenge Northern States Power Company, community organizations defeat the domed stadium, neighborhoods fight high-rise developments (finding out that what's good for Shelter Corporation is not always good for the city), antiwar activists continue to remind us that Honeywell designs bombs used to kill and maim civilians . . . through all of this, the UE remains the one union that can be depended upon to support these struggles. Only time will tell if organized labor resumes its place as a leader of the people against the bosses, but if and when it does, you can bet UE will be in the vanguard. As leader Jim Matles says: "Yes — we are one regiment, but by God, man for man, woman for woman, we'll make it count. Just one regiment — we'll keep on going until this labor movement is reunited.

"The Union that Kept the Faith"

A Homecoming for Odysseus

for Genya and the Greek Comrades

He had learned to be at rest on the irrational sea.
Alien shades preserved him from the stink of time.
In wars between wars and among barbarians
He sowed a salt alphabet and called it home.

Alpha was the coal mine of the one-eyed imperialists,
the Aliemani. Here he went underground.
In the revolutions of the zodiac and of nations
He had a gun called Omega: which he kept cleaned.

Now, the irreconcilable hero is coming home —
With an old dog, a son, a delegate from the poor —
And arrives where those singing sirens and happy colonels
Have eaten his house alive and turned his wife to a whore,

And now, from their secret places, the outlaw weapons arrive:
Magical. The exile enters. The blood-daubed names on the wall
Shout! And the Agora shouts! In an awful silence
The mode of the music changes and the gates of the cities fall.

—Thomas McGrath
(Anvil #9)

War and Peace

As the Vietnam war drew to a dismal close, several authors turned to the power of story and verse to voice the rage, sorrow, and guilt that still haunted the country. These emotions found expression in "Mai is the Name of a Flower," by Lowell Gomsrud, published in number 8 (1973) and in "The Enemy," by Emilio De Grazia, which appeared first in Anvil *number 7 (1973) and was republished in a somewhat revised form (used here) in* Enemy Country *(1984).*

Vietnam receded into history, but nuclear arsenals and the cold war persisted. Some in the peace movement had followed the call to Gandhian civil disobedience, accepting protest and prison terms as a permanent way of life. The Anvil *gave them ever-growing attention. One of the first examples was Jay Walljasper's reflective essay on an interview with Elizabeth McAlister, which appeared in number 32 (1980). A year or two later a new wave of popular antiwar feeling swept the country, as the Reagan administration plunged into a massive escalation of the arms race. One response was the nuclear freeze campaign. Its value and limitations were addressed by Eric Steinmetz in* Anvil *number 42 (1983). At the same time draft resistance again became an issue for young midwesterners, as discussed by Mordecai Specktor, also in number 42.*

In Vietnam Mai is the Name of a Flower

A Story By Lowell Gomsrud

In Viet Nam
Mai is the name of a flower.
It is supposed to bring good luck.
It is small and yellow
and blooms only once a year — at Tet —
and fades quickly.
In Viet Nam
Mai is also the name of a girl.

I looked for your grave this time, Mai,
my third trip to Viet Nam,
five years after we put you on board a helicopter
and flew you out of our surrounded camp.
Forgive us.
We didn't know it would mean you couldn't be buried
next to your home.
You see, we hoped you would live,
and no one would believe it
when the Sergeant said you had just died.
I couldn't look.
Now I would like to move your tomb
to the home I destroyed
and your parents rebuilt.
The monk at the Buddhist cemetery at Thu Duc —
Someone told us you might be there,
a quiet, leafy, rambling collection of whitewashed tombs
clinging to the top of a low hill —
wanted to be helpful to the blond, somber ex-soldier.
Yes, he said, as he offered us tea with ice,
I seem to remember a girl the name of Mai
was brought here at Tet of 1968.

My heart felt afraid.
He led us around the outside of the temple,
six or seven small, curious children following
whispering to each other excitedly.
We stopped in a moment
and they grew hushed.
I looked, and did not hear violins.
The tomb was large and covered by a portico with vines.
No, it said to us,
this is not the tomb of a poor young girl from the country.
The name belonged to someone else.
Ah well then, sighed the monk,
I must have been wrong.
There were so many then.
He smiled lamely.
We turned to go.

Mai
our moments in the five months before the great
offensive
were so full of promise.
I never thought the war would come to us,
how could I know they would be the only moments we
would have
for all time?
Vital to me then,
now I hunger after them.
Then
the future promised more moments,
now
it promises . . . nothing.
I've tried so hard to preserve those moments,
but Mai,
in the very act
I'm losing you more.

A wise friend of mine
says a memory is a chain of protein formed in the brain,
and that every time it is recalled
a new chain is formed.
But
influenced by the contemporary atmosphere —
thousands of new stimuli in competition —
the new chain cannot help but be different,
subtleties, shadings, blurring, mixing, blending, fading,
at best a fainter copy each time
like that made by a Xerox machine.
By the first anniversary of your death
I had written a book about you,
it chronicled every one of our moments.
When I wrote it
every one was real.
Now
as I read it for the thousandth time
I cannot be sure.
Was that Mai?
Was that what we said?
Was that just how she looked in her yellow dress
with the yellow flowers in her hair?
I feel helpless
and afraid.
It's like someone coming up, smiling, and saying
Hi
how's your family? Was your father's operation
successful?
Do you still have that old piano?
and you think you've never seen them.

Last year
on my second trip to Viet Nam
I found your picture.

It was your last.
It was a proof, and was fading fast,
but the photographer saved you.
He still had the negative.
Now I have it everywhere
my office, my den, my bedroom
the room for the little girl who may come someday
and have your name.
I even carry it with me.
I know it is you Mai
but instead of feeling you
I feel only emptiness.
If I could have found your grave
I could have at least had your coffin.
Now that must seem a morbid, grisly thought
but it would be something, something,
if time has not taken that too.

Mai
your picture is so incredibly young and fresh,
and I am growing so old.
Only eight years separated us then,
(John and Jacqueline Kennedy were twelve years apart,
and my best friend's parents are thirteen.)
Now, can you believe it, there are fourteen years
between us.
Last month I let my beard grow
and it came out all grey and white.
It was a shock.
And there are small wrinkles now around the eyes.
Now
my only hope for you is my death.
But Mai
when I come to you
I may be so old.
Will you still want me?

The Enemy

By Emilio De Grazia

WHEN HE LEFT HIS FOLKS to get married he saw Bill, not William, printed on the birth certificate his mother delivered to him in a cigar box. On his honeymoon he and his bride saw the Hollywood musical "Showboat," and for the first time he heard the song entitled "Bill." He could remember only a phrase or two — "An ordinary guy . . . And Bill took me Upon his knee, So comfy and roomy, Feels natural to me . . ." The tune stayed with him long after his love for his bride faded and this love faded right in front of him as he watched Catherine, the preacher's wife, the soloist in his church, break into tears as she concluded her hymn. Then one day it occurred to him that the song was written for men like him, all the ordinary guys in the world.

The tune eluded him when he tried to remember it while on a mission near My Tho, the effort to bring it back as stale as the taste in his mouth and as heavy as the heat hovering over the marshes like a yellow fog. With the others he looked up to watch a Cobra slide sideways into the sky and disappear into a dot. He felt the hot air weigh him down, and he breathed it reluctantly into lungs dried by dust and cigarette smoke. No one spoke, not even when someone at the head of the column ordered everyone to quicken the pace.

Along the side of the road peasants worked in the mud, their feet lost in the rice slough and their backs bent over the earth. A stooped old man near the road looked up from his hoe as the soldiers passed, his eyes invisible behind the shadow of his hat. Bowing, he smiled just as the sun caught a golden tooth. A few of the soldiers glanced at him, and one took off his helmet and waved. The old man, still stooped, turned away and resumed his slow work with his hoe.

He had been through it before, but he might be the one hit this time. The village was just a mile ahead. The jets were coming in, and three platoons from the Second Division were to clear the southern and western roads before his squad came to the village. After the Phantoms finished their work his squad had to hold the village until an armored division passed through. Then everybody got to go home, and he, like everybody else, would return to the barracks and booze and card games that never ended but just fell apart when too many men collapsed at the table or fell into bed.

He knew there would be no enemy waiting for him. Never an enemy after the Phantoms went in. The enemy disappeared, or crawled like rats into holes no one ever found. Or the enemy walked away to some other village. He had never seen the enemy. Except when they were heaped in trucks or laid out on the ground in rows next to stacks of weapons on display for the children and old men. All of the dead, the faces, looked small. They had to be boys, but no one was sure. A soldier near the bodies once told him that anyone dead was the enemy.

Though he had been afraid before, today he was not afraid. He might get hit, but anyone might get hit. As his squad came to a ridge overlooking the village, he saw that this one was the same. A dozen or so huts made of wood, straw, scraps of metal, a clearing resembling a road wandering through. Already a few villagers moving about, ignoring the smoke and dust still rising from the pockmarks of bombs dropped only minutes ago.

Orders were given for the squad to fan out and regroup five hundred yards ahead of the clump of trees to the right of the village. Then in minutes the excitement would die. Mortar rounds would fall on the huts. Then they would follow the barrage in on foot, firing into the huts as they ran. The villagers would scatter, finding paths in the clearings between the blasts.

Only when he came down from the ridge did he feel the earth shudder, even while the last of the Phantoms faded away into its own thunder. After rushing past the thicket where the enemy was supposed to be, his heart pounded wildly as he sprayed bursts of fire into the huts he passed. His heart leaped as he saw himself among the first wave overrunning the village. But suddenly the feeling abandoned him when he realized that he had run with them to the opposite side of the village, that before him stretched a broad bare field broken only by standing water and grass. Then, as the soldiers walked back together, he came upon the villagers, some fifty in all, huddled in a group outside the central hut.

They searched the women for weapons and found one dead boy curled in a corner of one of the huts. The lieutenant ordered him placed outside the central hut. No one looked at the boy's face, no one dared touch the hand dragging backward on the ground, and no one picked up the rubber shoe that fell from his foot as he was laid outside the central hut.

And no one turned away when the dead boy's mother started a wail that cried like an ambulance returning slowly through midnight streets. He felt good when another soldier finally slapped the woman and dragged her away. The soldier ordered two older villagers to keep her quiet.

He did not know how he ended up in the hut with the other boy and the boy's grandmother. He had heard stories at the base about what happened in huts during a sweep. The men who laughed had their reasons to laugh. In one village an old man stole a pair of boots after offering to clean them for nothing, and he complained when forced to bring them back. And in the bars the whores, who drank beer while repeating the few phrases of a strange English they had borrowed like the dresses they used to lure their men, gave the men diseases in exchange for dollar bills. He had listened to the stories unable to laugh, as if the need to laugh originated in a delicate crisis that flared when a slowly squeezed trigger lost its balance and exploded, the mechanism needing only a thin impulse to uncoil itself. And there was a yellow smell that never went away, sometimes passing into troubled sleep.

He wondered what the huddled group of villagers thought of him as he walked from hut to hut, his hand always ready on the pistol holstered at his side. But he did not know how he ended up where he did, and what urge possessed him to require the old woman to watch. He saw two soldiers push a young girl into a hut, and remembered thinking yes, the stories are true. And suddenly he found himself in another hut with the boy and the old woman, she at first whimpering until he slapped her across the face, the boy silent, his eyes vacant and hard.

He quickly looked around — the dirt floors and crude wooden table and chairs, an open bag of rice, clay pots and a tin pan. Even then he did not know what he would do. He pushed the old woman down in a corner and forced the boy away from her toward the wall made of flattened tin cans. As he tightened his grip on his pistol and saw the boy's eyes open wide, the old woman lowered her head to the floor. Then he drew the pistol out with its barrel and lifted the boy's chin up toward him.

He looked around once more to see everything — for to see everything again confirmed that it had not all happened in some dark, dim dream — and as his eyes wandered about the hut he returned to the old woman in the corner, whose eyes stared beyond the wall near which he stood.

In a different space and time he had met a different woman, Mrs. Festerson. In the supermarket behind a grocery basket heaped high with boxes and cans. They talked about the weather, about the reporter who came to her house. The next day he saw her name in the *Daily News*:

"Mrs. Festerson explained . . . she has mixed emotions about the December bombing blitz . . . But I really think . . . something to bring Hanoi to its knees . . . but in the long run . . . She does not believe . . . the U.S. should intervene again . . . it should be in the form of . . . rather than more of our boys . . ."

He saw her smile and say thank you. She gave him a polite goodday, then pushed her grocery basket down the aisle as if she was happy now that it was full of solid opinions. In the corner of the hut, the old woman, her eyes beyond conviction or accusation in their steady stare beyond him and beyond the walls of the hut, sat with her back humped wearily toward the ground.

He ordered the boy to his knees, waited for him to obey. Instead the boy stood his ground. When he grabbed the boy by the hair and wrestled him down, the boy yielded, not struggling except to turn his face up.

Breaths came in short heaves as a hand began fumbling at a zipper. The boy closed his eyes and turned his head away, avoiding even the face of the old woman. The soldier grabbed the hair behind the boy's forehead and twisted his head back, until the boy looked up with begging eyes. Then he struck the boy sharply across the side of the face, sending him sprawling across the dirt floor of the hut.

"You pay? You pay?" the boy asked, half-glancing at the old woman.

This time the soldier half-screamed in rage as he struck the boy across the side of the head with his open hand. "You goddamn money-fucking nigger-gooks!"

The boy drew himself up straight-backed this time, like an altar-boy serving a priest. Their eyes met for a moment, then darted apart.

"Do it!" he screamed at the boy. "Just do it!"

He did not see the confusion begin to clear from the boy's face as the soldier's meaning became clear. He looked down at the boy and saw that his eyes were closed. The boy did not look up, so the soldier looked away, groped for other thoughts, pleasant thoughts.

She came into view standing in an orange bikini on the brown sand, tall and warm and tanned, mouthing a sweating bottle of Pepsi Cola. I will pour it in your bikini and lick it, he said, and she said yes, yes in a whisper close to his lips, and then she laughed as she went high-stepping away, twirling a baton before thousands in a stadium. He watched her as she crossed a field. For a long minute he swayed with the rhythm of her hips and stared into the small space where her legs met. Around him everyone was screaming, but he was small and quiet in the crowd. He hated the crowd, the people, their mad screaming for no good reason at all, and he would not stand when they stood. He would sit quietly and wait until she came back for him. He was not crazy. He would never play football like those fools did.

Then suddenly she appeared again. He saw her at the end of the game walking out with number 87, the nigger lineman from Louisiana, the big nigger laughing as he let his hand slide down her ass, and she squiggling as she smiled up at the crowd while he, a lost face, wondered what this world was coming to.

His wife screamed at him. Would he please scrub the burn marks from the pan? No, leave me alone, you bitch. When's your next leave? Not for another six months? Oh I love you my dear, my darling. Goodbye. And even, almost, a tear as he walked toward the waiting plane, a tear as he looked back at her and waved. The airport looked like a tidy flat model from the air. Nothing like the shacks and strange smells in the back streets of Saigon. Then a pounding in his head, a furious driving back and forth. You've got to let yourself go once in a while, they told him. Four years, he thought, and now this. It had come to this. He had heard, but never, never did he think he. But he was free now. No longer afraid. It's the ultimate, they told him. How do you know? Degrading, he told them. The ultimate degradation. Degrading. The whole war's degrading. It puts you on their level. They're pigs. Yellow pigs. Never would I.

And soon he could say he touched me, oh how wonderful, he touched me. The yellow pig. He remembered how his wife sighed the first time he put his hand on her breast when they were parked near the high school. Lock the doors, she told him, because they say there's niggers cruising in these streets at night. After white girls. They don't like their own kind. Fuck them. Fuck them before they fuck you. Yes, lock the doors. I'll do anything you say if you lock the doors.

And years later he didn't care anymore. The niggers were moving closer and nobody said a word. One even started coming to his church, and no one said a word. He had white hair and a gray pinstriped suit. He didn't look like a nigger until he smiled. Then you could see that his teeth were small. He smiled at everyone and the first day he came to the church he thrust his hand at everyone. No one said a word even after they saw him sitting near the front of the church, and one Sunday he was on the platform with everyone else. No one said a word because it got out that he gave ten per cent to the church, and he had plenty. He came from somewhere in the South, they said.

It didn't matter to him anymore after that, because he knew that money could get you anywhere. He never listened to the preacher anymore, but only watched the preacher's wife, the soloist, who had big breasts and who, when she sang about Jesus, smiled as if he had spent the night with her. Almost every other Sunday, it seemed, she sang her favorite hymn, her eyes closed and her chest heaving with the hymn's last line: "He touched me, O how wonderful, he touched me."

It was a Baptist church, a low flat building made of painted cinder blocks, but there no longer was anywhere for the people to sit and the pastor said the Lord would see to it that they soon might be moving downtown to the big stone church once owned by the Presbyterians. He used to watch the melancholy in the preacher's wife's face pass as her eyes followed the words of the hymn fading from her, rising up toward the squares of tile that lined the low ceiling of the room the preacher insisted on calling the tabernacle. He had touched her, and she had felt it in her arms, breasts, lungs, and voice, all of them quivering with conviction, and, at the moment she lost herself in the song, with joy.

He had never felt that. He had never felt the conviction or the joy. During all the months he had been in the war he had only waited and moved about his duties as if in a foul-smelling dream. He had seen some of the dead, but death never would touch him. The men they brought in piled in the back of trucks were dirty and torn, and flies swarmed on their eyes and mouths. But he kept himself clean and the soloist's bosom was clean. She was one woman he would not dare touch.

And he remembered what happened right after he talked to Mrs. Festerson. Right in the supermarket parking lot. The nigger boy who threw himself at his feet and started to chatter while shining his shoes and rubbing the spit into them. And before he could walk away from the boy, he was trapped, late with the groceries. They wouldn't make the early show. As the boy shined and shined, spitting on his shoe, the chatter faded and the smile straightened. He wanted to kick him, do anything to get away, but there were people around. And when the boy, kneeling on a matted pad spread before him, looked up, the smile was gone.

"Two dolla, suh!"

He felt no rage now. The hut was too small to contain anything more than a memory of the madness that came over him when he not only could not refuse to pay but had to wait while the boy fumbled through a fat roll of bills, counting out eighteen singles to change the twenty dollar bill he had to give him. And now in the hut he could smile because he was getting his money's worth. He had seen the justice of it in the eyes of the preacher's wife. He remembered again how her voice quivered slightly as she sang the last line of the chorus for the last time. "He touched me, Oh how wonderful, He touched me." The words rose from deep within her and floated over heads bowed in sorrow and prayer.

"And now come," he heard the preacher say. "All of you out there who have been touched, come. Come, kneel at the altar and offer yourself to Jesus. With every head bowed and every eye closed, I want you weary sinners to come." And as he thought about the voice begging him to come forth, he saw the preacher with his arms outstretched facing not the congregation but the wall behind the altar. He could not see the preacher's face, recognize his voice. But he stood up and walked toward the front. "Come, you sinners," the preacher shouted once more, his back still turned.

Yes, it was time to give himself up. He felt his body giving in. He felt himself swaying now, and he let himself go. His whole body rose in that moment, and then he felt the rush again. Suddenly, as if his eyes opened as his heart skipped a beat, he saw himself in the hut, with its Pepsi Cola wall, the boy on his knees, and the old woman crumpled in a corner, her face turned away. In that moment he realized that nothing could stop him from surrendering or stop the rush that sent him running toward the platform, toward the preacher whose back was turned, and who whirled, showing him a black face with small teeth, the preacher who screamed like a wild man as he spread a pain as sharp as a spear through the room.

The pain spread through his whole body, and there was no more past, only the hut and the woman screaming, the boy still on his knees, and he vainly trying to fend the boy off with his hand as if the boy were a dog. Then the rush and the pain ended with the crack of the pistol, which his hand had wrestled from his holster. For a moment the boy seemed to hang suspended in the air as blood spurted over his face. He saw the boy's eyes in a last desperate moment asking why, and then everything collapsed as the boy fell to the floor of the hut.

There was no thought, only the pain and the blood. As his hand fumbled again for his zipper he saw, as he drew it away, his own blood on it.

The old woman in the corner had lifted her face, and as he ran out she began the old ritual wail for the dead, slow and quiet, warning everyone that sorrow was wandering the countryside again. The villagers had heard the wail before, so when the soldiers left they would leave their places of hiding to wail with the old woman beside their dead.

Talking with Elizabeth McAlister

By Jay Walljasper

ON PARTICULARLY HOT AFTERNOONS IN Iowa you can smell the corn grow. Warm gentle winds drift in from the southwest bringing with them a sweet, almost decadent, odor. It might really be alfalfa or freshly spread manure, but in Iowa they say it comes from green cornstalks pushing their way skyward.

The air was thick with that smell one July day as I walked around the Johnson County 4-H grounds in search of Elizabeth McAlister — one of the Berrigans' "co-conspirators." It seemed odd to interview one of the military's most tireless critics at a 4-H fairgrounds. But the whole event seemed odd; an Iowa festival that billed itself as a revival of a '60s style political concern for peace and justice.

A blues band played from atop a flatbed truck. Devotees of Maharaji-Ji sold macrobiotic sandwiches at counters where bills are usually swapped for corndogs. Long-haired boys drank beer. Others sucked on clay pipes. Official Yippies (card-carrying members of the Youth International Party), most of whom had once attended the University of Iowa three miles up the road, sat in a circle with guitars, singing "serious minded men are ruling the world."

Taking in all of this, along with the sunshine, gave me a good feeling. And it no longer seemed so unusual to be seeking out a woman who had once stood trial in Harrisburg, Pennsylvania, on charges of conspiracy to kidnap Secretary of State Henry Kissinger and blow up the steam tunnels beneath Washington, D.C. In the midst of this ad hoc community of bohemians, farmers, students, beer drinkers, radicals, poets, leftists and vagabonds, no one could seem out of place.

McAlister had once been a Catholic nun but now was married to former priest Philip Berrigan. Still, I almost expected her to be walking around the fairgrounds in a long black habit with a rosary dangling from her waist.

After several more minutes of scanning the crowd, it became clear that I had no conception of who to look for. A 6 p.m. deadline back at the newsroom was creeping up so I looked for Joe Grant, an organizer of the festival.

Grant is a controversial figure in Iowa City and I had gotten to know him while covering his political activities. His idealism, dedication, and energy had always impressed me. He was slated to go on trial the next day on vandalism charges. His crime was painting "no more war" on a jet fighter that was mounted at the entrance to the Iowa City Municipal Airport, two miles up the road.

A local VFW post had offered a reward for anyone who volunteered information leading to the arrest of the persons responsible. When Grant turned himself in, he suggested that the veterans send the reward to McAlister's Jonah House project in Baltimore. They, of course, didn't.

McAlister was sitting on the grass in the shade of a livestock pavilion reading a book about Marxism and the church, when Joe and I approached. The two of them had met while working on anti-war projects in Washington, D.C., and Joe had invited her out for the festival.

She looked very little like a nun and even less like a '60s radical. Yet she still had a religious aura, centered more in her gentle earnest manner than in appearance. Her voice was soft with an Irish brogue, yet it was compelling. There was none of the stridency in her manner that characterized so many political activists. Instead she conveyed a firm sense of commitment and dedication that made me wonder about my own net purpose in life. This woman had been to jail several times; her husband was there right now along with a number of her close friends, all because they opposed the military policy of the United States government.

Listening and watching her led me to an inevitable examination of my own beliefs and actions. I certainly agreed with her that nuclear weapons and nuclear energy were grave issues. But my opposition to both wings of the nuclear industry consisted only of signing petitions, griping and voting for progressive Democrats or socialists every other November. That really amounted to little more than just dabbling, out of some sort of need to feel hip.

On the newspaper I would do an occasional piece about political activities when I wasn't busy with cute feature stories or rock'n'roll reviews. It always struck me odd that covering left wing politics was considered a part of the music critic's beat. All in all, my political dedication matched my interest in reggae music. They were both interesting to discuss at parties and read about in magazines.

McAlister tapped right into these guilt feelings when she said, "Passivity is a cause of nuclear weapons. A willingness to pay for them (through taxes) is a cause of nuclear weapons. A person can do something about the causes of nuclear weapons. A person can make a difference." She added that the number of peace activists has declined since the early '70s, "but the people coming along now are coming along for better reasons. It's no longer a popular cause and people's commitments are greater."

My own introduction to the peace movement and radical politics had been during the popular cause era. I was in my mid-teens and although not actually in the front lines at every peace march, I did wear black armbands and buttons with dove symbols. I saw myself as a radical and was sure that I would never stray from that path. Sitting in the grass next to a woman who had not let the '70s mitigate her outrage or idealism, I wondered where my course had changed.

McAlister was saying that after her experience with mass-scale protest in the '60s, she thought war resistance executed by small groups and individuals was more effective. "I'm sick of arguing politics, arguing tactics. I've seen too much in-movement fighting. People should be more in touch with what they really believe and act upon that."

Unlike many others — fatigued and disillusioned by "the movement" — McAlister continued the struggle for peace and justice in a personal way. The Jonah House is an embodiment of her beliefs and hopes — a communal household which is run according to the principles of Christian radicalism. The house sits in one of Baltimore's poor neighborhoods and community projects and war resistance consume the householders' attention.

"We have done a whole scope of things at the Pentagon," she said, "from picketing to digging a grave which we called the nuclear grave, to planting a garden."

She added that a network of similar communities — some guided by religious ideals and others by the philosophy of humanism — has sprung up. It is these communities which will be the most effective force, she said, in the fight against nuclear weapons and nuclear energy.

The lengthy interview, which had turned into a Socratic dialogue between McAlister and a small crowd of festival goers, ended when she felt the obligation to talk with some old friends. Walking away, my thoughts were not on what angle to take for the lead of my story or which quote best summed up her attitudes. Rather, I was still concentrating on what she had said — with her words, her presence, her conviction and her example. Fully realizing that my deadline was near, I sat in a quiet corner of the fairground and sipped a solitary beer while thinking about the loss of my own idealism and commitment. I didn't remember when I had lost them, but I had.

Back at the newsroom, I quickly pieced together the usual patchwork of quotes and commentary while the managing editor impatiently marked my progress. But after the final page was handed over to the copy desk, this interview didn't just fade away like those with Frank Zappa or Chuck Mangione or the Democratic hopeful for Iowa's first district congressional seat.

The Future of the Freeze

By Eric Steinmetz

THE IDEA OF THE FREEZE, which surfaced in the fall of 1981, was an immediate, mutual, verifiable halt in the testing, deployment, and production of nuclear weapons and delivery systems. The Freeze, its advocates argued, would create a climate in which nuclear arms could be reduced, even abolished. It would head off planned development of dangerous new weapons — weapons for a "first strike," weapons that would be easier to transport and conceal, weapons that field units might be tempted to use first in a crisis. The Freeze would be an essential first step in reversing humanity's flirtation with self-destruction.

It was an appealing idea. But I doubted whether such an idea could gain an effective national following. The activist groups that would support it are extremely at odds on many issues. A coalition would have to hold together in an election year, with the usual short-term deals, back-stabbing among factions and disagreement on local issues and candidates. The voters would have to be convinced, educated, frightened enough by the abstract idea of their own extinction to vote in large numbers and take to the streets. All of this would have to be managed in spite of the sure retaliation of the Reagan administration and the military-industrial establishment.

Somehow it all held together. Through the caucuses and primaries early in the year, through Ground Zero Week, through legislative sessions, petition drives, party conventions, town meetings, the Freeze kept growing. And it began to attract the attention of the mainstream media and politicians. On June 12, more than a million people demonstrated at the opening of the U.N. Disarmament Conference in New York City. Millions more had signed petitions. Freeze resolutions had been adopted by a dozen state legislatures and hundreds of local governments. The Freeze was on the ballots of a dozen states and nearly 40 cities and counties, representing nearly a quarter of the U.S. population. And it won landslide approval nationwide, failing only in Arizona and two small counties elsewhere.

In a very short time, the Freeze has achieved incredibly wide acceptance. Combined with the European disarmament movement and a new critique of nuclear morality by American religious leaders (especially the Catholic bishops), the Freeze has produced the most serious debate on nuclear weapons since they were developed. Yet there is reason to be less than euphoric.

For one thing, the Freeze movement has been showing signs of organizational rot. It is natural that there be some indecision and confusion, after the immense effort of the last year, about what to do next. But there have been hints of rivalry between local Freeze committees and the national coordinators in St. Louis.

At the same time, a debate is building about how to put some teeth into the Freeze proposal. So far, resolutions have simply "urged" the government to propose a Freeze, and that's not likely under the Reagan administration. The movement risks a loss of its credibility if something can't be done before the impending deployment of a new wave of weapons and delivery systems. Yet, it is argued, forcing the administration's hand — by a cutoff of funds for new weapons, for example — would amount to a unilateral, not a mutual, freeze. And that would cost the movement much of its broad support. Others argue that the movement is already being manipulated by those who pay lip service to the Freeze while continuing to support new weapons deployment.

All of this tends to obscure the fact that the Freeze is wholly inadequate, in and of itself, to deal with the threat of nuclear extinction. The Freeze *really is* only a first step. The next step must be the dismantling and abolition of nuclear weapons, worldwide. This would require general disarmament and the abolition of war. For any nation fearing its existence jeopardized by an enemy's conventional weapons would want a nuclear capability. So the ultimate issue is how to dismantle the sovereign nation-state, with its power to impose its will by violence. This, it has been pointed out, is a major undertaking. Yet there is no way to do less and survive. The nuclear genie is out of the bottle. It will always hereafter be possible to make a nuclear bomb.

We must therefore devise a social system under which no one will again be able to threaten mass nuclear violence. Otherwise, through miscalculation or madness, we will become, eventually, the victims.

So while we are appreciating the very real gains of the Freeze campaign, we should be aware that we are not on the crest of a wave; we are at the foot of a very tall mountain.

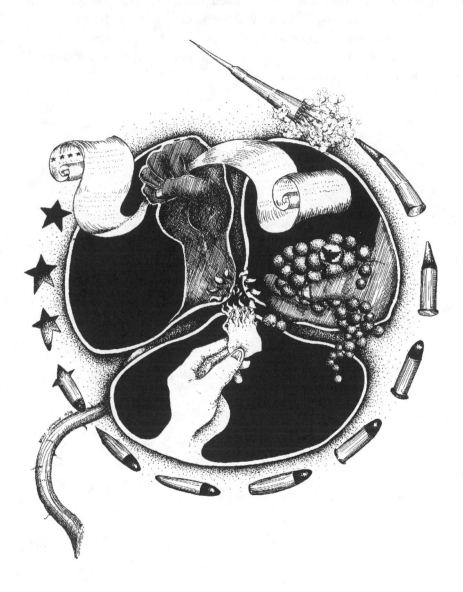

Drawing by Becky LaMothe

Draft Resistance in the Midwest

By Mordecai Specktor

FRANZ JAGERSTATTER, AN AUSTRIAN PEASANT farmer, refused induction in the Nazi army. Jagerstatter took a dim view of National Socialism and, unlike most of his countrymen, refused to assist the new Nazi overlords after 1938. He responded to greetings of "Heil, Hitler" with "Pfui, Hitler."

Jagerstatter was imprisoned in the military detention center in Linz. He was later transferred to Berlin's Tegel prison and then to Brandenburg prison, where he was beheaded on August 9, 1943. He left behind a wife and three little girls, the eldest six years. Today, many see Jagerstatter as a saint, "for he had sacrificed everything — his possessions, his family, and his life — for the convictions of his conscience."

In America young men again are refusing to cooperate with the government's plan for draft registration. Hundreds of thousands have failed to register, thus risking prison terms of up to five years. The government at last report had indicted 14 of the non-registrants.

Early in 1980 Jimmy Carter proposed draft registration in response to the Russian invasion of Afghanistan. President-to-be Reagan denounced registration, but upon becoming Actor-in-Chief, he switched his position.

There have been no indictments in Minnesota thus far. In Wisconsin, Gillam Kerley recently became the eighth indictee for failure to register. While in the Twin Cities, he said, "I felt compelled to resist, because I saw registration as being a step toward war, as part of a rising tide of militarism in the country." Kerley sees his actions in an historical context:

"Civil disobedience throughout the history of the country has been a real positive force, a force of innovation. The Boston Tea Party, the abolitionists who ran an underground railroad, Susan B. Anthony who voted before it was legal for women to vote, Martin Luther King, Jr., Rosa Parks, the freedom riders — we all look back and see them as having contributed a whole lot to society, and having been in the fore-front of social progress."

Phillip Beisswenger, from Nashville, Tennessee, a senior at Macalester College in St. Paul, wrote Reagan recently of his decision to "publicly refuse to register for the draft." He explained, "Mine is a conscientious objection, not to personal involvement in violence per se, but to the monopoly of power that a small syndicate of like-mind-ed, egoistic men have over our lives in this country and abroad."

Asked why he did not simply register and then wait to see if an actual draft developed, then cross that bridge, Beisswenger replied, "Registration is being used as more than a mechanism for a draft. It is also fulfilling a purpose of subservience to a military establishment, through force. It's making young men say, 'I'm in agreement with your purpose,' and giving the decision-making power then to the military concerning their own lives." President Reagan has not responded to the letter, but the Selective Service contacted him through a search of Tennessee driver licenses. Tax records, driver licenses and other means are now being employed by the Selective Service system to locate non-registrants.

In the Twin Cities, U.S. Attorney James Rosenbaum, who will bring forth any future indictments against non-registrants, said in a telephone interview: "All of the cases that have been handed out thus far have been essentially either self-reports, or somebody else reported that person. There has been, to my knowledge, no active effort to go out and obtain the names of people. Most of them have been people who've written letters or made public declarations." Such a situation prompted a federal judge in California to dismiss a non-registration case against David Wayte on November 15. Judge Terry Hatter ruled that the Justice Department was selectively prosecuting only those men who took public stands against registration.

A corollary legal development to registration was a law passed de-nying federal loans and grants to students who have not registered. The law has been scorned by many college and university financial aid of-ficers, saying the law would make them "policemen for the Depart-ment of Defense."

Tying educational aid to registration has been condemned by the Minnesota Student Association, and the Minnesota Public Interest Research Group has filed suit to block the law. The MPIRG lawsuit contends that the law, passed as an amendment to the 1983 Defense Authorization Act, determines guilt without a trial; forces self-incrimination by students; discriminates as to sex, age and wealth; and violates the Privacy Act of 1974, which restrains government agencies from excessive snooping or information gathering.

A lot of people would think if a student doesn't cooperate with the government, he doesn't deserve any help or financial aid. "The problem with that argument is that it ignores the constitutional provisions involved," repies Jim Miller, MPIRG director. "Non-registration may be a criminal act. There are in-place mechanisms for enforcing that criminal law; that is, indictment, trial and conviction, prior to punishment. What you have in this case is the government doing an end run around the whole constitutional framework. . . . You haven't complied with the act, therefore, you don't get financial aid. Well, there may be perfectly legitimate defenses to why the act wasn't complied with. Not to mention that you're going to have tremendous problems with folks who have registered, but nonetheless are not showing up on the government lists."

Draft resistance became widespread during the Vietnam war. Draftees went to Canada or underground. The Minneapolis induction center was bombed. Draft raiders trashed the Hennepin and Ramsey County draft boards (and were never caught). On July 10, 1970, eight draft board raiders were caught in the Winona, Little Falls and Alexandria draft boards late at night. Authorities learned of the planned disruption through an informant and were secreted in the three offices when the raiders entered, intent on destroying draft records. Don Olson, who lives in south Minneapolis, was one of the Minnesota Eight. He spent 20 months in the U.S. prison in Springfield, Missouri. Today he works with the Twin Cities Stop the Draft Committee.

Olson commented that in 1982 the public non-registrants are a thoughtful group who have analyzed carefully the role of the U.S. in world affairs and the implications behind their cooperation or resistance. "We had this phrase during the Vietnam war: 'Use your whole body to stop the war machine,'" Olson recalled. He sees today's outspoken resisters to registration acting on that concept.

St. Paul attorney Ken Tilsen, the "dean of Minnesota draft lawyers," who defended the Minnesota Eight, minces no words on what he views as the vileness of the Reagan administration: "There is a kind of obscenity about our nation today that is identical to the obscenity of the Vietnam war — the government's indifference to the suffering of people around the world."

Jagerstatter, the Austrian peasant, would not cooperate with Nazi power. From his cell shortly before his execution, Jagerstatter wrote a final letter to his wife:

"Greetings in God, my dearest, beloved wife and all my children. . . . I wish to write you a few words of farewell. I beg you again to forgive me if I have hurt or offended you, just as I have forgiven everything. I beg, too, that all others I have ever offended may forgive me. . . . May God accept my life in reparation not only for my sins but for the sins of others as well."

Korean Adoption, an Inside Story

As I brush my hair
Before the bathroom mirror,
I am thinking
About civil disobedience,
Thinking about
Making the world safe
For Korean babies,
Thinking about
Making the world safe
For everyone,
Parents and babies.

I plan a sit-in
At Lutheran Social Services,
Eight couples joined
Arm-in-arm singing
One thousand and one
Choruses of "We Shall Overcome,"
And the agency gives up
And grants us all babies,
Deciding everyone has suffered enough.

Then we shanghai
a Greyhound for DC,
The Minister holding
A hymnal to the driver's head.
On reaching the Pentagon,
We begin marching
Around the visitor's lobby.
We have made signs—
"Make Adoptions Not War,"
"Love Conquers All,"
"Babies Not Bombs."

One couple gets carried away,
Prints "Adopt a Commie for Christ."

"No, no," we say.
"The babies are South Korean,
Not North Korean!"
We change the sign,
"Korean Orphans Unite,
Adopt a M¢ommie for Christ!"
And begin a hearty round
Of "Nuke the paperwork
In the Microwave"
Sung to the tune
Of "Jacob's Ladder."
After 2000 verses,
The Pentagon agrees
To fly us for free,
Finding an extra few thou'
In a "Flush Fund"
Earmarked for overruns
On three martini lunches,
$500 coffee pots,
And $3000 toilets.

Our venture does more
For international relations
Than the last few junkets
And summits combined,
And soon
The Pentagon is promoting
International adoptions
As a last diaper effort
Against Cold War.
Uncle Sam, on the billboards,
Pushes a stroller,
"Nuclear families,

Not Nuclear War,"
Awards fat contracts
To the makers of playpens,
Fills silos in Utah
With rattles not bombs.
Everyone and their babies
Live happily ever after,
While I finish
Brushing my hair.

—Sandra J. Lindow
(Anvil #55)

Something Flies Out of the Cells

Something flies out of the cells
Where the doomed poets lie:
Something tells it like it is
In the bowels
Of the vast nervous amphibious powers.

Human nails day after day
Incise graffiti on the walls:
The legend of decades
Of the lions of silence.

If the poets are strangled
At puberty,
Generations will live in the undersea
Of the blind.

Even the secret police
Cannot change a fact:
Each state is a passing exhibit
In a small sad county fair.

The poet says what he has to say:
The giant does not fall at once
But he always falls,
Wondering why.

The poem has a half life
Of a thousand years,
The prison after a moment
Returns to sand and lime
While the word flies out of the cells
As a dove
From an ark of the drowned.

—Don Gordon
(Anvil #29)

Alternative Life Styles

Changes in life style were in many ways the central preoccupation of the Anvil. *Its broad challenge to industrial society demanded no less. Emerging from the '60s, those who read and wrote for the magazine looked with nostalgia to the rural hippie commune. The vision quickly faded, but voices urging a return to the land remained strong. For people dedicated to "doing it themselves," home birthing and home schooling held great appeal, and both issues were discussed repeatedly. Instructions for gardening, preserving food, managing wood lots, building homes, using wood stoves, raising milk goats, installing windmills, and other "how to do it" pieces were also enduringly popular.*

Stories and poetry touched on life style issues more delicately and indirectly, sometimes with humor. It was there that the personal questions got raised — the pain and frustration and sense of alienation from a culture that seemed blind to human values. There, also, one found reference to issues that proved awkward for some in the alternative movement — like the farmer's relationship to animals and the mystique attached to hunting in rural America.

To the first number, in June, 1972, a young Minneapolis woman who identified herself only as "Sun-Fire" contributed an account of life in a commune at Georgeville, Minnesota, which is just off Highway 55 in southwestern Stearns County. In number 3 (1972-73), a story by Curt Johnson posed a poignant question as to who is the real "Trespasser" on the earth. In number 5 (1973), an early testimonial from one of those who had tried living off the land concluded that "Homesteading in the North Woods" was no picnic. Interviewed by Michael Eliseuson, the struggling subsistence farmer preferred to remain anonymous. A brighter story of "Reviving a Country Store" in rural Wisconsin was told in number 17 (1976) by John Marks. Finally, in Anvil *number 57 (1988), Janis Thesing wrote a haunting recollection of life with a pair of other hippies in an abandoned farmhouse south of Winona and of her return to the place years afterward.*

Photos by
Brad Christian

The Georgeville Experience

By Sun-Fire

WE BEGAN IN 1968 AS a commune on the West Bank, associated with Stone Age Industries, a craft store on Cedar Avenue. We had chosen to live communally in order to share our lives, our interests and our possessions.

When we were evicted from our home by the housing authorities for having too many unrelated persons in one house, a man came into Stone Age saying he had a good building for a commune in the tiny town of Georgeville, 100 miles west of the Twin Cities. We went out to see it.

It was an old brick building which had been a farmers' cooperative; a general store and bank, a bar and dance hall during the '20s. There was no heat, no workable plumbing. Dirt and litter lay over the floors. Snow was piled to the second story along the north wall. But it was big and in the country, and there was an acre for a garden.

The first group moved in during January, 1969; five men who were so scared in the ratty, dark old building that one of them slept with a shotgun beside him. They put in oil-burning space heaters and got the plumbing together somehow, and soon more people went up.

There were about 30 of us in the beginning. The number swelled to 45 that first glorious summer. The brothers outnumbered the sisters about two to one. Our ages ranged from 17 to 28 — high school drop-outs, college drop-outs and graduates, and one PhD. A year and a half later we had half a dozen infants and a couple of post-30s.

Whoever came was accepted and blended into the group as well as possible. Some were expelled by a rising tide of personal and group outrage after weeks or months of anti-social behavior (refusal to relate to people or to daily work; social or material destructiveness).

At first we tried consciously to have group meetings. We found they didn't work well for us. So mostly we lived and worked together on a free basis, coming together when we happened to meet on common ground. This was more or less often between individuals, but pretty often on the whole since we became very close friends.

We never had a schedule or sign-up sheet for anything. Everybody did what they thought they should do. Everything eventually got done. If anyone thought someone definitely wasn't helping enough, they hassled him or her. Most people participated in daily work.

Like the rest of nature, Georgeville flowered and grew in the summer. Starting our own garden was an important step on the road to freedom; freedom from the prices and poisons of commercially grown produce, freedom from the necessity of working an 8:00-5:00 schedule to support ourselves.

We gathered horse and cow shit from the old manure piles and by cleaning barns for neighbor farmers. We spread it on our land, then plowed and harrowed. On a grey blustery day with a cold wind sweeping in from the northwest about six of us strode out across our seemingly vast expanse of dirt. We stopped about two-thirds of the way across the garden and began our first work with Mother Earth.

One woman stood calling directions from Robert Rodale's *Organic Gardening* while the rest of us struggled with the seeds: How deep do they go? How far apart? Few of us had ever done anything like it before.

The Georgeville family spent long hot hours working in their field to raise food for themselves and for what they called their "quiet revolution."

We learned to garden by the moon, planting such crops as greens or cabbage or broccoli in the first quarter. Planting crops which carry their seed inside the fruit such as tomatoes or melons in the second quarter, and planting root crops like carrots or potatoes during the third quarter. The fourth quarter was best for cultivating or destroying weeds or pests. One year we were running late and planted some treasured yellow watermelon seeds in the fourth quarter. Not one came up.

The days grew warmer and, wondrous surprise, the garden grew abundantly. The West Bank faded out of existence. Our world became a carrot patch needing to be thinned, weeded and watered.

We tied about 50 tomato plants on stakes. We got bales and bales of straw for mulch, laying down six inches of straw between rows and for paths through the garden. This way the weeds didn't grow up again, and moisture didn't evaporate so quickly during what turned out to be a long very dry summer.

Amateurs though we were, we had one of the best gardens in the county. There were carrots and onions and corn, green beans and peas and tomatoes, melons and summer squash and winter squash. And we had lettuce, sunflowers, cauliflowers, cabbage and beets. We ate a lot, gave a lot away, sold some, and canned nearly 800 quarts.

There were good times too, when we went bicycling, or on picnics en masse, swaying down country roads in an old one-ton truck. We sewed and cooked and washed thousands of dishes, hayed, fixed cars over and over again, and most of all, talked, sang, smoked, and drank beer . . . with anyone: friends and strangers, wandering hippies, motorcycle gangs, farmers, runaways, and even sometimes some very nervous visiting relatives.

The neighbor's pond was our summer's delight. At dawn people would go loping off down the quarter mile of gravel road to the pond. As the hot hours of summer wore on and our clothes wore out, we took to swimming naked. You'd just slip out of tattered shorts or dresses and slide or splash into the cool water. What a joy to be free of that final barrier between eye and skin, or skin and skin, and to laugh and play like guiltless children!

The pond was several hundred yards off the road. Passers-by still managed to see by driving back and forth and craning their necks. Our neighbors finally firmly requested we keep our bodies draped.

We brewed our own beer, made dandelion wine, and grew our own weed. We did psychedelics but no hard drugs, no speed, no hard liquor. The grass became more a group ritual than anything else. I can remember sharing three joints with 28 people and getting high.

Sometimes there was too much dope and too much loud music brought up from the Cities. Then the Georgeville people would O.D. (over-dose) and go sleep it off, leaving the others to amuse themselves.

The women were very close that first summer. We used to go to a field near the railroad tracks where we couldn't be seen from the road and sunbathe in the nude. The railroad men started coming around in their little cars, asking if we had any beer and if we wanted to party. We didn't. So we stopped our sunbathing.

Though there was a lot of talk, mostly by men, about communal sex, it never happened. Couples were monogamous. Most who had children have remained together for years now.

When winter came, the group narrowed to about 12 people. Winter was like being on the edge of a cold distant planet. We huddled around a wood stove, talking of gods and gardens, of governments that must fall to be replaced by peaceful cooperatives. And finally, we learned to love and trust each other.

Our winter sport was taking saunas. We built one in the basement using two oil drums for a woodstove. We'd build a roaring fire, then we would sit and sweat until the heat was unbearable. Finally we would hose each other down or jump into tubs of cold water. Some even rolled in the snow, following the Scandinavian custom. Some of us loved the sauna and gained great vitality from it. Others complained that it felt good only when they stopped.

When we first came to Georgeville, we were still into white flour, white sugar, and meat. The meat went first because we couldn't afford it. Later on many of us became principled vegetarians. We were already baking our own bread and eating brown rice, so white flour was just gradually replaced by more nutritious whole wheat flour. We went from white sugar to brown sugar to only honey in our quest for good health. Herb teas replaced coffee. We bought a grain grinder from the *Whole Earth Catalog* and ground fresh flour for our bread. The women did all the baking and meals at first, but after a year at Georgeville most of the men made bread and began to cook too.

Communal meals were a time to share both our lives and the cooking we'd learned. For breakfast we usually had oatmeal with raisins or apples cooked in. Sometimes there were pancakes. I liked to get up early and mix a batter of water, whole wheat flour, brown rice flour, oil, sesame seeds, and salt. The woodstove had to be blazing hot for the griddle to be just right for the pancakes. By the time I'd cooked a nice stack, the kitchen was warmed and several people would be milling around getting out plates and forks, filling water or milk jugs, or cleaning off the low table and setting out honey and butter.

On Sundays we'd take hours making waffles, just a few at a time. We'd scrounge up a couple dollars and send someone into town for the big Sunday paper and maybe even butter and frozen orange juice. Then we'd sit, read, and talk while the waffles came off the griddle.

After breakfast two or three batches of bread were begun so there'd be hot bread and vegetable soup and, in summer, salad for lunch. When we rang the gong, people would come streaming in from the garden, the yard, or the road, or we'd hear them come thumping down the stairs from the second story. Rice, beans, and vegetables were standard fare for supper. The vegetables were sliced and stir-fried in a bit of oil in the wok (a large bowl-shaped Chinese frying pan). We had eggs and cheese only occasionally, and never enough fruit. A good friend once brought a whole case of apples from the city on his visit. A delicious surprise!

Birthdays were always special occasions. We'd have an especially delicious meal with whole-wheat birthday cake and candles and wild flowers on the table. People would bring in beautiful little hand-made presents: a shirt, a dress, beads, a god's-eye, a pot, or flowers, or drawings, or an astrological chart, or a book or a long-treasured object. Love came beaming from every face as we sang the traditional birthday song.

There were hassles too.

Whose fault was it when the old cars broke down? Why so few trips to town? There's a pile of dirty dishes no one wants to wash. The goddam dogs are bugging the neighbors again. And the cats are shitting around the house. And money was a problem sometimes. We argued with the landlord over his politics; he claimed to want a free state, Utopia, he called it, but he still insisted we pay the $100-month rent.

We put up a sign, "Wash Your Own Dish and a Few More." And there was "The Great Animal Dispute" between animal lovers and people who wanted to get rid of the pets. And there was the everlasting problem — relating to tourists and guests.

We would get up to 500 tourists on a Sunday in the summer. They came to buy our crafts and sewing, pottery and leatherwork, woodwork and beads. But they came more to stare at psychedelic stoves, barefoot woman hippies, and our wild-haired men. What with crash-ers and tourists some of us often felt like underpaid staff of a Hippie Hilton.

We got along all right with the local people. The kids were happy and excited to have us there. The older folks were more wary but still curious. We would work for some of them if they asked but would not accept money. They'd give us eggs and milk, and one farmer for whom we worked a lot gave us a cow.

Only one sour couple across the backyard refused to accept us . . . They called the county sheriff several times for real or imagined in-fringements of the law. The old fellow wouldn't sell gas to us from his station. And his wife became dramatically offended if we spoke to her at all. She would lift her nose, rush into her house, slam the door, and pull the shades. We shattered their reality. They never forgave us. One of our communards painted "LOVE THY NEIGHBOR" in huge let-ters high on our wall facing their house.

In the spring we began our gardening and pottery work in earnest. There were several good potters at Georgeville. We had two wheels and built our own kiln. Firings were always tense and magic evenings, with the potters hurrying in and out with smoke smears on their faces. We would go out to the kiln shed and squint through a tiny hole into the raging fire inside the kiln. Would we have beautiful new pots or a mass of sagging muddled lumps? The firing would take nearly 18 hours, then the kiln had to cool for a day before it could be opened. The potters were never satisfied with the results, except for a special pot or two. The rest of us were delighted. The tourists were delighted too.

In the spring of 1970 my child was born on a Saturday night. It was a high, holy time shared only with the family and friends. Most went quietly on with their daily work. Some sat meditating outside my room. I could hear flute and guitar music drifting through the evening.

Two other babies were born later that summer, each echoing the joy of the first-born.

The summer after the babies were born we decided to separate. The children needed more attention than could be given them and the commune too. Some people felt they were being psychically seduced to give more of themselves and their property than they wanted to give. Gradually we have all drifted back to the city.

Georgeville was more than an isolated living experience: it was a seedbed for communalism. On April 14, 1970, the first meeting was held at Georgeville of the people who were to become *Hundred Flowers*, the longest existing alternative publication in Minnesota. Other people from Georgeville started the People's Pantry and helped with five other food co-ops in the Twin Cities area. And other people yet helped found the People's Company Bakery and a West Bank fabrics and notions store, Northcountry Dry Goods.

The big building has been pretty much abandoned since the fall of 1970. There are three people in a small frame house we bought. They should be headed east soon. After that the garden will sit rich with three summers' composting, untilled. There will be apple trees, an herb garden, a strawberry patch, and grape vines waiting . . .

American culture emphasizes our differences. Georgeville showed us how alike we are: the human family, manifestations of The Spirit in different bodies. We learned to be a part of the cycle of nature, a part of the ebb and flow of the seasons.

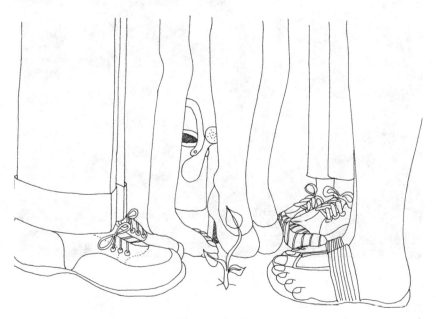

Photo by Jack Miller

Trespasser : A Story

By Curt Johnson

IN DE VALLS BLUFF, ARKANSAS, they brag about the White River fishing. The White River runs east of town and there is supposed to be some of the best fishing in the world there: blue channel cat and bass and bream and — for those who want them — alligator gar. Fishing for alligator gar is done for the sport of it. You hook a gar and it comes boiling up out of the water and fighting all the way in. It sounds and then runs at you, gills open, and surfaces again and sounds and so on. But when it's landed all you have is a long, heavy, ugly catch of scales. You don't ordinarily eat gar; you do eat bass and channel cat.

Occasionally the White River crowds over its banks and floods the low lands. It used to be that at times even the old highway into the Bluff got flooded over. When the river subsides it leaves ponds and small lakes behind and these hold captive fish which are easy feeding for those gars also left behind.

The Bluff itself is situated on high ground, so its citizens don't have to worry much about being flooded out. In fact, many of them look forward to a flood now and again because there is less food in the ponds left behind than in the river and, therefore, better fishing. But there are people on the east bank of the White, the low side, who are inconvenienced very much by the flooding.

One old man, elderly at least, had a shack in the timber a little over 200 yards from the east bank and every year he had a wet time of it. In the really bad years, ever since the new highway, you could get to his cabin by land only two or three weeks out of the fifty-two. This man, Thomas, had been in France during World War I. When he came back he first worked as a handyman in the Bluff. Then the Depression forced him to move his wife and belongings out of town across the river to government land, where living was free.

He built a house from mill scraps and next to his house he placed an eight-foot-square tank made out of old metal road signs. He stocked the tank with worms and went into business. Every day he sat beneath a tarp stretched between his house and the tank, waiting for customers. He developed an extraordinary sense of patience; his wife, with him.

When the old highway was still in use and a fisherman wanted a nickel's worth of worms, he turned off the highway to "Buzz's Place" — spelled BUS'S PLASE on the old man's sign.

At the bottom of the Depression, the White River, during one of its floods, threatened to change its course entirely. When it finally went down again the army engineers were called in. The engineers lined the banks with rip-rap and sank rock on mats in the river and drove pilings and after that the river held its course. Then the engineers paved a section of new highway paralleling the old on higher ground to the south and finished their project by constructing a new bridge into the Bluff.

During this construction Thomas worked fifteen hours a day. Other than his service in France during World War I, it was the only steady job he ever held. When the work was completed he went back to his post in the chair under the tarp, only now — from the new highway — there was no convenient turnoff to his stand so his business dropped to almost nothing.

The next year, the army, as a reward for its efforts in checking the river, was permitted to use the abandoned section of the old highway in a demolition exercise. Its experts buried several tons of high explosive under the old highway and moved Thomas and his wife into temporary quarters over the rear of a tavern in the Bluff and then they set off their charges. There was a loud explosion and many fish in the ponds next to the old highway were killed by the concussion, but not much real damage was done except that the reinforcing rods of the 39-year-old highway were left jutting from its surface.

When the Army left, Thomas and his wife moved back to their home. They cleaned up the litter in their yard and shored up the roof of their house, which had been left with a slight sag by the force of the explosion, and things went more or less back to normal for them. Except that now their house was completely cut off from the new highway by the snarl of reinforcing rods in the abandoned section of the old road. So Thomas got rid of almost his whole stock of worms and turned for a livelihood to turtle-trapping and fishing.

In time he and his wife became accustomed to their isolation. Their life was somewhat lonely, but they were content with it and with each other. They got their food from the river, their fuel from the timber, and the occasional sale of a turtle or fish supplied the little cash they needed. They bothered no one and no one bothered them.

Their days had a careful pattern and they depended upon each other to see that this pattern was not disturbed. They arose, they worked, they ate, and they slept. They made do with their lives and they were happy enough.

When his wife died Thomas considered burying her in the river but decided against that because of the gar and the turtles. He did not take her to town and the cemetery because he could not afford to bury her there. He finally decided on a site beside the house.

He took a mattock and dug a grave for her in the center of the enclosure made by the rusting metal sheets of the old tank. He was not a young man and it took him some time to finish and when he did and had buried his wife he sat down in the chair by the tank and rested. He smoked a pipeful and then, after a time, he got up and went to the river and set the snag-line he put out every evening. When he came back to the house he went to bed.

The dry summer was very hard on the Southwest. There was no rain in some areas for as much as eighty days, and it was very hot. Around De Valls Bluff the rice farmers were sitting tight and hoping. Their hope was that their wells would carry them through, the dire possibility being that they might not. This feeling of apprehension was shared by the goldfish-farmers in the area. They raised crops of goldfish for the market just as the other farmers raised rice — with plenty of water. And water was hard to come by that summer.

Unfortunately, it was that summer in which the telephone company brought to fruition three years of planning for a coaxial cable between Memphis and Little Rock: through the conduits of Memphis, underground across Arkansas, and into the conduits of Little

Rock. It was a big project and the telephone company had spent much money and hundreds of man-hours preparing for it. They did not look kindly upon the dry summer; it interfered with their operations.

The telephone company's right-of-way agents were sent out in the early spring to obtain easements. These right-of-way agents were fine fellows. If we cross your front lawn, they told you, we put down a canvas and take up the sod in rolls and put the dirt on the canvas very neatly and when we're done, every particle of dirt goes back in its proper place. Sod too.

The cable-laying itself was done by a plowtrain led by an oversize tractor upon which was mounted a giant share, two smaller caterpillars ahead on either side, pulling. The share on the big tractor ditched out an opening slightly less than a foot wide and about five feet deep. The coaxial cable was reeled out into this ditch and then the ditch was covered over by other cats and dozers. Under ordinary conditions the plowtrain was a marvel of efficiency and speed.

The other side of Forrest City the plowtrain ran into trouble. Twice it became mired for a day at a time, once in a rice field and once in a field of goldfish. The most serious delay given the train, however, was the day-to-day obstinancy of the rice farmers. This was what proved to be the most unfortunate consequence of the telephone company's bringing their plans to fruition that dry summer.

More than once it happened that the plowtrain, in going through a field, lost almost all of the field's water. Word of these local disasters spread quickly ahead of the train along its intended route and then, in spite of the fact that easements had long before been obtained by the right-of-way agents, it was not uncommon for the telephone company to be met at a fence by a farmer with a shotgun cradled across his arms.

In some cases these gun-bearing farmers had to have it explained to them many times over that the men from whom they rented the land had already legally granted the company the right to cross over the field and that therefore the train had a legal right in the field. And most of the time, in spite of these repeated explanations, the farmers would not budge out of the way.

Because it is difficult to assess the amount of damage done to a field of rice by the loss of its water in midsummer, even if that loss is only for a day, the telephone company faced with some reluctance the prospect of a multitude of claims against itself at harvest time. As a result, the plowtrain slowed to what for it was a crawl, taking extreme care of the dikes in each field that it was allowed to enter.

For several weeks the cats and dozers sat in a fallow rice field watching with mechanical indifference the herons in the next field feasting upon goldfish and frogs. The splicers behind the train were almost out of work and the General Manager in the telephone company's area headquarters in Kansas City had begun to hope for rain almost as fervently as the farmers.

When the train came to a halt, the only ditching going forward on the Memphis-to-Little Rock coaxial anywhere was just outside of De Valls Bluff in the timber next to the White River. There it was too thickly wooded, overgrown with scrub, and too uneven for the plowtrain to maneuver, and the ditching had to be let to a private contractor who worked with a dragline. So when the plowtrain was halted and its equipment left in the fallow field, the train's crew was sent to help the private contractor.

Cable had been laid across the White River, on top of the Engineers' mat, and it was the contractor's job to join this White River section with the section paralleling the new highway, which had also been placed. The contractor had to work through the snarl of the old highway as well as the underbrush and the timber and it was slow going.

The private contractor had his trench almost completed after three weeks' work — all but a stretch of about sixty feet, part of which was up and over the swell of ground on which Thomas had built his house. The contractor had worked his dragline without haste and dug a deep and a wide ditch. Deeper and wider than was necessary. He had worked slowly. At his own pace, that is, until the day that the management group from the General Manager's office in Kansas City came to the Bluff to look into the reasons for delay there and everywhere else.

When the group from Kansas City arrived, the private contractor — a citizen of De Valls Bluff — proceeded even more slowly than before, because he wanted no mistake made: He considered himself his own man, and the only operator between Little Rock and Memphis who would risk his equipment in the White River bottoms, even in a dry year.

But the arrival of the management men from the General Manager's office in Kansas City did produce a flurry of activity among the train crew. They wished, naturally enough, to make a good impression upon representatives from the front office. Preceding their accelerated work tempo there was, of course, a great shaking of hands when management met labor the first morning of the visit. Management in the telephone company — as perhaps elsewhere — operates on the theory that they are part of a great team. The team theory holds that the lowliest switchboard operator in the smallest exchange in the country is no less important than is the president of the entire system himself. Management has a saying which is often repeated in its offices to the effect that One Doesn't Meet Finer People Than Those Who Work for the Telephone Company. Since management seldom meets any telephone people other than those from its offices, management considers it an important part of any field-trip task to Meet and Make Friends with the Men. Thus, the shaking of hands.

Particularly was this spirit of camaraderie shown by the senior member of the group from Kansas City, Mr. Stanton, a tall, well-built gentleman of around forty-five, head of the area's personnel department but being groomed for an even more responsible position in the White Plains main offices. Mr. Stanton made a special point of being friendly and cordial to members of the train crew, even going so far as to pitch several spadesful of earth upon one occasion.

Before leaving Kansas City, Mr. Stanton had taken the trouble to have it ascertained for him who, among the train crew, owned stock in the company. At the river site, when the opportunity presented itself, he let it drop, man-to-man, that he also owned a few shares of stock and wasn't this delay a dirty shame. "We're all in the same boat, aren't we?" he said. "Have to watch our dividends next year if we're not careful" — this last, with a confidential, low-throated chuckle.

The men from Kansas City had made their field trip to determine at first hand the causes of delay in placing the cable. They had talked with the splicer foremen along the route, looked at maps and reports, and were concluding their investigation with a two-day stay at the White River site. By noon of their first day there, the private contractor's dragline had reached the bank of the swell on which Thomas had his cabin.

Thomas had observed the approach of the dragline with interest. He had pulled his chair to a place in front of the old tank at the side of his cabin and he would sit there smoking his pipe and watching in front of and below him the huge claw of the dragline gouging away roots and dirt. He was reminded of his work for the army engineers during the Depression.

After lunch of the first day that the group from Kansas City was on the site, the dragline operator began to trench up the bank of the swell upon which Thomas's cabin was situated. By two o'clock he was up the barranca and there he was forced to stop. Thomas was in his chair, quietly smoking, and directly in the path of the dragline. The group from the general manager's office was standing to one side of the cab of the dragline in conference with the foreman of the train crew. The operator called to them and pointed at Thomas. The senior member of the group, Mr. Stanton, understood the operator's gesture and clambered up the bank.

Leaning against the cabin was the faded sign from worm-selling days, BUS'S PLASE, and the senior member glanced at it as he smiled and extended his hand. "How are you, Bus?" he said. "My name's Stanton. I work for the telephone company."

Thomas shook the hand and nodded, not rising from his chair in front of the abandoned tank. The dampness of the bottoms had worked upon him so that he looked and moved as if he were older and more decrepit than he actually was.

"Guess you'll have to shove over if we're going through," Mr. Stanton went on in a friendly and ingratiating tone. "Comes pretty close to your shack, I guess." He indicated the path of the ditch. "But we'll have it back-filled in no time." He waited but Thomas made no sign that he had heard.

After a silence of a minute or so, Mr. Stanton bent forward at the waist and said in a louder voice, "I guess you'll have to move, Bus. We don't want that dragline taking a chunk out of you." He laughed and slapped the elderly man on the shoulder.

Thomas looked up at him. He said, "Can you go round?"

The question apparently surprised Stanton because he replied somewhat sharply. He said, "We've got an easement through here. That cable can't go around, the trench has to go through. Right here." He pointed down the center of the enclosure behind Thomas's chair.

Neither spoke for several moments then, and finally Stanton turned and went back down the bank to where the AT&T foreman stood. Two of the train crew had returned from the riverbank where they had been repiling rip-rap over the strip where the cable had gone into the river. They were perspiring and hot and the foreman was lighting a cigarette for one of them when Stanton came up. He related his conversation with Thomas and the foreman replied, "Well, I guess we shoot the old man and tell God he drowned."

This statement seemed to puzzle Mr. Stanton, so after a moment's further consideration the foreman volunteered that the cabin was on government land and that Thomas was, in fact, only a squatter. After making certain that his foreman knew what he was talking about, Stanton climbed back up the bank and again approached Thomas.

"Listen, Bus," he said, "we've got to go through here. You'll have to move, that's all. We're not going to hurt your cabin, just get out of the way."

But as before he received no answer. Thomas had refilled his pipe and sat smoking, relaxed, and looking levelly ahead at the dragline.

"Did you hear me?" Stanton said. "We're going through. We've been held up long enough as it is."

At this Thomas looked up and said, "If you don't mind, you'll have to go 'round." He seemed now somewhat concerned by the insistence of the man who stood over him.

Stanton turned and looked down at the foreman and the men from the train crew. He no longer tried to conceal his anger. "Couple of you men get up here and move this old buzzard," he said. "And pull out this." He pointed to the old signs which formed the enclosure that had been used for worms.

The private contractor shut off his dragline's engine and climbed down from the cab to smoke a cigarette and stretch while he waited for Thomas to move. When the foreman and the two men from the train crew started up the bank, he followed them. The other representatives from the general manager's office in Kansas City stayed below. They were studying a chart of the White River.

When the foreman and the two crew members and the operator had gathered around Thomas, Stanton repeated his instructions. There was then a brief period of uneasy silence because the two men from the train crew did not seem to comprehend their instructions. At last their foreman stepped forward. He grabbed Thomas by the arm. Thomas stood up slowly then, but he did not move from in front of his chair. It was clear that any man there could have moved him easily. Still, he stood there, not aggressively, but seemingly worried now.

Stanton attempted to reason with him once more, but when he received no reply he gave up and motioned to the foreman. It was then that the dragline operator intervened. The dragline operator spoke quite slowly but he kept his eyes fixed upon Stanton's face as he spoke. He said that it was almost three o'clock. He reminded Stanton that in an hour they would be quitting for the day, anyhow, and he said they might as well quit now. He said that living alone for so long had not been good for the old man and that in the morning, if they let him alone for now, he would probably be ready to move of his own accord. He said he did not believe in man-handling the elderly; it didn't look right. He suggested that they drop it for the time being, go into town, and give it a fresh start in the morning.

Mr. Stanton attempted to interrupt the dragline operator several times, and he grumbled at the suggestion that they go into town before quitting time, but in the end he gave in. Not, however, before vowing to bring the sheriff with them in the morning.

Thomas remained standing where he was until they were all out of sight. Then he went into the cabin and returned carrying his mattock, moving as if he were very weary.

When the train crew and the dragline operator and the group from

Kansas City and the sheriff arrived at the site of operations the next morning, Thomas was gone. The sheriff made a short search but could not find him.

Around the enclosure next to his cabin, on the side opposite the cabin, they found a newly dug trench, about two feet deep. It started where the dragline operator had stopped his ditching the day before, skirted at right angles the rusted metal signs which formed the front of the enclosure, paralleled the side of the old tank, made another right angle turn at the rear of the tank, and picked up the original path of the ditch with another right angle.

The discovery of this trench was greeted with laughter. Then Stanton told the foreman to get going before the old man showed up again. The train crew pulled up the rusted metal sheets of the tank and the dragline operator began his day's work. In an hour and a half he had trenched across the swell of ground upon which the cabin stood.

The Little Rock-to-Memphis cable was completed in time to handle part of the heavy Christmas traffic that year. But today — many years later — there are men of the telephone company who still speak of the difficulties they encountered that dry summer.

Mr. Stanton did get the more responsible position in White Plains, where he often related some of the many exasperating incidents which took place during the laying of the Little Rock-to-Memphis. He usually brought in, somewhere, the story of the detour ditch dug by the squatter. As if, as he said many times, you can bend coaxial cable at right angles.

Sometimes he injected still more humor into his narrative by quoting, drawl and all as best he could, the crew member who said of the ditch that if a snake were to urinate in it he would float away. But Mr. Stanton's many new responsibilities did not leave him time for such tales.

In De Valls Bluff they still talk of the dry summer. And still brag about the fishing on the White River, although the year after the dry summer an eight foot, 190-pound gar was caught at Stuttgart. This gar still holds the record for size, and Stuttgart is not even on the White River.

Sometimes in the Bluff, when the dry summer is brought up, someone will mention the cable-laying that year. Whenever this is touched upon the talk comes finally to the digging up of the woman's body next to Thomas's cabin. One who spoke to someone who was there has it for a fact that the claw sheared her in two just at the chest. They agree in the Bluff that it was a terrible thing.

But since Thomas hasn't been seen by residents of the Bluff since the afternoon of the day he stalled the dragline, indignation is usually short-lived. To change the subject, there is always the latest fishing innovation. Some of the natives go out at night now with a flashlight fastened to their boat. The goggle-eyes, in jumping at the light, flop right into the boat.

Photo by Brad Christian

Homesteading in the North Woods

By Michael Eliseuson

IN NORTHERN MINNESOTA, a "down on the farm" life may be impossible. The dream you have of a small self-sufficient farm cuddled betwixt pine and birch may be just that — a dream.

The family in this story is real. The father ran away from the Good Life and the American Dream. Where once he had been a PhD candidate pruning his way through the halls of ivy, now he and his wife would farm and cultivate a life of freedom and fulfillment.

They bought 80 acres of land in Itasca County for $3,200. The home they made for themselves and their four children, ages 8 to 13, is a two-story cedar log cabin, 12 feet by 24 feet. The original cabin on the place had burned down in the 1920s and they rebuilt it. Some of the original logs were used and more were cut from the nearby forest. When it was finished they had bedrooms above, pantry, tool room and combination dining room-kitchen on the ground floor. Heat is furnished by a woodburning cookstove; another woodburning stove stands nearby to provide extra heat in the winter.

For milk, they bought a cow and planted hay to feed it. A few chickens, ducks and geese were added. over the next three years they acquired another cow, two pigs, a donkey and a goat. Two calves and six piglets followed, and they were able to butcher some animals. They wanted to live as people did a hundred years ago. They wanted to "live off the land."

"Is subsistence agriculture possible up here?" I asked.

"No! — only for Troglodytes!" responded the father. "You can't make it without some form of welfare."

He poured coffee and I asked if it was Folger's.

"Yah. Mrs. Olson comes over every day. We're coffee freaks in the winter. We drink 50-60 cups a day."

He believes welfare is anything given to you. Whether it comes from your parents or the government doesn't make any difference.

"The only thing we take is food stamps. I wish we could get along without them." He stood up to pour coffee and added: "You have to rip off the land to survive. The soil is only four inches deep on top of clay. We can't raise enough grain for the cows and pigs unless we mechanize — and we don't want to."

They considered buying a team of horses but gave up the idea. "You become a slave to the horses. They make you work and it takes half an hour just to harness them. You can't just switch them off and on like a small tractor." I drank some more coffee and listened. "People don't realize the hours and hours of boring drudgery and hard work — day after day — just to survive this way. You have to do it, though."

We talked about what it's like to have a number of dreary, repetitious chores to perform:

"I fantasize while I'm shoveling the shit in the barnyard. I fantasize while I'm cutting brush. I call it swamp sculpture. I've been cutting alder out of the swamps with a brush axe. I want the cedar to come back in. Somebody cut the cedar out in the 1920s and the alder grew in. Alder is bad because it's so shady and drives everything else out. I feel it's my responsibility to the land to improve it where I can. I spend four to five hours every day after morning chores just cutting alder and piling brush. I've been doing it for two months . . . I make trails everywhere through the alder. The kids can wander around on their own mystery tour and don't have to worry about getting lost. Doing something like this keeps my head together."

He sat down again with another cup of coffee. Every cup brought forth another topic:

"The peace movement is in pieces. Dope is a rip-off and dealers are profit-motivated." He feels closer to the establishment than to longhairs, hippies and freaks. "If you want something done, see the shorthairs. I went along with a hippie to look at 160 acres of tax-forfeited land he wanted to farm. It was in the late fall — cold and crisp. We saw one grouse on the way in. The freak started shouting, 'Food for the Revolution!' . . . No, they don't realize the boring drudgery of farm work. If freaks from the West Bank of Minneapolis think they can come up here and live off the land they're crazy!"

He offered some examples of the problems involved in ecological farming:

"For $15 we could have bought enough grain for our pigs, but we tried to grow it ourselves. We planted one acre of oats — it's not supposed to grow well here. Anyway, we grew a beautiful field of oats. Then we raked it together and bound it into sheaves. We flailed it by hand — we did everything by hand — the whole family worked hard, but we couldn't get the husks off. We tried everything and all we got was poor oatmeal. When it was all over we got about three cents worth of oats for every hour of labor."

Over another cup of coffee he told me about the hog pasture:

"Instead of buying grain we put our two pigs and six piglets in a two-acre pasture. Doing it this way I'll probably come out ahead in 25 years. So, you don't do it for profit, you do it because you think it's better. We try to be as self-sufficient as we can. We butcher our own cows and pigs. As inflation increases, subsistence farming becomes more practical.

"We have no debts. We built our cabin for less than $100. The roof is shingled with plates from printing presses — they cost five cents each. If the house falls down in 20 years, what the fuck! I'll build another one for $100."

I watched with fascination as he poured another large cup of coffee.

"Middle-class Americans will be paying on their mortgages until 1991. They pay on a car for three years. When the car finally gets paid off it breaks down. They have to work when the boss says — they have to keep working just to stay ahead. That's insecurity."

I still wondered if it couldn't be done, but he had the answer:

"The Finnish land co-ops of the '30s didn't make it. They worked hard and were organized. Everybody worked together — cousins, uncles, brothers, and sisters. What happened? The co-ops got bigger and fought the Farm Bureau and in the end the Finns got ripped off."

Finally, I could drink no more coffee. I asked the final question: "Do you feel insecure — like the middle class?"

"Yes, but we have more options. The first thing to learn is that you are the cause of everything you hate. This is the first step toward self-realization."

Katie Mc Mahon

Reviving a Country Store

By John Marks

KATIE MCMAHON AND I DIDN'T move to the land with the idea of starting a country store. We started out on separate farms in this very rural area of southwestern Wisconsin east of Winona and north of LaCrosse. Katie had come about the time the first back-to-the-land "hippies" moved in, some six years ago. Katie got to know a lot of people in the area by working various jobs — especially by cooking at the supper club in Ettrick. I've lived in the area more than three years and have come to know a lot of people by working for farmers and by clerking the monthly consignment auctions at Franklin, three miles up the road from the hamlet of Hegg, where the store is located. Katie and I each had part ownership in farms a few miles from Hegg. In 1974 she and I lived together and did subsistence farming.

This area of Wisconsin is pretty remote, but a large number of alternative culture people have moved in. The Stephen Gaskin communal farm — one of the largest communes in the country — is just four miles from Hegg. And there are many other new homesteaders in the surrounding area. We've all hit it off especially well with the local people, and partly as a result, the place is becoming a thriving new community. In the year our store's been going, it has become a community center, with space for people to meet and talk. There are weekly men's and women's meetings, a political study group, a weekly painting get-together, a community sauna bath and a lot of work-exchanging. We're also starting up a bakery at the store and hope some day to have a restaurant upstairs. We're talking about having a farmers' market on the front porch of the store this summer. People at an Amish community nearby have started making bulk food orders through the store. A number of people are unhappy with the local school at Blair and several households have begun sending their children to an alternative school at the communal farm.

Hegg is on a county road off Highway 53 between Ettrick and

Blair. It has 16 houses, a blacksmith shop and the store. This area along the upper branch of the Beaver Creek Valley was settled in the 1860s, and in 1880 a group of farmers got together and built the Hegg store. After a few years the store was sold, and it had a number of owners before 1906, when Lars Underheim bought it and ran it for 42 years. With Lars in charge, the store became the main shopping point for people from a wide area between Ettrick, Blair, Taylor and Melrose. People now living here remember, when they were kids, carrying a basket of eggs over the hill to the store and trading for groceries. A country store, is, of course, a general store, and in those days the Hegg Store sold groceries, notions, clothing, material, nails, bolts and other hardware items, gasoline, kerosene and motor oil. It also sold pipe, cutting and threading it until the blacksmith shop took over that business in the 1930s. For many years the post office was in the Hegg Store. For a while, there was a room fixed up in the store where you could get a haircut two afternoons a week.

But the times changed. Horses gave way to cars, and Lars got old. In 1948 he sold out to his son Casper. By the mid-1950s the business had begun a slide that forced Casper to work outside jobs. By the mid-1960s, the store was open only a few hours a day. People drove by Hegg without stopping, taking their business to other towns. The entire area was losing population to the cities, where there were jobs. Chrysler was hiring in Illinois, A. O. Smith in Milwaukee. Young people not interested in farming were moving away and as the marginal hill farms became vacant, no one moved in. Prosperous farms absorbed the less prosperous. There were a lot of windowless houses and leaning barns around.

But now, the population trend in this area has reversed. According to the former chairman of Ettrick township, which includes Hegg, there are more people than there were four years ago. With jobs scarcer now in the cities, fewer people are leaving. In Hegg there are two families with a total of six children who have finished high school, and four of the young people are living at home. In addition, there are now about 75 newcomers living within seven miles of Hegg. These folks have living and working arrangements that include one communal farm, one collective and several partnerships. You might think that such an influx of alternative-culture people to such a small area might create friction with the local folks. But this has not happened.

It is true that during that first summer six years ago, when a woman from Minneapolis moved onto a farm with her 18-month-old son, some local people would drive back and forth to look at the "hippies" they had heard about on TV. The sheriff even showed up one day and said there had been a complaint about co-habitation. But none of the neighbors would sign anything, and the woman and her friends were not bothered anymore.

Since the first summer, there has been no major problem between the long-haired, blue-jeaned newcomers and the local people. This seems to surprise some people. Maybe there are some reasons for the smooth relationships. For one thing, this area of Wisconsin is fresh — there has not been another period when large numbers of outsiders moved in. Also, you need neighbors in the country, and the relatively prosperous local farmers appreciate having more people around to help get in the bales before it rains or to drive an extra tractor during silo filling. Another thing that helps is that all the local people over 40 can remember the last residents of the abandoned farm homes and they can understand that we newcomers are trying to do the same thing, to make it on the land. And finally, the farmers around here are just plain friendly people.

In October of 1974, a woman from Hegg told Katie that the Hegg Store was for sale. At this time, the young newcomers in the area were talking vaguely of creating community, but the only getting together was the occasional potluck suppers or gatherings at the community sauna. When Katie and I went to see the owner of the store we talked about renting the store to start a food co-op or buying club, but for various reasons the Underheims wanted only to sell it. Casper showed us around the building, and it captured us. He told us that other parties were interested. One wanted to turn the store into an antique store, another wanted to sell car parts. We thought it would be a shame if it ceased to be the general store for Hegg.

We talked with friends, but no one seemed able to make the

necessary commitment of energy or money. We thought that if 100 people gave $100 each, that would be enough for a down payment. But the people we spoke to didn't think the store would make it. We then wrote to our relatives, and the response was good. To our surprise. we found that we could buy the store. Katie sold her share of the farm for $6,000; I was able to borrow $6,500 from relatives, and we had about $2,000 between us. That gave us enough to get a mortgage for the rest. The purchase price was $25,000 and our mortgage is for $18,000 over 20 years at 10.5% interest.

We bought the store on January 2, 1975, and the next day began work to clean up the store and the basement. It hadn't been cleaned thoroughly for many years. The color of the main store room was dull grey. After dusting and washing, we painted the ceiling and one wall white and painted the two walls with shelves and the front window wall yellow-gold. We refinished the floors and the shelving. By the end of January we were ready to make our first grocery order, of $2,900, which we had delivered. During the first week of February we put the groceries on the shelves and organized the weekly deliveries of bread, dairy products, wheat, frozen foods and ice cream. On February 7 we opened for business.

Neither of us had ever been in business before, so we had everything to learn. Our idea was to make it so people could buy all of their groceries here, and we kept open long hours to accommodate the farmers. Our hours were 8 a.m. to 9 p.m. every day, with an hour off for dinner and supper. Since that first big grocery order we have used our Volkswagen van to make weekly shopping trips to LaCrosse. We make stops at a fruit and vegetable house, a bakery wholesaler for our flour and molasses, a grocery wholesaler for our canned and packaged items and a clothing wholesaler for gloves, rubbers, caps and socks. We decided to mark up the groceries at cost plus 15%, the frozen food at cost plus 20% and the meat and produce at cost plus 25%. After five months we saw that we were falling behind, so we increased our markups by 5%. At this time we had to get a loan from the local bank of $3,000 to pay our debts.

Now, a year after we started, the business appears to be supporting itself. We do not seem to be falling further behind. A grocery store is a nickel-dime business, and it still amazes me that all those nickels and dimes are enough to cover the $300 checks we write every week. It is apparent that the store will not support much besides itself. If no money were taken out for personal, nonstore expenses, then all the bills could be paid painlessly, with money left over for expansion of the inventory.

Katie does our bookkeeping, and she has finished a rough profit-loss statement for 1975. Our total sales were $52,916; our gross profit was $7,031; net profit — $573. Total money that went into the store is $70,916; total expenses were $68,908. The difference of $2,008 is what we took out of the store for ourselves in food and gas.

We are extremely pleased with how things have gone this year. One of the nicest aspects of a country store is that it becomes a community center. We have a big table with chairs in the front of the store and have plans to buy a wood heater. Many of the people who have moved into the area are used to buying bulk foods from co-ops in the cities, so we have a bulk food counter with such things as flours, beans, oil, peanut butter, molasses, honey and sorghum. People can come in with their own containers and help themselves. Folks come from 15 to 20 miles away to buy these things. We also will order bulk items for people. If someone wants a case of toilet paper, or a 100-pound bag of flour or a pail of sorghum, we charge cost plus 10%. A small nearby cheese factory buys carraway seed and other spices through us.

The next big development at the store will be the bakery. A friend is buying and setting up equipment, and, if the room passes inspection, we should be turning out bread by March.

For the future, we hope that the store can help focus the community's awareness of itself. People here feel that what they are doing is important; that we are on the crest of a breaking wave, and that whatever the future social and political changes, we will be helping to shape events.

More or Less

By Janis Thesing

I DON'T EVEN EXACTLY REMEMBER meeting Walken, just that it was years ago in Winona, Minnesota, and probably at Famine Foods Co-op or the Riverbend Cafe. He told me right off his name used to be Ken, but he changed it to Walken after years of living and "walken" in the hills of Oregon. Well sure, I said, far-out and groovy.

Anyway, he had no car and promised me two kinds of homemade ice cream if I would give him a ride home. I said yes, of course. I love ice cream. I phoned the community of folks I lived with to say I would not be coming for supper, a courtesy that was expected whenever I would be away. It was already dark when we left town. Eventually, we turned onto a narrow gravel road and my '63 Valiant, heaving and coughing, crawled up two miles of deep ruts and craggy rocks.

The farm was at the very top of the road and I could see that the yard was large and grassy and bounded by trees. Then I noticed an odd structure which looked like it could once have served as a wooden wheel on Paul Bunyan's oxcart. It had been cut in half, rounded sides placed on the ground parallel to each other. The pieces were connected on top with wooden benches. I found out later it was a hand-fashioned toy for rocking and teetering. To my left was a junker car and a small square building which looked like a child's playhouse — the sauna, no less. Pretty classy. The house lay straight ahead. It was a cool night and the two-story relic looked warm and inviting. Besides, all that bouncing had made me uncomfortable.

"I'm glad we're here," I said. "I have to use the bathroom."

Walken pointed to a vague shadow I had missed.

"There's an outhouse over there. Or you could just squat." He was urinating on the ground. Geez, we had just met. I fought the stinging nettles on the path to the outhouse. It was a four-seater.

Walken waited for me, then we climbed the shaky cement slabs to the house. I pulled on the porcelain spool handle of that crooked screen door, gave the warped wooden inside door a hard push, and stepped in.

"Hi. I'm Happy."

I believed him. Happy. A tall thin man smiling delightedly, like a child keeping a great fun secret. His shoulder-length hair and unruly greying moustache and beard covered all but his eyes and cheek bones, making him look ancient, yet ageless. He reminded me of an elf, or a Hobbit.

"How 'bout a beer?"

Walken busied himself with making popcorn and I had a chance to indulge impressions of that wondrous kitchen.

On the floor were two hand-crank ice cream buckets, a promise of good things to come. The table was a huge wooden spool, the kind utility companies use to hold cable, and it was littered with bottles of Old Milwaukee and Special Export and a half-empty gallon jug with a homemade label which said "Summit Farm Cider." Next to the jug were a rolled-up baggie full of pot and a pack of cigarette papers, a pouch of Drum tobacco and a bottle cap with a butt in it.

The bare bulb hanging from the ceiling was harsh, but it was softened by the light from a floor lamp in the corner. The wooden floor boards were old and dull. Peeling paper dangled in coils from the walls. The wainscoting was festive in bright rainbow stripes.

To my left was an electric stove blackened and crusty from years of neglectful use. Beyond, in a small pantry, I saw *The Vegetarian Epicure*, *Betty Crocker* and the *Tassajara Bread Book* propped next to each other on a shelf inside the door. Strange bedfellows, I thought.

On the north wall was a single porcelain sink and drainboard. The faucet was missing its handle, but I supposed the pliers hanging on a string nearby was for turning on the water. There were no drainpipes: a bright green five-gallon plastic pickle bucket under the sink served the purpose. On a jagged mirror above were old pictures of Walken, Happy and another fellow I learned was Tom. High school pictures, I guessed. Next to them, on a high shelf, stood four glass gallon wine jugs, each with a partially inflated balloon on its mouth.

I moved to the south wall and the warmth of the wood stove. Hanging from a line above were tansy and herbs and clumps of sumac berries. The wall itself was covered with mirrors. So many mirrors! Kaleidoscopic fragments reflecting everything in broken, infinite fractions, cloudy, like an opium dream. The best one, I decided, was a huge round mirror cut in half by a long uneven crack. Someone had painted a big yellow rising sun on it. A newspaper caption clipped to its side said, "if you want less, tell me."

We ate two kinds of homemade ice cream — pumpkin and apple-cinnamon — and popcorn with butter, and tamari soy sauce and nutritional yeast. We drank cider and beer and listened to Beethoven's Sixth.

"Where's Tom?" I asked.

"He hasn't been around for a few days," Walken said.

"Does he call if he isn't going to be here for supper?"

"Hooome for superrr?" Happy teased me. "When is supper? We don't have any expectations like that. We don't have a phone, either."

Beethoven blended with the quiet. It was so satisfying.

"It's good to be here."

"Yeah."

During the winter I stopped in once in a while, often staying longer than I had planned. I was glad to be stranded there on snowy evenings. It felt good to sit in that warm, wood-smokey kitchen with Happy, Walken and Tom the Vagabond — earthy, mellow men all. We talked and read and listened to Beethoven and ate popcorn. When winter passed, I moved in. I just put my things in an empty room and I was home.

That spring was glorious — the earth erupted in life. Lilac and plum and apple blossoms smelled luxurious. Elm and walnut and shag-bark hickory unfolded in sumptuous new growth. Even the air had an extraordinary energy, a real and tangible quality. There was so much, an abundance of abundance.

Like a loving mother, the soil took seeds and gave back in such profusion — peas and okra, melons and parsnips, beets and Jerusalem artichoke — that we couldn't use it all, though I suppose we tried. Parsley and basil and thyme took their places on the line to dry. Chutnies, relishes and zuchinni pickles, apple butter, blackberry and mulberry preserves and plum jam moved in on the shelves next to the jars of dried beans and lentils and brown rice. The apple press and the two-person saw came out of their dusty corners.

Walken and Happy and I (Tom had wandered off sometime) rotated the neighbor's chores and split the "hired man's" wage of $500 a month, with milk and meat to boot. During quieter times, we meditated and chanted and took saunas or went "walken" the eight miles over ridge tops to town. (My car objected too strenuously to the rough road.)

Then there were the books: Alan Watts, numerology, massage and yoga, Dylan Thomas, Shakespeare, Ram Dass and Swami Rama, the *Tao Te Ching* in three versions and the *Lazy Man's Guide to Enlightenment*. And there were people: friends and strangers. They stayed for an hour or a week. For a time, we wanted nothing. Life was good.

I wonder now why any of us moved on, but we all did. We've taken mates and jobs and mortgages. We're making families. We're still friends. This is good too.

My son is nine. He tells me the best things in life are Reeboks and Fieros, things which cost more than I'm willing to spend. He says what's cool is stonewashed. I tell him I prefer stone-ground and he says I'm weird. His hero is the quarterback of the Chicago Bears. What happened to Kahlil Gibran?

I went back to Summit Farm once, a long time later. The nettles and brush lining the outhouse path had reclaimed the yard. The teeter-rocker lay in broken pieces. The junker car, crumbled and rusty had sunk into itself. The sauna was charred and ashy from a fire. The house, now gutted, stood lonely as a ghost.

I walked into the house and stood in the pile of broken wood and plaster and glass. Some of the sumac and herbs were still hanging upside down on the line, dusty and fly-specked. I saw a piece of paper on top of the pile of rubble and I smiled. I knew even before I picked it up what it said. "If you want less, tell me."

Outhouse Poem No. 1

Lac qui Parle County, Minnesota

The white schoolhouse lies anchored near the road.
On each side, floating, two white outhouses,
like delicate outriggers.
Two thin paths worry away to each.
How marvelous to think of the two sexes,
each with their separate bottoms,
out here on the treeless plains!
There are two sexes! It's a fact!
It's a fact with a white door.
It's a fact with a hole underneath.

—Robert Bly
(Anvil #3)

Now I Know Grouse

Know the legs muscled flat
against their fleshless backs;
know their heavy flight
as I snap ribs, blood
from the thick dark breasts staining my hands;
a shot clinks in the sink.

Know too why you hunt them:
walking tense beside you through the trees,
all of us in line, scanning the gray grass,
ears strained for the clucking rush,
the shotgun butt, the blast,
the tumble of feathers.
They hide well in the grass,
bundles of meat and feathers,
quivering with fear of death.

Know too your squint at the sun,
how you carry a shotgun easy like a pistol
in one hand,
know your shoulders between the rows,
know how you fire without aiming,
eyes on the gray thing you love and kill,
know your brown eyes, crinkled from looking
at the sun, horizons, bottoms;
know the blue firelights in your black beard,
its crispness to my fingers.
Know how you love, and kill.

—Linda M. Hasselstrom
(Anvil #14)

The Drowning

Oh, the winds of November are sharp and chill;
Snow seeps from the sodden sky;
The icy gusts on the rocky hill
Make the barren trees cry.

Ed Brown is leaving with little Bill;
His wife begs him to stay:
It's much too lonesome here until
You come back late today.

I do not think the weather will
Be good upon the lake.
The dozen ducks that you might kill —
Let other hunters take.

Without a word the tank they fill
And get into their boat;
The boy drives fast: it's such a thrill
He doesn't stop to note

How logging for the paper mill
Has left a deadhead where
His small swift craft with whining shrill
Scrapes, tips, and crashes there.

The surface of the lake is still;
A boat drifts to and fro;
It has no master, has no will;
It goes as dead boats go.

Oh, the winds of November are sharp and chill;
Snow seeps from the sodden sky;
The icy gusts on the rocky hill
Make the barren trees cry.

—Florence Mead
(Anvil #16)

Wild West

Trouble is, it's getting harder
and harder to find a good horse —
even the stage to Tombstone is a
Chevrolet. Posses and Indians
will only work for union scale,
the cavalry is fighting hostiles
on the far side of the moon.

Good whiskey must be part of
someone else's dream — most folks
in this town roll funny cigarettes.
You ever hear of dancehall girls
in pantsuits? A schoolmarm
teaching sex education classes?
Wagon trains don't stop here anymore.
There hasn't been a squaredance in years.

On the other hand, the mayor's still
the sneaky little dude who owns most of
the ranches and the only good hotel.
You don't have to travel far to find
a poisoned well. Snake-oil shows and
public lynchings happen almost every day.
There's always a gunslinger or two
ready to prove whose innocence is best —
out along the windy Interstates,
where shadows stretch for miles.

—Mark Vinz
(Anvil # 25)

Blood Plasma Center

1.

"Earn $100 dollars a month!
Help hemophiliacs part-time.
Ideal for students, housewives and clubs.
Become a professional donor now."

If any club has answered this ad,
it's the drunks who meet all day
behind Addison's Bar on Franklin.
They're here like me because they're broke.

Aisles of donors in easy chairs,
their arms attached to plastic tubes
draining into pouches of blood,
the music over the sound system
is the disco version of "Let It Be."

2.

As a nurse sticks my needle in,
I concentrate on "Bobby Sherman Always"
tattooed forever on her wrist,
then stare at the man across from me
as my blood spurts through the clear tube.

He is getting settled in his chair,
leaning back like someone's dad,
adjusting his glasses, reading the paper.
When his needle is inserted,
I expect him to shake his head and say,
"I work all day and come home to this."

He reminds me of my friend Will:
Will who fought in three wars,

was bayoneted in the Philippines and Korea,
Will who is jobless and owes support,
who gave blood here twice a week for months
until it screwed up his gamma globulin.

3.

Why am I here — I'm not broke like Will
or the Indian woman in the hallway
trying to keep her children quiet.
She has already given once within two days
and has hours left to wait.

I thought it would be easier than work,
just show up and do as they say:
let the receptionist assess my veins,
prick my finger for blood,
stand when the doctor checks my heart.

But there is a tiredness I didn't expect
that makes this ten dollars hard to spend
a tiredness that won't be relieved by sleep
like after a day of unloading trucks
or by the steak dinner the doctor recommends.

—Kevin FitzPatrick
(Anvil #34)

The Man Selling Pencils
Outside the B. Dalton Bookstore

I blink, but there he sits, unreal
As an organ grinder or a breadline
In some jerky thirties newsreel.
I thought we had schools for the blind.

His cane looks like a stick of chalk,
But he advertises Pencils, 10 cents.
The shoppers balk. Some stop to gawk.
I wonder if he has a license.

He's creating a disturbance,
But he's oblivious or bored.
He squats there like a dunce
Staring at the blackboard.

I've heard that some can see you
As a shadow or a silhouette
And others make out curlicues
And figure-eights of light.

So maybe he envisions patterns
Like meiosis, weird and lovely,
Like the spiral tracks of protons,
None of us can see.

The window at his back displays
Books no one would read in braille.
The fountain gurgles. Muzak plays.
And he offers pencils for sale.

Some of us buy. Just for kicks.
They don't cost much.
And none of us exist
Unless we speak, until we touch.

—Barton Sutter
(Anvil #43)

Walker Church

"People's Clothes" Co-op

From Communes to Co-ops

Out of the communal spirit of the 1960s and a lifestyle based on serving mutual needs rather than profit, came a "new wave" of co-ops. The beginnings, philosophy, and organization of the alternative food collectives that sprouted during the early '70s in Minneapolis were described in several Anvil *articles. One was an account of "The People's Bakery," by Bob Malles. It appeared in number 9 (1973-74).*

Almost unknown to their founders, these enterprises built on a long north country tradition rooted among farmers and immigrant communities of Scandinavians and Finns. The Anvil *was quick to point this out. In numbers 11, 12, and 13 (all 1974) it ran a series of three articles by prolific contributor Paula Giese, who outlined the 19th-century origins of cooperatives and the rise and fall of successive waves of co-op activity in the upper Midwest. Reprinted as a pamphlet, they were widely read and are regarded as something of a classic among local co-op people. Here they have been combined and condensed into a single essay.*

A watershed event, both for the new wave co-ops and for the alternative movement in the region, was the so-called "co-op war" of 1975. Jack Miller hoped that someone closer to the action would write up the story for the magazine, but no one did. So he himself undertook to pull together the various threads, gleaned from a number of sources. His account appeared in Anvil *number 15.*

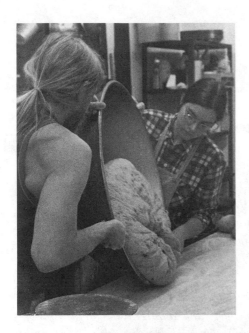

People's
Bakery

The People's Bakery

By Bob Malles

THE MOST SATISFYING WAY TO get good, wholesome, fresh bread is to bake your own, using stone ground, whole-wheat flour. But for the many people who can't, or would rather not go to the trouble, the People's Company Bakery in Minneapolis is making it for them, and at a price folks appreciate.

The People's bread is made from wheat grown in Minnesota by farmers who don't use chemical fertilizers or chemical-spray poisons. This wheat is ground into 100 percent whole grain flour on a small stone mill at the People's Warehouse. While the flour is very fresh — no more than two or three days old — it is taken to the People's Bakery. There it is made into various breads worthy of the name, "the Staff of Life." The other ingredients, in addition to some other whole grain flours, are honey, vegetable oil, yeast, water and salt, with a little slippery elm bark to help hold it together.

You can buy these breads by walking into the bakery at 1534 E. Lake St., Minneapolis, or at any of 11 food co-ops in the Twin Cities and at many affiliated stores throughout the Upper Midwest. The price, considering the premium quality of the ingredients and the process, is amazingly low (even after a recent price increase) — 34 cents for a 1½-pound loaf!

How is it possible for a small bakery to offer bread of much greater nutritional value for much less money than the white breads fed to America by the capitalistic giants? It's easy, really. The new (young people's, hippie, freak) food co-ops do it by working together to serve the needs of the people. The big companies try to exploit every resource — human and environmental — in a constant war for wealth and power. In the co-ops, there are no profits. There are no high-interest loans to be repaid to banks or other institutions: loans have come from people who believe in the co-ops. There are no high wages: people who work in the co-ops for pay get a little more than $1 per hour. And there are no expensive administrators: the co-op workers make all policy decisions collectively at regular weekly meetings and they rotate the task of "coordinator" so that nobody (everybody) is in charge.

This country is blessed with such great natural wealth that even though monopoly capitalism controls almost all of it, a few people can still get together and, with a little hard work, organize an economic sub-system whose basic assumptions are the precise opposite of the big companies'. And because these little co-ops are self sufficient, within a network of mutual support, they can multiply without limit. Maybe it's a little early to be talking about displacing the entire capitalistic economy, but it is entirely possible. The people's co-ops are part of an alternative culture that is challenging every aspect of current American life. The co-op people are offering a vision of collective life that is so much more spiritually satisfying that, to those in the movement, it is the difference between heaven and hell.

The People's Bakery had its birth with the first component of the Minneapolis co-op movement 3½ years ago: the People's Pantry. The pantry began on a back porch in the Cedar-Riverside West Bank area of the University of Minnesota. It soon moved two blocks away to the People's Center, which had been created out of the Andrew-Riverside Presbyterian Church building.

The first baking was done by three Pantry people in the church's two big ovens. They turned out 20 to 30 loaves of bread and about 90 pounds of granola four times a week. The granola was an immediate, flashing success. Sweet and chewy; made from whole grains, nuts and seeds, and costing 45 cents a pound, it soon became a symbol of the movement.

The operation grew. The three bakers were making a "people's wage" of $25 a week. The big gas range at the old church wasn't enough any more. (The range is now in use at the New Riverside Cafe.) So, sometime late that winter it was arranged to rent night-time use of Nebel's Bakery on Lake street near Cedar for $25 a night. A $500 deposit was borrowed from community members and was put up in case the machines were damaged.

Community loans have been our means of raising money ever since the movement began. The People's Pantry began on a borrowed $50, the People's Warehouse on a $1,000. Tens of thousands of dollars have since been borrowed from members of the community — and paid back — for purposes of expansion and in times of special need. Such loans, and the commitment and faith of the leaders, are important to our community as a cultural, economic and political unit striving for complete realization.

In order to pay this large overhead (no rent was paid at the People's Center), it was necessary to increase production and sell the bakery goods at several "straight" grocery stores around the West Bank and Southeast Minneapolis. The granola was packaged in one-pound plastic bags, as was the bread, and delivered to the stores in an old, borrowed panel truck.

During the same winter of 1970-71 the North Country Co-op store had been organizing too. It opened for business on April 8, 1971, at 22nd and Riverside, and grew rapidly all that summer and fall. It wasn't long at all before the Bakery was operating seven nights a week, instead of its initial three, to keep bread on the shelves of our new store.

Soon, more than $500 a month was being paid to Bernie Postuma, the owner of Nebel's Bakery. It was time to get a bakery of our own. So it came to pass that the Dai-Paul Bakery at 1534 E. Lake St. went out of business, and an agreement was signed June 21 to buy the business for $5,500. The down payment was $2,500 with the remaining $3,000 to be paid off at $100 per month.

A two-year lease was signed with the owner of the building at $300 per month. The agreements were in North Country's name, although all the money had been raised by the bakery in a big campaign throughout the community for loans and donations. This was because the co-op was already larger and wealthier, and "established"; it didn't make much difference whose names were on the legal document, as long as we got our bakery.

The bakery opened on July 1, 1971, and expanded so rapidly that on November 1 it was able to pay off the remaining $2,300 to Dai-Paul and own the business outright. At this point the co-op and the bakery wrote an agreement turning over everything to the People's

Company. Looking back, this bit of legalese is an anachronism in the co-op food movement.

The Bakery quickly found itself making more money that it needed to cover costs. It wasn't sure if it should lower the price of the bread and granola, or let the money accumulate and use it to help out where it was most needed, like starting up new projects. The matter was resolved by putting a little card along with each loaf of bread explaining the problem and asking the shopper what should be done. People said overwhelmingly that the bread was pretty cheap the way it was, so we might just as well leave the nickel a loaf in the bakery.

So we did.

The co-ops spread rapidly, and in a matter of months the bakery was employing 30 people and operating around the clock. Several kinds of bread were made: raisin, apple cider, date nut, Russian rye. And goodies like oatmeal cookies, carrot cake, and sesame-date bars became favorites in the community.

The basic operation hasn't changed a whole lot since then, although the flow of dollars varies greatly from month to month and season to season. The wage has gone up to $10 for a day's shift, or $30 a week. It had been $8 for the first two shifts and $9 for the third, making $25 in a week.

In an average month the books might look something like this: $6,000-8,000 gross income, with $2,000 going for wages, $4,000-5,000 for ingredients and $600 for rent, utilities and overhead. The expansion margin of two years ago has been eaten up by continuously rising food prices, which recently forced the Bakery to raise its prices for the first time, to 34 cents for a loaf of bread and 45 cents for a pound of granola. Now the Bakery is satisfied if the checking account stays right near zero. The $1,800 per month in wages means 15 people getting $120 per month.

The work force at the Bakery is usually more than that, say 20 or 30 when you count the people coming and going and not working a full three shifts weekly. There is a list of "regulars" who get three shifts weekly and substitutes who take the remaining shifts on the calendar. The difference is seniority. If a person quits or just doesn't show up for four weeks, the substitute with the most seniority becomes a regular. A person becomes a substitute by just coming in, getting to know the people and the work, and doing volunteer tasks like sweeping the floor and working the "front," relating to customers. Gradually somebody becomes familiar enough to start working shifts.

The $10 per shift rule isn't the only compensation that may be paid. An extra $10 per week child-rearing allowance is provided to those who feel they need it, although only a very few have taken advantage of it. Pregnant women get eight-week paid leave to have their kids and there is a workman's compensation of half pay for bakers unable to work due to sickness or injury.

Each week two people are paid $20 to coordinate the business and they also get one shift. This is just taking care of details such as ordering from the warehouse, getting the store's orders, signing checks, answering phones, etc. The task rotates, with all the workers getting their turn at being management. The ultimate manifestation of management is the weekly potluck suppers and meetings held every Sunday evening at the Walker Church.

The coordinators are just that — coordinating details of the shop's operation. All important decisions are made collectively at the meeting. During the week anybody who sees a problem or wants to change a policy writes the topic down on a sheet of paper that's taped to a cooler in the Bakery. This comes to the meeting and becomes the agenda. Some person will read off the items as the meeting progresses, but there is no chairperson.

A consensus is necessary to decide any matter, which is the way all the co-ops have done it for two and a half years. This is one of the very most important aspects of the movement, I believe. When you don't vote, you don't create winners and losers, majorities and minorities. We are all one faction, one spiritual body, and this is the way we work, in all of our contrasts, to form the whole. Sometimes it's a lot of work coming to a decision that all can live with. The meetings aren't all pleasant, but we couldn't stay together without them.

So, what does it all mean? In the face of corporate monsters like Pillsbury, General Mills, Cargill and International Multifoods, what significance does this one small bakery have?

It might sound as if such co-ops are fine for hippies but not the kind of thing normal people would want to be a part of. This is true at least in the sense that most people can't make their ends meet by working for about $1 an hour (though the co-op counter-culture has developed many services and support mechanisms that make a dollar go a lot farther than in the "normal" world).

But the most radical premise of the co-op movement is that the entire society can be run by people the way the co-ops are, as a kind of anarcho-socialism that envisions a cooperative commonwealth. Whether or not you think such a dream is possible (or desirable), you have to admit that people's control of the biggest industries and the government in this grass-roots sense would make some big changes in the economy. If General Motors and the government weren't wasting billions of our dollars on things we don't need, $1 an hour might be plenty for anyone to live on.

And whatever the possibilities the co-op model may hold for transforming the whole society, it's a fact that right now, the People's Bakery is providing good, whole-wheat bread for thousands of people, including a lot of normal suburban folks.

I believe that the bakery and the other co-ops are living, breathing proof that ordinary people can get together wherever they are and satisfy their basic needs much more completely than the whole range of capitalist institutions. It allows a significant number of us to earn our livelihood doing vitally useful tasks in a creative, cooperative way. It brings us together so we can feel the brotherhood and sisterhood of shared struggle. We have a growing movement that is becoming more and more able to provide basic needs. We started out with nothing but our wits and a spirit of cooperation and built from them a true alternative to bad food and exploitive jobs.

If we can do it, anybody can.

How the Old Co-ops Went Wrong

By Paula Giese

PEOPLE'S COOPERATIVES HAVE THEIR ORIGINS in working-class struggles in the 19th century. The first co-ops represented a peaceful attempt to build an alternative, people-controlled system of goods distribution, an attempt which often looked beyond that to an entirely people-controlled political economy. Most of the present co-ops see themselves that way, too, not only providing a little help in individual struggles for survival, but actively working for an end to exploitation, profiteering, and the hostilities and wars a system based on these generates.

Some historical understanding seems necessary, because the first several waves of co-ops were either destroyed or so thoroughly co-opted as to have become parts of "the system." Yet these often started with strong, hardworking people who well understood the nature of the struggle and had considerable ideological unity among themselves.

The co-op movement started in early 19th century Britain. It developed out of industrialization and the forcing of small farmers from "the common lands," which were enclosed and claimed by the wealthy. It accompanied and sometimes provided the center for labor union and political power struggles. Small farmers who were not making it, unemployed ex-farmers, and small craftsmen were all struggling to organize themselves — to become a self-conscious class — and to survive. Women were in the forefront of struggles around food. Marches, demonstrations, and "bread riots" at marketplaces were common and were commonly led by women. The working class strove to bargain collectively with employers (though often they did not have a clear idea that this is what they were struggling for). Women sought ways to use collective purchasing power to feed and shelter their families without paying huge profits to landlords, owners, grain millers, and middlemen.

Early strikes by stillborn unions were easily broken, because there were large numbers of unemployed people near starvation who would work, or send their children to work, in the mines, cloth mills, and factories. Political action and petitions to government were ignored. Militant demonstrations, marches, and attempts to destroy factory machinery to force employer bargaining brought heavy repression.

At the end of an unsuccessful weavers' strike in 1843, 27 men and one woman (Ann Tweedale) found themselves blacklisted; they could not get any kind of work. They formed a collective discussion group, "The Equitable Society of Rochdale Pioneers," which spent months discussing how their political beliefs could best be translated into action.

From Ann came the suggestion that if they could not organize producers to bargain for living wages, perhaps they could organize them as consumers to obtain food and other necessaries at a better price. From such a beginning, more effective and sweeping changes might grow.

The group was ideologically diverse — Owenites, Chartists, Socialists, Radicals, religious dissenters — and they did not arrive at an ideology all could agree upon. But they did agree on a program. Starting with $140 and a shabby store, ("the Ow'd weaver's hut in Toad Lane") they established an organization that has grown into a worldwide movement.

The store was to be only the beginning. Ultimately they envisioned a society that would "arrange powers of production, distribution, education, and government — in other words to establish a self-supporting colony of united people, and assist other societies in establishing such colonies." (By "colony" they meant a politically and economically independent group within the mother country.) Their goal was a people's state, whose economy was democratically controlled by those whose work produced its wealth. The means to this end — the immediate operating principles — they set down in three "first principles"; experience soon led to others.

We should look closely at these "Rochdale Principles." Virtually every co-op that has grown and flourished has organized itself around them:

(1) *Democratic control* — one vote per member no matter how much capital is put up or how many stock shares are held, and no proxy voting.

(2) *Returns on invested capital* of members shall not be more than

the prevailing bank interest rates; dividends do not fluctuate; and co-op stock is not to be speculatively traded.

(3) *The patronage refund.* After operating expenses are paid and reserves for member education and expansion are set aside, the remainder of earnings is paid out to patrons as a percentage of how much they have bought at the co-op. This principle is generally considered the most important in the success of presently-existing large co-ops.

Of the "secondary" principles, three are particularly important in terms of financial success. They had been drawn from the bitter experience of an earlier Christian Socialist co-op movement, which had grown to several hundred stores, then failed:

(a) *Business for cash only — no credit.*

(b) *Current market prices shall be charged — no price-cutting.*

(c) *Adequate reserves for depreciation, expansion, and unforeseen difficulties shall be regularly set aside.*

The "patronage refund" principle and the three secondary financial principles all have slightly different rationales, but all stem from the same basic problem which faced co-ops then as it does now: how can a poor, weak, and undercapitalized enterprise survive under capitalism?

Cash-only business derived from the trouble co-ops got into when they extended credit: they piled up debts they couldn't pay out of accounts receivable they were unable to collect. Rarely could co-ops rely on the means of the establishment to extract payments from the poor to whom they extended credit. Co-ops that gave credit, therefore, went under. They still do.

The "market value" pricing policy was an attempt to avoid two dangers. One danger was price wars, which the under-capitalized co-ops always lost. Large enterprises could always undercut them and wait them out. The second danger of "lower than market" prices (immediate savings for member-customers) was setting prices too low because of inexperience to cover actual costs.

The "adequate reserves" principle was an attempt to plan for unexpected costs. What is "adequate" is hard to determine, especially if you are trying to expand. But "unforeseen events" might include having your store smashed up by police or burned by a mob led by a government agent. It might include having all your goods stolen, or being cheated on your orders or payments by merchants out to get you. All of these things frequently happened to the early co-ops.

This also supported the patronage refund method of operation, because that allowed co-ops to hold onto their sales revenues and "profits" long enough to tell what true expenses would be, and to have some cash reserves in case of emergency. It also led to an expansion principle: Where possible, co-ops "shall combine their strengths in democratic association for the purposes of wholesaling, manufacturing, and providing services too large to be undertaken by local organizations."

Yet if a co-op is to expand, it must draw in new members and not alienate potential supporters, whatever their politics. So another principle was added: the principle of "political neutrality." As we shall see, in Minnesota this was a double-edged weapon. "Neutrality" is itself a political concept; it favors the existing social order.

The success of co-ops organized in accordance with these principles has been considerable in some ways. In England, by the start of World War II co-ops controlled fully one-sixth of all British retail trade. They owned a bank which lent money, held savings, and financed new co-op ventures. It was next in size to the Bank of England. But these British co-ops were just another bunch of chain stores by that time. In the U.S., co-ops affiliated with National Co-operatives, Inc. (NCI), have millions of members and do several billion dollars worth of business yearly. They include supermarkets, rural electric companies, Land O'Lakes Creameries, and the National Credit Union. The St. Paul Farmers Union Co-operative, started on less than $1,000 raised by members in 1927, distributed to its members in 1970 more than $13,000,000 in patronage refunds from savings made by collective purchase of farm supplies.

Evidently the Rochdale weavers were onto something, in terms of "success" as defined by growth and money. But something got into the co-op movement which drained it of all its early militancy and idealism and which now casts doubt on whether co-ops can be a force for social change at all.

The large establishment co-ops are surely not such a force. Their own literature makes this plain. They repeatedly assert that co-ops are part of "the free-enterprise" system, not opposed to it. NCI co-ops are madly opposed to "communist subversion." During the early Cold War years, Minnesota's commissioner of agriculture praised co-ops to the legislature. He called them a "bulwark against Socialism and Communism." That is what they are now.

The early co-ops certainly didn't start out to be bulwarks against socialism, but to be peaceful means of bringing it about. Yet they became nearly indistinguishable from the institutions they were supposed to replace. A closer look at the American — and Minnesota — record helps to show why. The purposes of the Rochdale workers — for whom co-op operating principles were to be a means to the end of a people-controlled economy and society — those purposes were forgotten entirely, or actively denied.

❖ ❖ ❖

The first important American co-op movement was started by a society of farmers in the agricultural depression that followed the Civil War. It was called the "Patrons of Husbandry," better known as the Grange. Minnesota was one of the first states to have a Granger co-op; an exchange was established for buying and selling farm goods in 1869.

Politically the Grange had little internal unity. There was nothing like the visionary statement of purposes of the Rochdale society, and there was no thought of building a society around collective ownership of the means of production and distribution. Granger farmers were highly individualistic. Granger marketing co-ops were simply a more efficient way than individual marketing to sell produce, providing some chance of more equal footing in dealing with rail and mill robber barons.

As for collective buying of supplies and other needs, there appear to be two financial reasons for the Granger failure. The Granger co-ops did not follow the Rochdale principle of delayed patronage refunds; they passed on savings immediately in lower prices. Grange stores and warehouses were undercapitalized and had no reserves, so they could not survive price-cutting and other attacks launched by well-heeled capitalists. Moreover, several Granger organizations moved into direct manufacture of farm equipment before they were able to handle the technical, financial, or organizational parts of such a venture. Bankruptcies weakened the whole organization and destroyed many farmers' confidence in it.

The next large venture into co-ops was made in the late 19th century by America's first industrial union — the Knights of Labor. The Knights had a broad utopian socialist vision and an ultimate goal of economic and political power for the working class. At the height of their growth, in 1885, they had a million members, and in Midwest urban elections they could call out a much larger vote to support the candidates they favored.

The Knights set up both producers' and consumers' co-ops. The producers' co-ops were intended to give jobs to laid-off and striking workers; the stores sold at a discount to union members. Profits made in sales to nonmembers went into the union strike fund. There were about 300 stores and about 200 small factories in 1885, as the Knights entered the battle to force the steel industry to recognize the rights of workers. The co-ops were seen by the union — and unfortunately, also by Big Steel and Big Rail — as an integral part of the struggle.

Demonstrations and wildcat strikes were met by troops, arrests, lockouts, imprisonment, blacklisting, and murders. By the end of the century, the Knights of Labor had declined to a small group of aging men. Their co-op stores and factories had been burned out, bombed out, wrecked by company agents, forced out economically, or abandoned.

The third American wave of co-operatives — the one that lives on in the NCI group with its "circle pines" emblem — began in the Midwest, with some of its strongest, deepest roots in Minnesota. Farmers and Iron Rangers started this movement. Unlike the Grange and Knights co-ops, this wave did not begin with a large national organization which had broader purposes, but with small groups of people.

There were two kinds of co-ops. One kind tied itself initially to left political thought and action. The other kind — the type of group that has flourished — was primarily interested in economic advantage (or survival) for its members. This second sort of group avoided ideology and politics and saw co-ops as a means of using the capitalist economic system, not as a means of changing it. Farmers' marketing and supplies purchase co-ops were mostly of this type. Let's look at the growth of two such co-ops: Midland Oil and Farmers' Union Central Exchange-Grain Terminal Association.

In 1921 a group of farmers in Cottonwood, Minnesota, organized a gas station co-op, selling oil and gasoline from a rickety pump at a back-street location. The gas co-op was able to return about 20 percent of the purchase price to its members. The idea of gas-oil co-ops instantly took hold among midwestern farmers. Gas, oil, and fertilizer (around which a battle was also being fought, mainly in Indiana) are the main farm operating expenses.

As the small gas-oil co-ops spread, the oil wholesalers began refusing to deal with them. The arrogance of the oil monopolies in not dealing with "those bunches of farmers" provided a spur for the otherwise individualistic farmers to get together. They got mad. In 1926 a county agricultural agent, E. G. Cort, organized 13 oil co-ops into Midland Co-Operative Oil Association, the first wholesale distributor for gas, oil, kerosene, and grease. By 1936 Midland did the largest volume of gas-oil business in Minnesota.

Unfortunately, Midland and other gas-oil co-ops, such as Union Oil of Kansas City, soon showed up a weakness in the percentage patronage refund principle of operation: it favored the larger purchasers at the expense of the smaller and poorer ones. Not only was this true because the larger purchasers got back bigger refunds; it was usually also true that the larger farmers could afford to wait until year-end for their savings in the form of refunds. The smaller farmers were often in desperate straits and could have used the immediate savings of lower prices. Sometimes they had to have credit.

Thus, the gas-oil co-ops, with their very rapid growth, became a factor favoring the growth of large, highly mechanized farms and the decline, failure, and loss of smaller, "less efficient" ones. The gas-oil co-ops fitted slickly into the network of economic forces in capitalism which concentrate ownership of the means of production.

With the sort of rapid growth exhibited by Midland Oil, there was no possibility — and little pretense — of a "democratic co-op society." Professionalized management became an immediate necessity, and there was a rapid, sharp separation between the owner-consumers and management. This was all right with most of the farmer members. They weren't looking for utopian societies; they wanted cheap gas and oil. They were uninterested in running the co-ops as long as the co-ops delivered.

The Farmers Union Central Exchange — a co-op purchasing outfit which stocked oil, fertilizer, and other farm supplies — and the Grain Terminal Association, a collective grain marketing outfit allied with FUCE, had a similar story. In 1927 the Farmers Union Terminal Association, which marketed livestock, set aside $1,000 to get the wholesale Central Exchange going. In 1929, it had 20 member associations, sold 425 tank-car-loads of gasoline and 31,875 gallons of lubricating oil. By 1935, it had 227 member co-ops, was selling 4,150 tank cars of gasoline, 1,144,604 gallons of oil, and $137,936 worth of tractor tires. Again, the patronage refund principle favored larger farmers.

The Grain Terminal Association became the biggest part of the St. Paul Farmers Union Central Exchange. It was a collective marketing group, originally for Minnesota wheat farmers; other grains (rye, corn, soy) were added as these became economically important in the state. The advantages of collective grain marketing were considerable for all farmers. When the railroads owned the elevators and worked with giant milling establishments like Pillsbury and Washburn-Crosby to control the entire grain marketing system, farmers were always in debt.

It didn't matter whether there was overproduction (which presumably lowers prices) or underproduction (which is supposed to raise them); the market was controlled, and the farmer got just enough to get by on, if that. So co-operative marketing, which gave farmers control of some grain storage elevators and better bargaining positions with shippers and millers, was a help.

Nevertheless, the FUCE-GTA tended to be a conservative organization, even given the social limits of what the co-op movement can be expected to do. The farmers had collective marketing, storage, and shipping arrangements. They benefited a great deal from these and in some cases were able to cut out certain middlemen entirely. Why not go the next step and set up co-op milling and baking enterprises, controlled by farmer-producers, or perhaps jointly with consumers, who were working "back" toward the origins of production by organizing their stores into regional associations and larger wholesales?

Many of the FUCE-GTA farmers saw this as a logical next step. Producers and consumers could between them have organized at least the food production sector of society without middlemen, and controlled it by themselves. The leadership of GTA, however, turned them away with statements such as: "When we take our grain to market, our job as producers is finished. We shall welcome the day when the consumers reach the point where they come out here and build a flour mill next door to us. But it is up to the consumers themselves to take this step."

Why? Well, there were quite a few reasons. The producer co-ops sold to everyone, and the farmers produced in such volume that consumer co-ops and small enterprises were only a small part of their market. Mainly they sold to the giants who could do national and international selling. And the giants were always out to get them. They couldn't rock the boat too much, or they'd be thrown overboard. Their small gains and small challenges to capitalist power placed them under constant attack.

For example, the National Taxpayers' Equity Association had been organized by mill undustry hireling Ben McCabe of Minneapolis. NTEA was always howling to the state legislature and Congress about the "unfair" tax breaks co-ops were getting — namely not having to pay corporate taxes on the "profits" co-op members saved by collective buying and by using their own labor. NTEA directed a lot of its attention to FUCE-GTA, until some deals were made.

The main deal was legislation on the federal level setting up two categories of co-ops. One is "non-profit, tax-exempt." Such co-ops' memberships are limited to farmers only, mostly large ones at that. The other category is "non-exempt" co-ops, which have non-farmer members (as most consumer co-ops do) and have to pay tax on "corporate profits" — a tax which reduces the savings refunded to members.

These laws form a permanent barrier to producer-consumer market organizing that cuts out capitalist middlemen. The criteria in existing legislation are — and are intended to be — mystifying, even to insiders. For instance, a non-exempt co-op, which is given certain small advantages over a "for profit" corporation, is defined as "a business operating in a co-operative manner." The complications and uncertainty leave plenty of room for deals via legalistic "interpretation."

I talked to a "survivor" of those early, nonpolitical farmer co-ops. She and her husband were still small dairy farmers and still belonged to a small co-op. Several levels "up" in the hierarchy, their co-op is affiliated with Land O'Lakes Creamery.

"Did you find the co-op an advantage?" I asked.

"At first it was," she said. "But the bigger ones took over very quickly. Now, in our co-op, about all we have to co-operate on is paying for the truck that picks up from all of us. We have nothing to say about prices or policy.

"Recently there have been some rulings about the kind of storage tank you have to have to be 'Class A,' which you have to be if you are going to sell milk at all. The requirement is for a very big storage tank — it would hold three times what we produce. We just bought our new storage tank three years ago. It isn't paid for yet. We can't afford a new and bigger tank, so we are quitting."

While the nonpolitical co-ops were following the precepts of economic growth, "buying cheap and selling dear," and getting co-opted in the process, there was another and quite different group of explicitly activist, "political" co-ops developing in the northernmost parts of the Midwest. It had its origin early in the century, when a wave of Scandinavian immigrants — Swedes, Norwegians, and Finns — settled in Minnesota, Wisconsin, and Upper Michigan, where they were employed at first in logging and mining. Later many started small farms on the poor, logged-off lands known as "the Cutover."

The Finns, especially, brought with them strong beliefs in unions and in consumer co-ops, both of which had lightened their oppression in Czarist-controlled Finland. They also brought strong commitments to the achievement of socialism. Oppressive conditions in mining, logging, small farming, and urban factories strengthened those commitments. Co-op stores, housing, and community halls were set up in northern Minnesota, and especially on the Iron Range. The first such co-op — as best we know — was organized in 1908 in Nashwauk. It was named the Elanto Company, after the semi-underground, repressed and harassed Elanto Society of Finland.

Many of the co-ops were associated with workers' halls or socialist halls, set up as places for social get-togethers and discussions to develop political consciousness. Class struggle was well understood by these miners, farmers, and workers. But they were an ethnic and linguistic minority, having relatively little contact with others in the region. The main newspaper of this group, *Tyomies*, was very radical, as many will tell you, but unless you could (can) read Finnish, it was (is) closed to you.

In 1917 representatives from 19 of these small Minnesota and Wisconsin co-ops met at Superior, Wisconsin. "Private" wholesalers and merchants were combining to attack them, refusing to sell to their stores, cheating them, and raising prices. So the group decided to fight back by forming their own wholesale.

A collection from those present raised $15.50, starting capital for the Central Co-operative Wholesale (CCW), which used space, labor help and some financial donations from the Communist Party, whose members were well represented in the small co-ops. Printing was done by the *Tyomies* newspaper staff, at first on an informal basis and later by a formalized arrangement providing that *Tyomies* would set and print the CCW newspaper, *The Co-operative Builder*, which was written in English.

By 1920, CCW was doing almost half a million dollars' worth of business. This was the point at which a serious split began. A few people who remember the fight are still around, but it is obvious that their accounts of it are highly partisan. I am unable to unravel the connections between the co-op movement, with its communist-socialist-opportunist splits, and the internal turmoil that eventually destroyed the left direction of the Farmer-Labor Party in the late 1930s. It is evident that there are many interconnections.

It is clear that the Communist Party (CP) controlled or partly controlled many of the small co-ops. Its membership was fairly large in northern Minnesota, where it was vigorous and respected as an organizer among miners. The CP had given CCW much support over its first critical years: office space, loans, labor. It is not clear whether loans were repaid, but apparently no payment was contemplated by CCW for office space and other services.

From Erick Kendall, an anti-Communist, red-baiter, and former editor of *The Cooperative Builder*, comes this version:

"In 1920, the CP demanded a $5,000 loan from CCW. This was refused; it was contrary to the Rochdale principles to involve the co-ops in this kind of direct politics, as opposed to the political implications of 'economic democracy,' which are inherent in their existence and nature. The demand was defeated by those who well understood that it was destructive. Then the CP demanded one percent of the gross (which would have been about a $10,000 donation from CCW to them). They tried to pack the boards and vote this through, but we defeated them."

From a former CP member who was involved comes this version:

"When the wholesale was just getting started, we were very much a part of it all. As they started to succeed, we were forced out, amid a lot of accusations that we had 'infiltrated' that which we had started ourselves. At first we saw the co-ops, and they saw themselves, as part of the general class struggle. If it had not been for our support and our work, there would have been no CCW. When they grew successful, the bourgeois opportunists moved in fast. They engaged in smear tactics, packed board meetings and attempted to split the younger people from the older ones, saying theirs was 'the new way, the American way, not the old country way.' We were pressed financially, especially for legal defense funds, as our people were getting arrested all the time. We thought they might repay us at a time when we needed it as much as they had at the start when we helped them."

The conflict was very bitter and sometimes violent. It divided families, especially on old (radical) versus young (conservative) lines. In the course of it communists, fellow-travelers, and some red-white-and-blue reds were "purged" from the co-ops. Those organizations that survived all the in-fighting have become supermarkets indistinguishable from Red Owl, except that they have member-directors, and each year they refund a percentage of sales slip totals to members who save their receipts.

While the sectarian battle was going on, the capitalists were taking hostile note of the co-op movement and getting it on to get it off. One entire volume of Minnesota statutes, laws regulating co-ops (Volume 20A) was passed, unnoticed, while the left and sort-of-left were fighting each other. Additional legislation, since passed, fills two more volumes. Minnesota is one of the worst states in which to incorporate a co-op, from the point of view of legal restrictions. In general, this legislation favors bigness and professional management. It sets various standards of operation that small groups cannot meet and standards for some things that most groups would not want to meet (for instance, phony "health regulations" which can be met only with expensive equipment). There was no unified fight against this legislation; none is shaping up now.

❖ ❖ ❖

The "new wave" of '60s and '70s co-ops is mostly little stores, with an emphasis on "healthy" foods of various kinds. (This was also an element of Ann Tweedale's plans for the Rochdale cooperative; she was particularly annoyed with the dangerous habit of stretching and whitening flour with chalk and lime.) Many "new wave" folks have their eyes on "extending back" to the land, to becoming, or joining with, producers. They should study the "unpolitical" co-ops and try to figure out ways of gaining volume savings and collective market power without building in structural features that lead to bigness and centralization. It is not at all clear how this can be done, or if it can be. At the same time, they must recognize that existing legislation amounts to a total weapon that can be used against "new wave" co-ops if they ever grow enough to be seen by food capitalists as a real or potential economic threat. Member-customer consciousness-raising and unified plans of political action would seem to be a must if they are to escape the fate of the old co-ops.

Counter-culture co-operators may feel confidence in their collective commitment to building for change as a protection from co-optation. I think this confidence is wholly unwarranted. We should not be contemptuous of those who went before us. Often they seem much more together than we are.

The British Rochdale co-operators had a clearer view of what they were trying to do than do modern local folks. Their principles were agreed on, written down for everybody to see and work toward, not merely tacitly understood as vague ideals springing from "life style." But clarity did not protect them. They faced the need to "grow or die." This led to their adding the principle of "political neutrality," that would make it possible for anyone to join without being turned off by politics. They added a lot of stuff about internal education, because they hoped to convert member-supporter-customers into political-supporter-activists. Status quo "neutrality" won out, because it's not really neutral.

Co-ops cannot be politically neutral, for there is no such thing. Nor can they make revolution — or any kind of significant change — merely by existing and growing. It is important to recognize the criticism made clear back in the 17th century by pre-Marx British "Levelers": namely, it is not possible to build an alternative society quietly and peacefully, wholly outside the mainstream society, for the latter's rules control most of the wealth and the means of producing new wealth (land, minerals, energy supplies, factories, tools). If an alternative looks likely to threaten this, they fight. If you cannot defend your "alternative," they win.

Struggles for control must go on inside existing institutions, where most of the resources are located, and most of the people are working. "People's co-ops" can serve as small "utopian" models and as survival centers for such struggles. But the food industry will not become "people controlled" by the building of co-ops. Not while there exist the A & P (world's largest retail network), Tenneco (oil, factory farms conglomerate), Pillsbury, General Mills, General Foods, Green Giant, Ralston Purina, International Minerals and Chemicals, IT&T, International Harvester, and the U.S. Defense Department. Co-op people should ask themselves how they can best aid struggles within such power-controllers as those corporate giants. This may lead to more fruitful strategies which would achieve the Rochdale pioneers' purpose: not a "people's store," but a people's world.

Midland Co-operative employees, 1939

Co-op Crisis in the North Country

By Jack Miller

THE NEW CO-OPS, SOMETIMES CALLED the "people's co-ops" and sometimes known as the "hippy co-ops," are the center of the movement in this part of the country for the creation of an alternative society. Begun in Minneapolis four years ago with a single back-porch food store, the co-ops now have grown to 35 units throughout the Minnesota-Wisconsin-Dakotas region. They include bakeries, a warehouse, several cafes, a garage and much more. The warehouse alone did close to $900,000 in business last year, and a number of the co-op stores do in the hundreds of thousands. But what really makes the North Country co-ops distinctive is that they are so numerous and diverse. It is the most extensive alternative system in the nation. And while the co-ops all work together and make some policies together (particularly for the central warehouse), each co-op is independent, run by a collective and in most cases directed by its members.

But all has not been well with the co-ops. Many of them have been too much dominated by a single cultural group — notably the pot-smoking, easy-going counter-culturist, or "hippy" — and have been slow to bring in other people, especially average working people. And the co-ops have failed to build strong links to other people's struggles in the region. They have seemed for some time, too, to lack a strong, commonly felt set of ideas about the point of their efforts and how it related to other people's struggles.

In the last few months, a heavy debate has been going on in the co-ops about who they are, what they're doing and how they can do things better. On Monday, May 5 [1975], the controversy went beyond debate. . . . Members of a group calling themselves the Co-op Organization (CO), some carrying pipes as weapons, took over the Peoples Warehouse in Minneapolis. They told the 11 people who were peacefully gathered in the warehouse, "Work with us or get out!" — that they had 30 minutes to decide.

The occupation lasted for a week. In that time, most of the 30-plus co-ops that get food from the warehouse were getting it through a new network they had set up. The occupation ended in a negotiated settlement between the CO occupiers and representatives of the co-ops. But the occupation dramatically revealed crucial weaknesses in the co-ops, and the struggle over their future direction will probably go on for some time to come.

The CO is a recent name for a group of people who have been organizing in and around the Twin Cities co-ops for the last year or so and decided this spring to take action to re-shape the co-ops in what they said is the interest of the working class. They issued several papers criticizing the leadership of the co-ops as being hippy, middle class, bourgeois; they said "class cliques" had taken control of the co-ops and that the predominant philosophy was Utopian Socialism, which the CO identified with dreamy idealism, escapism and "puritan" ethics that keep people in the movement from getting involved with evil in order to overthrow the present system. They said the "cliques" in control of the co-ops have been running them as their own private property — ignoring the needs of the "working people" and "the masses."

For their part, the CO people have identified themselves as anti-imperialists working for the overthrow of monopoly capitalism. Toward this end, they have raised the cry of "good, cheap food for the masses." In their analysis and approach, they seem to be old-fashioned Communists. They purport to believe in democratic centralism. They clearly are convinced that the revolution will be led by a tightly organized vanguard party in the manner of the Bolsheviks after the 1917 Russian Revolution. Several of them have acknowledged Stalin as one of their mentors, publishing and distributing one of his papers. And in one of the later rounds of the debate they began, they justified Stalin's destruction of millions of kulak families (well-off peasants) on grounds that they were hoarding food during their resistance to the forced collectivization program of the Bolsheviks.

At the same time, the CO has operated secretively in many respects. Its first organizing, during the last year, was through semi-secret study groups. When participants left a study group they were asked not to tell about it. The main leader of the group, Bob Haugen, has remained in the background most of the time. Many of the group's papers have been unsigned.

The CO has come wading into the diverse, loose counter-culture milieu of the Minnesota co-ops with a rigid line — essentially the old Communism. It has presented ideas that seem to deny that the Russian Revolution, and the events since, have happened. The group quotes Marx, Engels and Stalin and talks about class conflict as if this were still the turn of the century. I remember thinking that it is a wonder they were taken seriously at all in the anti-authoritarian, decentralist territory of the Twin Cities co-ops.

But it has become clear that the CO is not to be taken lightly. It has demonstrated a powerful ability to win converts — and these include several of the most dedicated worker/organizers in the co-ops, people we considered, and still consider, to be our brothers and sisters in spite of basic differences that have driven us apart.

The CO didn't come out of nowhere. By most accounts, Bob Haugen and a few others began to develop their analysis while working at Winding Road Farm, a small collective farm near Boyceville, Wisconsin, east of the Twin Cities. Most of the group were former Minneapolis co-op workers. They say their study, going back two years, included an attempt to understand the co-ops and find out how they could be made into a force for the "working class struggle." Returning to the city, Haugen and others took jobs and started organizing in the People's Bakery, the People's Warehouse and in co-op stores. "By last fall, an analysis of the co-op system had been pretty well completed and we knew what we had to do," the CO said in its much-disputed "History of the Twin City Food Co-ops."

The account continues: "First we needed a model, a place to test out our theories in practice. For this, the Beanery was chosen. It had the reputation of being the worst store in the co-op system, was so far in the hole economically that the warehouse wouldn't even deliver to it, and the atmosphere reeked of hippy cultism." After "going to the people" and finding out what the masses wanted, the group transformed the store into "a center for working class discussions and organization. . ."

Then came the opening round of the debate that became a struggle: the issuance, unsigned, of the CO's paper, "The Beanery Policy." The paper includes analyses that run thus: "It is a historical fact that anti-imperialism was the motivating factor behind the creation of the co-op stores," as shown by such present policies as the grape and lettuce boycott and (earlier) the boycott on Farah. But, it asks, "do the co-op stores' politics correspond to its political context? . . . The answer is NO!! In order to understand why, we must look at class ideology. From the inception of the co-op stores, they took on class snobbishness, elitism and upper class domination of the lower classes. For instance, the capital that was used to set up the stores came from the middle and upper classes. . . . As you can see, the one who holds the money bag is the one who calls the shots. In order for the bourgeois leadership to maintain their class ideology and control over the co-op system, they instituted a deceitful line — community control." And so on.

If the masses were unmoved, the direct targets of the CO assault were not. At Mill City Co-op, one of the supposed strongholds of "Utopian Socialism," Jeb Cabbage and Emma Evechild issued a response — the second in a flood of mimeographed papers that spread through the co-op system in the weeks ahead. Rejecting the co-op history presented in the Beanery paper, Jeb and Emma called the assault "a pseudo-Marxist revision full of generalizations and accusations delivered in a divisive and vindictive tone."

Jeb and Emma acknowledged many poor practices in the early coops, saying: "Some came from good motives such as the desire to break through the stifling employee-customer relationship most people are used to in a store. This often resulted in a careless and flippant attitude towards people using the store and those people, especially the elderly, felt confused and unwelcomed. The intense dislike of conventional business practice led to attitudes about money and accounts such as, 'let things flow, be cool, it'll all work out.' And often the decision-making process was not spelled out carefully enough to those using the store. Many co-op workers didn't (and don't now) fully comprehend the responsibility to relate to their neighbors' unfamiliarity with the unique situation of a co-op. Caught in the hassles of just maintaining the day-to-day operations, people let down in explaining what the store is about and how it works, the type of food carried, its nutrition and politics."

But they said, "many changes in the nature of the stores and the people working in them have occurred, mainly as a result of co-op workers also being residents of a neighborhood. A maturity, reflecting criticisms and analysis and a serious understanding of what we are about, is evident."

Taking up the Beanery paper's accusations, Jeb and Emma said, "One of the most general and sweeping charges is that the 'bourgeois leadership' in establishing its 'class ideology as supreme,' tried to establish the priorities of doing your own thing and eating organically. Now really. This sounds like so much bombast. Where exactly is the policy of 'do your own thing' evident, unless one means the view that the individual should have the final say over what occurs in his/her life and not the State or the Party or even the Co-op."

Here the line was drawn. Jeb and Emma established themselves as liberationists — as believing in people acting freely, together, under *their own* leadership. "The co-ops were born of the spirit of all liberation movements — to hell with the rich and the bosses — people working together can do it and do it better," they said. The CO, by contrast, has shown that it believes in tight central control, in order that "the leadership" can take decisive and effective action *"for* the working class" (emphasis added).

In early April the CO formalized itself as a group, announcing, "People who have been waging a lonely struggle against class cliquishness, snobbishness, isolationism and escapism, now have comrades. Their struggles are being unified into a common front. This is the Co-op Organization."

On May 3, there was a meeting of the Policy Review Board (PRB), the policy-making and co-ordinating body for the region's co-ops. Before the meeting, the CO had sent out an 8-page proposal for restructuring the co-ops. This paper should have made it clear, if the other material hadn't, that the CO was preparing to effect a coup d'co-op, seizing the co-ops' power, including their "means of production." Acting (of course) *for* the working class and the masses, the CO was prepared to override the will of the co-ops in the name of "democratic centralism" and forcibly establish itself as the new "revolutionary" leadership. The last page of the proposal invited people to attend a meeting on May 4 at Walker Methodist Church to "discuss this transformation." That's when the PRB was supposed to be in the second day of its two-day meeting.

The People's Warehouse (by this time having a majority of CO people) was first on the agenda of the May 3 meeting of the PRB. Michael Biesanz of the PW collective (and the CO) presented a report on the financial position of the warehouse, suggesting, through the use of a number of capitalist business measures, that the warehouse was going broke. The report concluded that the warehouse was going to have to cut its expenses, just like any other business operation, either through wage cuts or layoffs. The PRB people were stunned.

On cue, as obviously planned, the CO began to provide the answer to the crisis. Michael Rachlin of the CO began reading from the CO paper on the co-ops' history in the Twin Cities. She read for a while, was interrupted by PRB people protesting the thing, then went on for another half an hour. Then she started reading the CO paper "Economic Facts of Life vs. Co-op Fantasies." In this paper the CO argues that the co-ops have to get over their anti-profit ideals — otherwise they are going to collapse economically. There's nothing wrong with profit, say the revolutionaries; it's just a question of how it's used: either it will be used for the benefit of the working class or it will be used to perpetuate the ruling class. There are no other possibilities.

Got it? Because the co-ops haven't built up ready-reserves, the CO says, they have to borrow from members and friends — and the people who lend the money (class clique) call the shots. Nobody who can lend the co-ops several thousand dollars can be "working class." (The collective that does *The Scoop*, the newsletter/magazine of the co-op movement, says flatly in its 48-page special issue on the controversy: "It is blatantly false to say that those persons who have loaned money 'own the co-ops' or have had 'exclusive control over the future of the co-ops.'")

Back at the meeting, people were walking out, and the session was adjourned with a whimper. The PRB was impotent, if not ridiculous, and it didn't take any great talent for the CO to dramatize the fact. In the hall in the back of the meeting room at the Oddfellows Hall, CO members were drumming up support for their meeting the following morning. And while many of the PRB people were having a boogie that night, members of the CO went to the warehouse and grabbed the financial records and checks.

When the second day of the PRB's regular two-day meeting opened on Sunday, Mark Larson announced for the CO that the leadership of the PRB had failed to respond to the warehouse crisis. Therefore, he said, the CO — with a mandate of 600 signatures on petitions demanding an end to private ownership of the co-ops by class cliques — was taking over the warehouse. The PRB members were stunned, then outraged. But it took these 60 people until late afternoon to act. What they did was make a public statement; pick Tracy Landis, Terry Hokinson, Kris Olson and Randy McLaughlin as "executive officers" to act in their behalf (while seeking guidance), and — if all else fails — to take legal action. *To take legal action . . .* that the co-op people would even consider such a move, especially in a dispute within their own movement, can hardly be seen as anything but a measure of its weakness as a part of the human liberation movement. Before long, the PRB "execs" would call the cops.

From here, I turn over the account to the *Scoop* collective:

". . . Word spreads that the stores will be gathering at the warehouse to hold a 'tactics' meeting. By dark, the PW is awash in people, with phone calls going out to notify more people of the meeting. Ken Baker from People's Bakery arrives in a cowboy hat brandishing a black banner of anarchy in one hand and a bag of popcorn in the other and wearing a 'make love not class war' button.

"People try to pull together a meeting to consider just what they are doing there. There is some feeling that people should spend the night in the warehouse so that, come morning, the warehouse can be kept open for business as usual. There is a question of what preparation should be made for possible confrontation with the CO during the night, but most people are not intending to stay the night anyway. Instead, a party atmosphere resumes, as Seward Cafe arrives with food.

"Upstairs the PRB 'executive officers' try to sort out what needs to be done the next day. By midnight the PW settles down. Eleven people decide to stay the night. A sleeping room is set up. The party is kept downstairs.

"Monday, May 5th, 1:45 a.m. Word has reached people in the CO that something is going on over at the warehouse. Gathering what people they can, they make preparations to 'retake' the warehouse. Plans are made for various people to assume particular tasks once at the warehouse. Expecting a struggle, some CO people arm themselves with makeshift weapons. Plans are even made for the possibility that guns might be used in the struggle, though the general plan is to use only the force necessary to overpower the people in the warehouse.

"Armed with clubs and mentally hyped for struggle, the CO enters the PW without encountering any resistance. Instead, they find their 'enemy' just as they always have — sitting around talking (ironically, the 'enemy' had just finished doing a dramatized reading of the 'Invasion of the Stalinoids,' a co-op comic created by Jon Havens) or upstairs asleep.

"No matter. They disconnect the phones and order the 11 into the warehouse proper where the ultimatum is delivered — 'Work with us or get out. You have 30 minutes to decide.' But even total control over the situation doesn't abate the momentum that the CO has been priming in themselves over the months.

"They have brought along a woman, Vee, a member of the Selby community. Vee is riled up, lacing her rap with threats and epithets. She rails on at the 11, 'We want food. Give us food, not this wheat germ crap.' 'Right on!' comes her back-up from the CO people.

"'Ah, I don't understand,' says Michelle, one of the 11. 'Why don't you go to the co-op in Selby?'

"'You shut up while I'm talking.'

"Eventually Vee gets into it to the point where she hits Marcia, another of the 11, with a steel pipe, for not jumping on command. Though the resulting injury is slight, the incident crystallizes the atmosphere created by the CO attitudes that night. The 11 are evicted. At the last moment two are permitted to stay and talk.

"Inside the question is asked, 'Are you going to refuse to sell food to the in-town co-ops?' Kris Garwic thinks a moment and then, quietly: 'I think the stores will have to realize it's all different now.'

"*8 a.m.* Word spreads that the warehouse was seized during the night. People from the co-op community gather in the PW yard and at nearby Whole Foods co-op. Ed Winter from the PW collective shows up at the warehouse only to be told 'You're not coming here for business as usual. Come in if you're coming to get involved in the restructuring.'

" 'I've come for the PW collective meeting.' The collective, he is told by occupiers, has been abolished.

"Out in the yard, Mike Dunn, grizzled, aging, decides to break into the warehouse. Mark Sherman of the CO tries to intervene and catches a glancing blow off Mike's shovel. Dunn threatens and rails as friends pin him, kicking, to the ground. He calms down just long enough for people to let him up. Then he grabs a 4-by-4 and climbs up to a stack of pallets to stand over the crowd. Bob Haugen (the leader of the CO) moves toward him.

" 'Get back you fucker, or I'll kick you in the mouth,' says Dunn.

" 'Mike,' calls Haugen, 'I'm not after power for myself.'

" 'See these hands,' says Dunn, trembling, 'I work with these hands. You work with your mouth,' says Dunn, his voice cracking, 'and it's full of shit.'

"Then he climbs up onto the roof of the warehouse and begins smashing windows. CO people charge back into the warehouse.

" 'If he gets hurt,' someone shouts to the people in the warehouse, 'it's your ass.'

"Within moments people from the warehouse charge out onto the roof and manage to wrestle Dunn down."

After that a lot of things got kind of ludicrous. The PRB execs went to the bank, found out that the warehouse occupiers had already withdrawn $6,000; then they talked the bank into returning control of the account to the four of them, as legal respresentatives of the PRB. Later, two of the original incorporators of the PRB, both CO sympathizers, proved to the bank that *they* were the rightful trustees of the account. The bank froze the funds.

Later on Monday, the PRB "execs" took the advice of a lawyer and told the occupiers to give it up immediately or legal action would be taken. The occupiers said no. So the PRB execs went to the Model Cities Police Precinct to file a complaint. The cops were doubtful, but they agreed to send around a squad car. When the squad car arrived at the warehouse, co-op people put heavy pressure on the PRB execs to keep the dispute "in the family."

At 7:00 that night co-op stores all over the Twin Cities held urgent meetings. The places were packed. The verdict came back: Don't call in the police, but use "civil action" if you have to. Score a point for the occupiers.

Late that night the "Third Force" came in with a proposal, supporting the CO criticisms, denouncing the CO tactics and calling for a structure in which "principled political struggle" could take place. It all got nowhere.

On Tuesday, a significant thing happened: An alternative distribution system started to form. This, together with a boycott of the warehouse by most of the stores, isolated the CO occupiers. The co-op "masses" (Or were they mostly "bourgeois elements"?) had failed to rise to the call of the revolutionary leadership to seize power and create the new co-op movement.

But the CO people weren't giving up. The warehouse had been given a large quantity of potatoes by Red River Valley growers who decided to distribute potatoes free rather than sell at ridiculously low prices. So the CO set up a "cheap food" sale at the warehouse and sent trucks into poor neighborhoods to distribute food free. And on two days' notice, they announced a plan to dissolve the CO and create a new Mass Organization (at a mass meeting, of course) to carry on the transformation of the co-ops. On Monday, May 12, the "Mass Meeting" turned out about 100 people, many of them part of the CO. The (now former) CO people got through the appointment of a steering committee of seven to carry it on.

By Tuesday the alternative distribution was getting food to the Twin Cities co-ops without the warehouse. Presumably this would have meant that the occupiers were beaten. But agreements reached during the next two days, ending the occupation, appear otherwise. CO people still controlled the warehouse, where they were in a majority in the collective. And the warehouse was, and is, *the* power in the regional co-op system. On Thursday, the occupation ended with the signing of a joint statement between the warehouse collective and the Steering Committee (both dominated by the CO people) and the PRB. And the statement endorsed the "restructuring" undertaken by the collective and steering committee and said only that these actions were subject to approval by the PRB at the June 21-22 meeting.

Though "restructuring" was not spelled out in the statement, it seemed to mean turning over the leadership and power of the co-ops to the several strong-handed CO leaders, notably Bob Haugen. And that presumably would mean making the co-ops at once more like profit-making capitalist businesses — and a centralized instrument for pressing on to revolution in the name of the working class. But what if the "masses" in the co-ops and the neighborhoods don't want to be "restructured"? Will it be necessary to get out the pipes again?

A major thrust of the CO effort after the occupation was the establishment of committees to carry out restructuring: Food, Farm Distribution, and Purchasing/Expansion. According to the *Scoop*, the purchasing/expansion plans are the most important. This committee is considering the addition of canned goods and meat. But this is part of a larger plan to expand the financial base of the warehouse (and other co-op units) and make it possible, among other things, to raise the wages to two or three times the $40-$50 a week now being paid in most of the co-ops, and to create more jobs. This would require large new sources of capital, and the Expansion Committee has been looking into the possibilities of foundation grants and government money through the CETA program. Of course, the people who hold the money bags call the shots. So it would seem important to pick foundations and government agencies that are interested in smashing monopoly capitalism and helping the working class seize the means of production. Right?

Photo by Cheryl Walsh

The Crisis in Agriculture

The 1960s and early '70s were reputedly good years for agriculture, but hardly so for small farmers. Faced with the relentless industrialization of agriculture in all its aspects, those who made their living on the land were told to "get big or get out." Then came the '80s, when anger and desperation among those who had hung on rivaled the years of the Great Depression.

In Anvil *number 13 (1974), Marjorie Dorner's story, "Last Harvest," dramatized the human costs of giving up the family farm. But as Jack Miller pointed out in number 43, the bell that tolled for farming as an American way of life only concluded a process that had begun with the country's earliest years. In the same issue, published in the spring of 1983, associate editor Paul Schaefer turned to economics and politics and held out hope for a "Resurgence of Populism" — at least among Wisconsin dairymen.*

Meanwhile, small-scale agriculture had acquired new and vocal allies in the environmental and back-to-the-land movements, but few farmers welcomed them. Reflecting on the ubiquitous mercury vapor lamps that dispel the soft darkness of country nights, Paul Gilk, writing in number 52 (1986), discussed the cultural rift dividing rural America. And in number 56 (1988) Steven Schwen wrote of the barriers facing the new breed of organic farmers in a society geared to government regulation and mass markets.

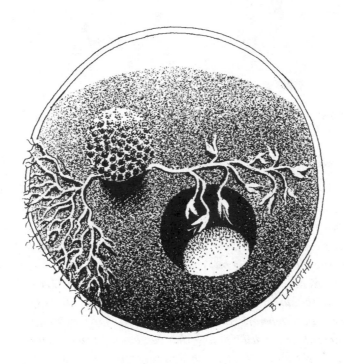

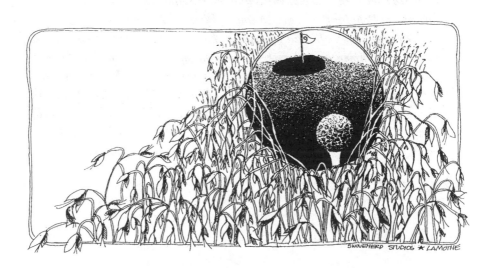

Drawings by Becky LaMothe

The Last Harvest

By Marjorie L. Dorner

CLOUDS OF WHITE DUST ENGULFED the shining blue car within a quarter mile after it had turned off the paved county highway onto a narrow gravel road.

"Jesus Christ!" she thought. "I always forget. Whenever I'm away for more than three months at a time, I forget what it's like. A hell of a lot of good it did me to have this car washed and polished before I left. I guess this is what I get for trying to flaunt my latest status symbol."

She slowed the car to a crawl and the grinding of the gravel under the new tires diminished to a low growl. As the solid state radio became audible, a voice was proclaiming Coke as "The Real Thing." Outside the windows, the stripped fields drifted away, the tinted glass making the oats stubble look greenish-brown in the late August sunshine. A sagging wreck of a house floated into view outside the right window. The doors were boarded up and two front windows, their glass long shattered, turned a baleful, resigned stare at the passing car. Among the waist-high weeds of the lawn, two apple trees drooped under the weight of the fruit no one picked anymore. Once she had played here, soaring skyward on the unpainted board swing which still hung from one of the trees, squealing in mock terror as her godfather postponed his afternoon chores to push her, for hours it seemed, on the hot summer days. But like his house, he, too, was dead now, and her father's brother owned the land.

"It's such an eyesore," she thought irritably, fighting the memories as the house disappeared behind the car. "Uncle Peter should just tear it down."

A stand of corn on the neighboring farm, her cousins', seemed forest-high surrounded by the flattened fields, yet it was in turn dwarfed by a huge, shapeless machine, gleaming red and bristling with power even in its repose.

"Their latest status symbol," she thought, catching sight of her own wry, intelligent eyes in the rear-view mirror as she turned her head back toward the road. Instantly, she made the gesture which had become habitual whenever she saw herself in a mirror, lifting her head sharply to tighten the skin along her cheeks and jaw. At 33, she was already beginning to exhibit the characteristic family features, the heavy lower face, the thick body bequeathed by generations of peasant farmers. In the mirror, the thin vertical line between her eyebrows was exaggerated by her carefully acquired summer tan.

She translated the sudden flash of irritation which passed through her into annoyance at having to make this trip on the very day she was expecting delivery of the new loveseat which would put the finishing touch on her living room. How she loved the peace and order of her suburban apartment, furnished piece by piece over the past five years; the tasteful study with bright rows of books forming a background for the gleaming expanse of the oak desk; the elegant little dinner parties for friends whose shop-talk was never boring because their shop — the world of books and theater — was her shop, too. But it was just like Henry to do this, self-importantly calling a family conference, making an imminent crisis out of a question whose answer was self-evident and had been for three years. Sooner or later the farm would have to go and everyone knew it; she had told him so on the phone, but he had insisted that they had to gather in force, and in person, or Papa would certainly "blow" the best chance of his life. She had stalled, but he knew summer session was over and that I-90 was finished at last; in the end, she simply ran out of excuses. So four and a half hours ago, she had hung one of her tailored pantsuits in the back seat of the car and started east.

Except for the obligatory appearances at Christmas and Easter, she had gotten out of the habit of going home. In recent years, she had even deliberately avoided extra visits. For the most part, her work was accepted as a valid excuse for long absences. Summers were harder, until she discovered the trick of traveling. She could almost see her mother's face, soft and mildly hurt, explaining to puzzled relatives, "Oh, Fran spends most of the summer traveling with friends." "Friends" was actually Julia Peterson, a fortyish divorcee whose thin energy bustled Fran through Italian museums, German libraries and Mexican markets.

To Julia and other colleagues, Fran always said, "I have so little in common with my family any more; we haven't more than three days of things to say to each other at any one time." She always said that, because she couldn't tell them the real reason she avoided the farm. It was the memories. Whenever she was there, memories so clear that they had the quality of vision came upon her like blows struck when she wasn't looking. Anything could trigger them — a scene, a word, a gesture — and she was helpless to stop them. They had none of the pleasant sadness of nostalgia about them, but seared her like physical pain. Her present life and her work were pleasant, steady, soothing. "Happiness" was a word she had rejected as "sentimental" when she was twenty-six, but her life now was one of contentment and she didn't want it disrupted by these hauntings.

The car crept up over a shallow hill and the homestead came into view. The T-shaped farm house sat with stolid confidence at the top of a sloping lawn whose summer grass was always faintly brown, except under the gnarled apple trees. The red roof was slightly sway-backed and the aluminum siding, she knew, covered solid logs. "Not a straight line in it," her father used to say, and she could never tell if he said it with irritation or with secret pride. From one corner of the house, an ancient fence, made of uprooted stumps stacked with their roots interlacing in a permanent embrace, wandered downhill toward the outbuildings. Among them, the dominant structure was the dairy barn, its wooden planks weathered to a pale bluish-gray, its steeple roof towering above the hayloft where she and her brothers had walked across beams thirty feet over the threshing floor, pretending they were a high-wire act in the circus.

As the car turned into the graveled driveway, she felt her hand and arm go taut as she remembered what it felt like to touch those rough, splintered barn boards. Only yesterday she had caressed the glassy surface of the newly refinished oak table which had been such a steal at an estate auction and which was just the right size for her telephone. "A very nice distressed antique," Julia had called it.

Her mother met her at the back door — within her memory, no

one had ever used the front door for coming and going. Anna Himrich was a short, plump woman whose clothes were forever in eclipse behind the bibbed aprons she always wore and made from a pattern handed down from her own mother. She had begun to gray early, and now her short, softly curled hair was almost white. Her daughter's periodic insistence that coloring it would make her look ten years younger was always answered with a smiling, "But I'm not ten years younger," and there the discussion would end.

"Frances," the mother smiled. "Come in." Her hands fluttered in front of her round body, telegraphing once again her uncertainty over whether she ought to embrace her daughter. Distressed and a little irritated as she always was by this uncertainty, Fran folded her mother in an embrace which was warmly returned.

Fran could not pinpoint with any accuracy how and when it had begun, this distance. Certainly not when she had gone away to college, an event without precedent in the family. Then, so homesick that she could not eat, Fran had taken every opportunity to slip home on weekends where the circle closed comfortingly around her and the chatter went on into the winter nights long after the bedtime of the early-rising household. Then, Anna had simply erased the absence which was, to her, so inexplicable, so unnecessary.

Perhaps it had begun during that Christmas vacation the second year of graduate school when Anna had found her packing on an icy December morning. From the doorway of the small room, the mother had said, "What are you doing ? Vacation isn't over for another week," and Fran had answered, "I know, Mama, but I have two papers to do and the weather is clear so I thought it would be a good time to start for home." At the last word, Anna had turned and walked quietly from the room. Yes, perhaps it had begun from something that small, but somewhere the circle was broken and Fran had gradually come to see her life as a straight road leading away, always away.

Now, the embrace over, the two women walked without touching into the large, airy room which was both kitchen and dining room.

"Henry is here already," Anna said.

"I know. I saw the station wagon."

Fran frowned sideways at a littered table-desk as she looked for a place to set down her bag; her eye caught a flash of silver.

"Isn't this the watch Paul gave Papa for Christmas?"

"Ya," Anna smiled half-apologetically, preparing an excuse for her husband.

"He broke it, didn't he?" Anna nodded.

"That was an expensive watch, Mama. Why can't he keep a watch? He's broken dozens, lost scores."

"You shouldn't exaggerate, Frances."

"Well, I suppose it's symbolically appropriate," Fran said, tossing the watch back down again. "Papa never did have any sense of time."

Anna's round face grew thoughtful. "I don't think that's quite true, Fran. He always came in when he got hungry and we never had to wait meals for him. You remember that, don't you? He's just one of those people. He goes to bed when it's dark and he gets up when the sun comes up. And he's never needed an alarm clock either."

At her mother's words, the memories began to clamor at the edges of Fran's consciousness. She beat them back with a toss of her head.

"Where's Paul, then? He certainly doesn't seem to have a built-in clock."

"Oh, I think it's the city traffic that holds him up."

Fran smiled secretly. The "city" was the nearest town, a community of some 55,000 souls.

Anna seemed to feel the need to change the subject. "How was summer school?"

"Hot and tedious as usual. The regents still haven't released the money for our air-conditioning. And my students! I swear, only regular session failures ever go to summer school these days. It would be one thing if I could teach Goethe and Schiller all the time, but those beginning classes —"

Fran broke off as she saw her mother's mild eyes drifting toward the stove and she realized that the question had been only Anna's way of asking, "How are you? Do things go well with you?" It required no direct answer and none was expected.

"I'll go say Hi to Papa and Henry. Where are they?"

"In the front room. Henry is being mysterious again, but Papa knows, of course."

As the two women walked together to the other room, Fran glanced quickly at her mother's face; it was unchanged, as open and gentle as ever. Where did it come from, this calm "knowing" that asked few questions and never even seemed to listen to the answers? Jacob Himrich strode to meet them; he was a stocky, barrel-chested man whose graying hair framed a long, deeply lined face. His eyes, Fran suddenly thought, were the same color as the barn boards.

"Frances," he said quietly, putting both hands on her shoulders. The sound of her full first name had an unfamiliar ring in her ears. No one except her family ever called her that now and she would tolerate it from no one else. She leaned forward to kiss the deep crease between her father's eyes and turned to greet her older brother. Henry stood with his feet planted wide apart to balance the weight of his spreading stomach and burly torso. Six years as foreman at a local lumber yard had imported an authoritarian air to his premature middle-age, yet he always faltered slightly in his sister's presence.

"Well, Fran. We haven't seen you since Christmas."

"Easter, Henry, Easter."

"Oh, yeah. You brought chocolate rabbits for the boys." He smiled uncertainly. "Louise and the kids stayed in town." Fran pictured the small frame house of which her brother was so defensively proud.

Over Henry's shoulder the massively-framed portraits of their great-grandparents dominated one long wall. The man's heavily bearded, unsmiling face had an expression of calm wariness, as if he looked at something he knew he would have to fight — an old enemy he recognized but no longer feared. The woman's downturned face, aged before it was old, looked sideways into the middle distance as if she saw there, always, the series of small wooden coffins she had followed to the church yard; three times they had made that journey together, two infant sons and one five-year-old daughter. Yet the eyes in the two pictures were the same — patient, kindly, in some strange way satisfied.

Between the two portraits hung the gilt crucifix which had rested on the cover of Jimmy's casket. Jimmy, the brother who had died when

Fran was eleven, was never discussed; the Himrichs refused to dwell on their dead. Fran turned sharply to her mother.

"Mama, I thought you told me at Easter you were going to put those pictures in the attic." She could not include the crucifix.

"I will, I will," Anna laughed. "I know they're not very modern."

Fran sighed. "Come outside all of you and admire my new car."

They all trooped out into the yard and Anna uttered exclamations over the now-soiled brilliance of the little car, speaking, as always in these matters, for herself and Jacob. Henry leaned against his own station wagon and brooded downward over folded arms. Fran looked past her brother at the small tractor parked near the east door of the barn. Without warning, the image sprang up before her eyes: the other tractor, her father's first. On that tractor, thirty years ago, her father had built an extra child-sized seat. Each of the boys in his turn had surveyed the farm from that perch before graduating to the driver's seat itself. This graduation was made into a real ceremony, with the family gathered and Jacob masking his pride by shouting counsel to the uncertain child maneuvering the jerking tractor around the yard, the huge, steel-lugged wheels digging down into the newly-thawed earth. Fran whirled back to her car, feeling raw and angry, fighting a sudden impulse to kick Henry out of his sullen silence.

The high-pitched, nasal chugging of a Volkswagen announced Paul's arrival. He stepped from the car, stretched up to his six feet two inches, and turned toward them. With his long body and his stylish clothes, his thick chestnut hair and modish mustache, he looked a stranger among his short, thick family.

"Snappy car, Fran," he said. "I'm putt-putting around in Cindy's little buggy 'cause my new one has been recalled. Something in the steering is haywire, they say." Then, before anyone else could speak, "Well, here we all are. What's for dinner, Mom?"

"Spare ribs, sauerkraut and dumplings."

"Oh, God! This ethnic cooking. Cindy says she'll have to let out all my suits if I eat here more than once a month."

"How is Cindy?" Fran remembered to ask.

"Oh, just fine. Getting more uncomfortable these last months, that's all. She's home practicing her breathing exercises right now. The doctor says it's a textbook pregnancy. Looks like everything is go for the natural childbirth."

Fran saw Henry turn away, a look of faint distaste passing over his florid features.

"Supper's almost ready to go on the table," Anna said, covering the silence with her usual bright efficiency.

Fran and her brothers sat at their old childhood places at the table. Combined with the absence of the wives and children, it made them all aware of something impending — some ritual they all expected and all were anxious to postpone. There was a great deal of chatter during the meal about the weather and teething children. In the silence which fell over coffee, Fran glanced at the bright yellow kitchen tile where four tiny holes remained as mute testimony to the childish rage which had once made her fling a fork at Henry's smirking, superior face. No one ever alluded to it, but Jacob had never replaced the tile.

"How was the harvesting, Dad?" Paul said at last.

"Hard," Jacob said simply; he was stating a fact rather than registering a complaint. "Peter couldn't help me as much as he thought he would be able to. And I don't have the machinery."

Henry saw his chance. "Of course it was hard, Papa," he said "and it won't get any easier. You're sixty-four, after all."

Jacob turned his slow gray eyes and held his eldest son in a long glance.

"I know my age, Henry."

The son flushed hot. "Well, I couldn't get away from the mill to help you, Papa. I asked, but I just couldn't get away."

Fran and Paul exchanged glances in the embarrassed silence. Henry drew a ragged breath and fumbled for a cigarette. After a long drag, he began again more quietly.

"Papa, that's just what I've been trying to tell you all along. I can't help, and the college boy there," jerking his round head at Paul and leaving the sentence unfinished. "Well, we aren't either of us farmers, Papa. I'm only thinking of you. It's time you sold."

The final syllable fell like a stone onto the table.

"Didn't take you very long to get to it, did it, Henry?" Fran said, an edge of bitterness coming into her voice.

"Now Fran," he said, the cigarette smoke haloing his head. "You know I'm right and you gotta help me talk to him. He can't keep on every year, planting and plowing and chopping and this is a chance, such a chance."

"Talk to me Henry, not to your sister." Jacob's voice was flat. "What exactly do you mean by 'such a chance'"?

"You know what I mean, Papa, so don't play it this way. Bill Connors told me about the new offer last Tuesday; it's better than last year's by twelve thousand. He wants all of it now because he knows that a housing development is a natural back along the timber stand if there's going to be a golf course here."

"Golf." Jacob prounounced the word out of the corner of his mouth as he turned his head away. Into the single syllable, he packed all of the cold disdain of countless generations for such foolishness.

"Papa, you gotta face it." Henry leaned forward, crowding the table with his shirt front. "The town is coming out to get you. Now sixty acres isn't much of a farm these days, but it's more farm than you can handle. And it's just right for this development. The county is going to blacktop the road next spring."

"I suppose that has nothing to do with Connors' brother-in-law being on the county board, either," Jacob said drily.

"Well, Papa, one hand washes the other."

"Must you talk in cliches, Henry?" Fran sighed wearily. Henry shot her a malevolent glance before turning back to his father.

"This farm, Papa, with the woods and the pond, why it's just a natural for a golf course, and I know how you feel about golf so don't look that way. You gotta be realistic. Connors is willing to pay you very impressive money."

Henry's right forefinger punched against the table to emphasize each of the last three words; a fine shower of cigarette ashes settled on the highly polished wood.

"I'm not impressed by Bill Connors' money," Jacob said in the measured tones Fran remembered from all her days at home. He never spoke loudly, never quickly; even now, as he spoke, he reached calmly to brush together the ashes which he knew were irritating his wife, just as he used to gather up the bread crumbs Henry would scatter around his plate to convince his mother he had eaten the crusts instead of shredding them.

"Well, Papa, you gotta be impressed by that much money." Henry was warming up now and he stubbed out his cigarette in a saucer, reaching for another at once.

"Not on the dishes, Henry!" Anna was indignant over the sacrilege committed on her mother's china. "I'll get you an ashtray."

"I'm sorry, Mama, but he makes me nervous talking about money that way. A farmer doesn't get a retirement pension, so what are you gonna live on with harvests getting harder and harder for him?"

"Talk to me, Henry." Jacob's voice was even quieter.

"All right, Papa, I am talking to you. I've been talking to you for three years, but let's face it, you never have been a practical man."

"Ah, of course! The best and soundest of his time hath been but rash," Fran pronounced sarcastically, feeling at once the familiar sting of annoyance as they all turned blank, uncomprehending faces toward her. "An allusion," she sighed. "Never mind," and they all turned away again.

"Paul, you talk to him." Henry spread his wide hands appealingly toward his younger brother.

Paul glanced at his father and faltered. Poor Paul, Fran thought. Of all of them, be was the most uncomfortable in this house. Handsome, amiable and successful: at ease in his office where she had once seen him with his long body flung back casually in the leather chair, he was nervous here, his face thrust forward in an earnest desire to please, but always thwarted, almost as if he and his parents spoke different, mutually unintelligible, languages. His defense, at last, in any serious conversation, was to agree with whoever had spoken last. He also had a wonderful trick of changing the subject with a shake of his thick hand and a flash of his perfect teeth. Football, the price of car repairs, the kids; these were his favorite topics during Sunday dinners at home. But this time Henry was not to be put off, or charmed, or distracted.

"Well, Paul," he insisted.

"Henry, I just don't know. If Dad doesn't want to sell maybe we shouldn't try to push him. And he's doing all right so far, aren't you, Dad?"

"Smart boy!" Henry snapped the words, enraged at the loss of an expected ally. "How the hell would you know how he's doing? You don't even remember what a harvest is like. Don't you try to make me into the bad guy in this, just because I'm the only one who's ready to say what has to be said."

Watching Henry's angry face, Fran felt herself accused along with Paul and she dodged the lash with her habitual retreat into irony.

"Dear Henry; always the dutiful son," she purred, taking a grim satisfaction in seeing his face redden into deeper rage. But, as usual, he was helpless against her tongue and leveled his heavy sarcasm at an easier target.

"Well, college boy. Maybe if we all try real hard, we can even understand what it is you do for a living. Insurance actuary! You're so smart about money and risks, you should tell him straight out what it means if he lets this chance go."

Paul shifted on the hard wooden chair and recrossed his long legs, sliding one hand along his bright, plaid trousers.

"Well, Dad," he said without looking up, "Henry may be right. These are different times. It's not like the days when you could make a living with a Ten-Twenty tractor and a team of horses. You and Mom need the security now and Connors isn't going to wait forever."

Horses. As Paul talked on, Fran saw with startling clarity a long-buried image. She and her brothers, swathed to the eyes in coats and scarves, lay on their stomachs on a large, flat-bottomed sled, clutching the taut tie-ropes normally used to secure a load of hay. Her father towered above them with his feet braced against a board, leaning back into the reins, controlling with arms and shoulders the lumbering canter of the team. The brittle winter air echoed with delighted squeals as powdered snow and Jacob's laughter were whipped backward into the children's upturned faces.

The mare had been sold when Fran was eight and the placid, dun-colored gelding put out to pasture at last. When the gelding died two years later, Jacob had refused to call the glue factory, but buried the horse instead. It had taken him six hours on a muggy July evening to finish the job and then he had never spoken of it again.

"Fran," Jacob interrupted Paul in mid-sentence. Startled from reverie, she looked up and met the quiet gray eyes. There was a direct appeal in the eyes, in the softened lines of the face. "You haven't said anything."

And she knew she would have to say it at last, say what she had thought she would never have to say because the inevitable decision would be made without her, while she was away and would not have to see it. She stalled for time, saying flippantly, "Well, I don't know, Papa. How many acres an hour do you think I could do strapped to a plow?"

Jacob's face remained unchanged.

"This is not a game, Frances."

"Of course not!" she snapped. "Nothing is ever a game to you, is it, Papa? Everything is always so damned serious, a scene from a tragedy."

She saw the wound strike home by the lowering of his eyes and the careful way he moved his fork to line it up with the knife on his plate.

"I'm sorry, Papa," she said feebly. "I'm sorry. That wasn't fair." And then Paul began talking again, quick and facile, smoothing things over, his horror of "scenes" moving him, almost, to eloquence.

Not fair, not fair. Of course not. There were the sleigh rides and the hayloft searches for newborn kittens when Jacob had held Henry's feet to prevent his getting stuck in the narrow passage from which the faint mewings came. And, that bright Saturday summer morning when Jimmy had committed the unforgivable sin of tracking mud onto Anna's newly-scrubbed kitchen floor; Anna standing on the back porch calling, "Jake! Jacob! You've got to do something about that boy," and her father, trotting in that odd way of his with his elbows held high and against his body, chasing Jimmy around the garage while she and Henry, dancing with excitement, cried from the hill, "He's coming the other way, Jimmy, he's coming the other way." Then the silence from behind the garage where father and child had surely met, broken at last by Jacob's roar of laughter and punctuated at intervals by Jimmy's breathless giggling until, at last, Anna, too, found her face crumbling into unwilling mirth before she turned back into the desecrated kitchen.

When had her father stopped laughing like that, Fran wondered; what had carved those lines into his face so that now he always looked serious? She knew, of course: the hatchets of pain and loss and grief. But what tiny knives were at work on her own face — that line already visible between her brows? Vexation, disappointment, "nerves." The instant the contrast occurred to her, she shrank from it, soothing the raw spot in her mind with the balm she kept always at hand: "I'm good at my work; I'm successful; I have a full life."

Paul's chatter had ceased and Jacob, lovable, inexorable, said again, "Well, Fran?"

"I can't help you, Papa," she cried. "I can't farm the land. What do you want from me?"

"I want you to tell me how you feel about all of this," he said. "That's all I want."

Cornered, she felt cold rage. "I think you must sell, Papa, and I have thought so for a long time. The farm is too much for you and mother alone."

Jacob winced visibly at the word "alone" and Anna made a quick gesture toward him, not touching him but putting her hand next to his saucer. Ashamed, Fran softened her tone. "And this old house is so big. Mama should have things easier now, too. You could have a lovely apartment in town. Much more convenient. Big enough, of course, for when we come to visit, but cozier than here. Wouldn't you have fun decorating and furnishing? And making new friends? It must get lonely here for you now with everyone —"

She trailed off because Jacob was slowly turning his face away from her. As his head moved, the blue shirt pulled away from his permanently sun-darkened throat, revealing the skin along his collar bone. The sight of that skin, as smooth and white as a baby's, filled Fran with an agonized tenderness.

"Papa, Papa. Forget the golf course. Why don't you sell the land to Uncle Peter so you and Mama can keep the house? Nothing much would be changed, but you wouldn't have to work so hard."

Jacob spoke from his averted face. "My brother, the gentleman farmer, I talked to him about that, but he tells me he's 'overextended.'"

"Uncle Peter said that?"

A sardonic smile twitched at the corner of Jacob's mouth. "I think it's his lawyer's word. Anyway, he's got so much money tied up in big machinery and new acreage, he can't see his way clear to invest in more."

"Then sell the land to the development and keep the house and enough for your garden," she said.

"That's a good idea, Papa," Henry said, shooting a conspiratorial glance at Fran. She turned away in distaste.

"I won't stay here to look at strangers tramping around on my land," Jacob said and though he didn't raise his voice, Fran recognized the finality in his tone.

"What's the difference, if the land has to go anyway, Papa?" Henry's distress was shrouding the table in cigarette smoke. "You're not making sense."

"Not to you, Henry," Anna said quietly. Forty years with Jacob had made a Himrich out of her in spite of her soft mildness.

"You're right about one thing, Henry," Jacob said at last. "I'm tired and there doesn't seem to be any other way." There was a kind of desperation on his half-hidden face.

Then he said, softly, "You make a very good living, Paul."

Paul jerked nervously to attention and looked around the table. "What do you mean, Dad?"

Without turning, Jacob said, "You could afford a country house. It would be nice for you and Cindy and the kids in the summer, right next to the golf course." His voice cracked on the last words and Fran felt slightly ill. All three children, puzzled at this latest turn in the discussion, looked at their mother; it was a habit from their childhood. Often Anna had acted as translator when Jacob could not, or would not, say what he meant.

"It wouldn't be so hard for us to move," she said. "If the house stayed in the family."

Paul was stunned — out of his depth. "Gosh, it would be nice, but this house —" He faltered. "Well, Cindy is used to more convenience. You know, a modern house and — and things. You know how women are, Dad." He grinned crookedly and fell silent.

"If I sell all the land to the development, they will tear down this house." There was an awful silence after Jacob's words. Anna spoke at last.

"His grandparents built this house."

"I know that, Mom. And I know you're fond of it, but it's not as if it were St. Peter's or something," Paul said. "It's an old house. It doesn't have that much real property value."

"Yes, Mama, it's an old house," Henry said viciously for he was angered by an old grievance. "But even if the property value is low, Papa would never think of asking me to buy it. I don't make a very good living like the college boy, do I? No, I went to work after high school so he could have his free ride to that good living."

"That's a typical non sequitur, Henry," Fran said drily.

"And that's another thing. The two of you. The educated ones. Always talking down to me. You, Fran, with your classy Ph.D., always sneering at Louise and me. You never ask me how my wife is. You two always had what you wanted — Papa's little girl and Mama's baby boy — but I never got to go to college."

Fran's nerves finally gave way.

"Oh brother! You've been harping on that theme so long, I think you've actually come to believe it yourself. You have that picture of yourself as the self-sacrificing big brother, but the truth is that you didn't go to college because you chose not to. You wanted to go right out and start cashing in on a fat salary, and it was fat in those days so don't snort. We never saw a dime of the money, Paul and I. And not Papa, either. College! I'll tell you how Paul and I made it on scholarships and by grubbing at dirty summer jobs. You were as selfish then as you are now. If you would speak truth in this house tonight, you would admit straight out that your real interest in this land sale is a tidy little estate for you to inherit."

"That is a dirty lie!"

Fran was moved to a little burst of hysterical laughter at the boyish phrase and the round-faced outrage she remembered so well from her childhood.

"It is a lie!" Henry raged. "I'm only thinking of them. But you! What have you ever done for this family? With your cushy job two hundred and fifty miles from any responsibility for anybody but yourself. You're too high class for the likes of us now, aren't you? Just who do you think you're kidding, anyway, calling yourself Frankie and driving around in a foreign sports car? You should be embarrassed to go out on the street in it, at your age."

Stung to tears, Fran said through her teeth, "Damn your Philistine soul, Henry."

"Enough." Jacob did not say it loudly, but his children recognized the tone. "This talk is at an end. I'll call Connors tomorrow and say I'll sell it all. It has to be."

He stood up heavily, pushing himself erect with his hands against the old table top, and walked straight out the open back door. Into the long silence that followed, Anna finally said, musingly, "Jimmy would have been a farmer, I think." Shocked at this unusual mention of their long-dead brother, the three children stared at their mother, who did not look up.

"We have no way of knowing that, Mama," Fran said softly. "He was so young."

Anna sighed and stood up. "Now I should get at these supper dishes. It's getting dark already. The days are so much shorter again. Hard to believe that summer's almost over." And she began to collect the rose-covered plates she used only for special occasions .

Ashamed, Fran began to help clear the table while Paul moved to the window and Henry reached for another cigarette.

"Henry, Henry," Fran said in a familiar, scolding tone. "You smoke too much. It's bad for you."

"I know, I know," he said. "I'm gonna quit one of these days."

Fran gathered knives and forks, thinking with half-guilty relief of returning the next day to her apartment to take delivery of the brown-and-gold striped loveseat. Suddenly Paul turned from the window and said under his breath so that Anna, running hot water over the precious roses, would not hear, "Jesus, I can't stand it! He's just standing out there, leaning on the stump fence and looking out over the farm."

The brothers exchanged glances.

"Fran," Henry said softly. "Go out and talk to him. I was mad before but you know you always were his pet."

Reluctantly, Fran handed the silverware to her brother and walked out into the gathering darkness. With the dew had come the fragrance of the earth, the dying heat of the brief northern summer clinging tenuously to the stubbled fields and the tangled tomato vines along the fence. When Fran came up to her father, he was resting both elbows in the smooth, upturned roots of one of the stumps, but he was not looking out over the farm. He was staring at the base of a sturdy old elm tree at the northeast corner of the house. Without looking at his daughter, he lifted one knotted hand and pointed at the tree.

"My grandfather died there," he said.

"What?!" Fran started, feeling suddenly chilled in her thin summer blouse.

"On a Monday morning. He'd come home from the churchyard where he'd just buried Grandma. Asiatic cholera. He had it, too, but he never let on. Didn't want to worry Grandma in her last hours. He made it that far and he died. When my Pa found him, it looked like he'd just sat down against the tree to take a nap."

"I never heard that story before, Papa," Fran said. "I wonder why you never told us." She gazed past Jacob at the thickening darkness under the tree, feeling suddenly frightened and young, unaccountably young and childlike. — "Imagine. Right there. My great grandfather."

Jacob looked at her now and she fell back before the concentrated bitterness in his face.

"My grandfather," he said and moved slowly back toward the house his bull-like shoulders sagging forward as he walked.

The Farm Bell Tolls

By Jack Miller

A YEAR OR SO AGO A University of Chicago economist who had recently won a Nobel prize emerged from the White House after a talk with President Reagan about the economy.

"Well, what's your view of the economic situation in the country," the White House press corps asked him.

The old economist began talking about the current "depression."

"You mean 'recession,' don't you, professor?" a reporter asked.

"No, I mean *depression*," the professor replied, annoyed. "I think I know a depression when I see one, and I see one."

In the cities, people continue to debate about whether the economic downturn is a depression or a recession. In the country, there's no debate. It's a depression, and everyone knows it. The only question is whether farmers are facing a serious crisis or full disaster.

By anyone's measurements, farmers haven't been in such bad shape since the 1930s. Some are being foreclosed by their creditors; others are selling out quietly; vast numbers are just hanging on.

What makes the current crisis especially serious is that great numbers of independent, family-sized farmers have *already* been forced off the farm in the last generation. In the period from 1970 to 1980 alone, *one-third* of our farm population got out. That left a tiny 2.5 per cent of Americans still on the farm. For all the political ballyhoo about saving the family farmer, the sober reality is that the family farm is already pretty well gone. What we have left are a few survivors — and unless something is done, soon, as many as half of them are going to be forced out by the current depression.

For those of us who live in rural America, the loss of farmers has been sapping our culture for many years. A healthy countryside needs large numbers of small, independent farmers, and we simply don't have them anymore. Solid old farmhouses have everywhere been torn down or left to fall apart. Country schools have been boarded up, bulldozed or converted. An occasional old town hall stands as a rotting relic of a brief period of self-determined rural democracy.

Lest we romanticize the recent past, it should be said that we are witnessing the final stage of a struggle that goes back a century and more in our part of the country. From the beginning settlers here have been up against combines of speculators, bankers, railroads, grain dealers and middlemen of all kinds. The history of the farmers' movements against these interests — the Grange, the Farmers Alliance, the Populist Party, the Non-Partisan League, the Farmer-Labor Association (and Party), the National Farmers Organization, the cooperatives, the farm strikes — all are filled with examples of vision, bravery and determination against awful odds. At their best these movements have fought not merely for a decent life for farmers and workers; they have fought for a society freed from the tyranny of a rampant commercial capitalism; they have sought to establish a different way for people to live and work together, a "Cooperative Commonwealth."

This tradition, too, has been ravished. The schools, even in rural areas, teach nothing of it. Other rural institutions ignore, or have forgotten, it. Agribusiness interests deny it. Most of the farm organizations reject it. Most of the farmers who have gone out in the last year to stop foreclosures at neighbors' farms had no idea — until it was reported in the *Wall Street Journal*, of all places — that their grandfathers had done the same thing at "penny auctions" in the 1930s. We can no longer keep track of our own history.

Would that we could look back to a period of unblemished, heroic history when American country folk stood strong against the forces of commercial culture; when they held to values of community and commitment to the land against the temptation to get ahead, to get rich, to leave their neighbor behind. Unfortunately, the picture is mixed. Some of our rural ancestors did indeed struggle both for a modest living and for the well-being of all. Others apparently succumbed to the lust for a quick profit at the expense of the land and the spirit of community.

The whole blame cannot be laid on our drive to conquer and subdue the land, nor on the "spirit of capitalism," nor on the exploiters and predators. Something deep and difficult to define has been wrong with our relationship to this land from the beginning.

One view is presented by the American historian Richard Hofstadter, who argues that the ideal of the self-made man "unleashed in the nation an entrepreneurial zeal probably without precedent in history, a rage for business, for profits, for opportunity, for advancement. ... What developed in America was an agricultural society whose real attachment was not to land but to land values."

While this perspective is not to be swallowed whole, we would do well to take a hard look at Hofstadter's assessment, put forth in his 1955 work, *The Age of Reform*:

"If a real culture means an emotional and craftsmanlike dedication to the soil, a traditional and pre-capitalist outlook, a tradition-directed rather than career-directed type of character, and a village community devoted to ancestral ways and habitually given to communal action, then the prairies and plains never had one."

No wonder a poet like Robert Bly, who grew up and has lived much of his life on the prairie near Madison, Minnesota, had to learn Norwegian, and finally Icelandic, in order to search out the remnants of his culture. It never took root in the new land.

Similar has been the experience of Erling Duus, a Nebraska-born preacher and folk culturist who has reached back to Denmark for the sources of his heritage in the folk-Christian movement of N.F.S. Grundtvig. Out of a belief that Americans have never come to terms with the new land in general and the great prairie in particular, Duus has written in *American Christianity and the American Earth* (1980):

"What we have mostly done in America is flee that immersion in immensity, that 'religious terror' .... The history of that failure is writ large in our treatment of the Red Man, our spoilation of the land, and in the slow retreat and devastation of rural America. We have refused to submit to the land to which we came as conquerors, but therefore too, it has refused us. We remain aliens. The failure of our religious institutions, specifically the Christian church, in this regard is tragic and extreme."

A number of church leaders, theologians and church commissions have made analyses in recent years of the problem of the land and of the people on it.

The Catholic bishops of the Heartland region (Minnesota, Wisconsin, Iowa, the Dakotas, Kansas, Nebraska, Illinois, Colorado and Wyoming) issued in 1980 a powerful statement entitled "Strangers and Guests: Toward Community in the Heartland." . . . They stressed that "Stewardship means caring for God's creation. It implies that civil title to a portion of the earth does not confer absolute ownership of it. That belongs to God alone. . . . The land is given by God for all people, not just for those who hold civil title to it."

The bishops found that the concentration of land ownership in the Heartland in fewer and fewer hands "directly contradicts the biblical concept of equitable land distribution." Further, they said, the heavy industrialization of agriculture is subjecting the land to heavy damage. Farm equipment has become so big and expensive that "farmers do not control but are controlled by technology."

The high costs and low return have forced many families into part-time farming, the bishops reported, with the result that both the land and family unity and stability have suffered. Many farm people have responded to cultural trends which contradict traditional religious values: "excessive competitiveness, consumerism, orientation toward profit maximization and an unquestioning acceptance of economic, political and legal structures that oppress people at home and abroad."

What to do about it? The bishops issued some strong recommendations, including legislation and policy to:

— Limit the rights of individuals and companies investing in land;

— Eliminate capital gains and investment credit tax writeoffs, and tax agricultural land according to its productive, not speculative, value;

— Tax bigger and more valuable farms at progressively higher rates;

— Set farm prices and farm labor rates at fair levels by public policy and law;

— Encourage farm producers, processors and handlers to bargain collectively for a fair return on their work and products;

— Give low-interest loans to aspiring, beginning and tenant farmers.

Finally, the bishops exhorted all people, urban and rural, to "recognize that their lifestyles, purchasing habits and expectations contribute directly and indirectly to the concentration of land ownership and the consequent abuse of the land. We are called as Christians to 'break with the frenzy of consumerism,' to 'find a simple way of living,' as we become more aware of how our consumption hurts people at home and abroad, depriving them even of life's necessities."

As the bishops make clear, we are not dealing here with "trends in agriculture" or "harmful farming practices" or "problems of erosion" or "the migration of rural people to the city." We are dealing with a fundamentally destructive way of being with each other and the earth. The "farm problem" is not separate from the threat of nuclear extinction. Our traditions have been co-opted into a political-economic-social system dominated by uncontrolled technology and run by a predatory elite. We have become stockholders in the system. We care nothing for this system's policies — we only want our dividends to keep coming.

It will do no good merely to pass legislation to lessen the destruction, though we must do that. We need to undergo a radical conversion and prepare to make whatever sacrifices are necessary to restore our wounded earth and create caring communities. This cannot be done without the spread of a new ethic of land and of life. Nor can it be done without determined struggle, courageous and nonviolent, against the tyrannical system that confronts us. This system and its agents must not merely be defeated and replaced, for that would only lead to a new form of tyranny; they must be transformed.

NORTH COUNTRY
ANVIL

No. 43 $2.00

THE FARM BELL TOLLS

The Resurgence of Populism   •   Bringing Education Home

Erosion of Land & Culture   •   A Lifelong Farm Radical   •   Rapture

Disarming Ourselves   •   A Mouthful of Grass

The Resurgence of Populism

By Paul Schaefer

ONE MORNING LAST FALL I stood in the desolation of a vacant Wisconsin farmyard. Toys and tools were scattered on the lawn, a kitchen window was cracked and taped, and several barn doors yawned uselessly. An awful emptiness existed where, three years before, a family had pursued the American Dairy Dream. The dream fell apart: they sold their cows and left the community; the farm was put up for rent.

As I examined an old hay rake, two semitrailer trucks pulled up to the barn. Another in a series of renters was coming, and I was there to help unload his hay. This man had been a tenant on a farm near Madison, on land owned by a wealthy professional. With little warning, the landlord had sold the place, forcing the farmer to leave. He had come to our area in response to an ad in *Hoard's Dairyman*. The farmer's dairy cows, some 40 Holsteins, would arrive later in the day and be milked almost as soon as they got off the truck.

While we worked, the two truck drivers, both from farm families, joked about how crazy the farmer was for shipping hay and a dairy herd around the state. They also laughed at their own plight: loads being scarce, they were reduced to hauling alfalfa in their sleek reefer rigs. "Shit," one of the truckers spat as we repaired the broken bale elevator, "it gets so a person doesn't know what the hell to do."

Not knowing what the hell to do is the perennial American farm problem. Most have responded by leaving. Between 1929 and 1965, more than 30 million people left the farm, a number greater than the total of European immigrants arriving in America between 1820 and 1960. Between 1970 and 1980, when all the woods hippies were moving back to the land, our farm population dropped by one third.

Many of the five and a half million people still farming are in tough shape, as is the land. Over half of the remaining farms are small, part-time operations dependent on off-farm employment. More than half of our farmland is worked by tenants. Farmers run ever-larger pieces of land with enormous machinery purchased at high interest in an attempt to counter low prices with increased volume. Like colonized peoples everywhere, they are forced to sell their raw materials cheap while buying manufactured goods dear. The difference is made up with injurious credit, resulting in no-exit debt and the eventual loss of farms through liquidations, bankruptcies and foreclosures.

Trying to forestall loss, farmers work the land more intensively, planting exportable row crops which open the soil to erosion losses up to fifty tons per acre. Looking over their shoulder, they see not only their creditors, but an increasing number of developers eager to urbanize prime farm land at enormous profit. And they see their families, educated to expect urban standards of living and leisure in a time when real farm income is lower than it has been since the depression of the 1930s.

Last January two attorneys spent most of an hour talking to a group of farmers in Mondovi, Wisconsin. The lawyers were telling the farmers how to combat foreclosures. Many of the farmers present faced the loss of their farms.

The meeting had been organized by members of the Wisconsin Farm Unity Alliance, a group formed in reaction to the latest farm crisis. Unity, which has a sister group in Iowa, is committed to a goal of fair prices for farmers. Until that goal is achieved, the organization seeks to prevent farm sales forced by creditors: hence, the Mondovi gathering. In related activities, Unity members had publicly protested the loan policies of a nearby Production Credit Association, one of the major sources of farm credit in the area. As a result of the protests, association officials were forced to renegotiate a loan with a distressed farmer. At the regional level of the association, officials then made an investigation of loan procedures, and the board of directors agreed to review cases where farmers were having troubles. In all of this, Unity has shown farmers that credit and other policies are not fixed in stone — but matters subject to debate and open to change.

While useful, the information conveyed by the lawyers at the Mondovi meeting was, I judged, not welcome. The arcane legalisms surrounding foreclosures were just further evidence of the baffling complications encountered by those who simply want to do a good job of raising food and being paid for it. To farm these days requires the aid of lawyers, tax experts, management consultants and financial analysts. Farming is now big business. Those who are unwilling or unable to adjust should get out, it is said, and most have done so.

When Tom Quinn, Unity President, and Tom Saunders, an organizer, began to talk to the sixty-some farmers, eyes brightened and the meeting livened. The response was partly due to the speakers' skills: Quinn told a good joke and Saunders has a forceful manner. People were also responding to the Unity message, which is that farmers need to organize, locally and nationwide, and to form alliances with workers and consumers. Of greatest importance, however, was the response of those at the meeting to one another.

The focus of the gathering left the head of the room, where the lawyers and organizers stood, and moved around to fix on farmers who spoke up about their difficulties, about the frailties and unfairness of the credit system and its bureaucrats, about the need to stand together. Several men noted that when a farmer is in financial straits, lenders make him feel that he is at fault — and singularly so. Embarrassed, farmers quietly go under without realizing that many of their neighbors have been, are, or will be in the same situation. The meeting's greatest value, therefore, was mutual awareness and the support and confidence that grow from such beginnings of community.

Talking to Quinn, Saunders and Craig Adams, Unity treasurer, several days later, I told them that I had seen some awfully fancy pickup trucks at the meeting. Weren't they, as some of my neighbors charged, simply helping the "cowboy" farmers who, having access to credit, bought everything in sight, including more land than they could reasonably work? They responded that, while farm foreclosures and price legislation are immediate concerns, their great hope is the creation of a radically different set of social possibilities. To create such change requires working with the diversity present in farm society. How is anyone, argued Saunders, going to be able to "back off" from cowboy farming without evidence of alternative ways, and the assistance to enact them?

Quinn, Saunders and Adams are dairy farmers. They differ from many other dairymen, however, in several respects.

The queen of dairy cows is the black and white Holstein, milked by most. Some hardheads milk and argue by other breeds. The Unity trio milk Jerseys, the small brown ladies with Bette Davis eyes and butterfat tests so high some claim that existing measures can't reckon them. Quinn and Adams, their wives Helen and Lucy and their children each own 30-cow herds of registered Jerseys. Their farms, close enough for the exchange of work, include modest acreages, silos, tractors, homes and debt. Saunders, his wife Pam and their children farm somewhat differently. Tom calls their place "the manifestation of Wendell Berry's vision." Berry is the poet-farmer who makes a compelling case for a return to small-scale, horse-powered farming. His vision, Tom Saunders version, consists of 80 acres, a new dairy and horse-barn built from lumber logged and sawed at home, an old house, 12 milk cows and a number of horses. Still working on the vision, Saunders recently revived an old threshing machine and used it to thresh his own and a neighbor's oats last fall.

None of the Unity organizers has a farm background, although Saunder's father was an agriculture teacher. Each went to college in the '60s and was involved in anti-war activities. Quinn was a founder of the food co-op movement in Minneapolis, attempting to create economic institutions that were part of the political process. In 1972, he and his wife and a number of others formed a cooperative farm near Connorsville, Wisconsin. As with other such communal ventures, most of the members eventually left to pursue separate lives. Tom and Helen stayed and worked in the area, bought some cows, and rented their present place.

The Saunders were also involved in cooperative, communal activities in St. Paul. Tom did a brief tour as a rural school teacher in Montana, then returned to the Twin Cities. After moving to their present place in Prairie Farm, Wisconsin, Tom became involved in an anti-nuclear movement that stopped Northern States Power Company from building a power plant at nearby Tyrone.

Craig Adams and his wife live with kin: Craig's parents and one set of grandparents. Previously resident in the Twin Cities, they all moved to Connorsville about the same time. A graduate of a Lutheran college, Craig has been involved with a Christian Land Stewardship study program. Unlike Quinn and Saunders, he uses a religious idiom in speaking of the farmers' plight and the social change needed to ease it.

The three organizers met socially as members of a large back-to-the-land community in the area. Perhaps because of their background, they are willing to think about, and act upon, the farm problem with some confidence that it can be solved.

"Bad management" is a common explanation for recent farm failure in my community. "A lot of people got into farming during inflation," a neighbor recently told me; "they weren't real farmers but increasing land prices kept their net worth up so they looked O.K. on paper. Now that land prices are falling, these guys can't make it, so we're getting rid of the chaff."

Farm Unity members charge that the "bad manager" epithet is a red herring. Price, they say, is the real issue. When farmers are not even paid for the cost of production, let alone able to realize a small profit, even the best managers go under. Hence their support for "parity," which is simply a means of keeping farm prices and costs in balance with one another and the rest of the economy. To ensure parity, the government guarantees loans on certain commodities at whatever a fair price is determined to be in line with a base period when equity existed. In doing so, it essentially places a floor on prices, in that farmers can get at least what the government is offering, thereby forcing buyers to offer that much or more. If the farmer gets his price, he repays the loan with interest. Failing to get a price, he keeps his loan and we, the government, get to keep the grain and store it against future shortages or sell it when the market goes to a point beyond parity. Because program participants are required to observe certain production limits and soil conservation practices, problems of oversupply and soil erosion are controlled.

The replacement of price supports with credit has a source in government and corporate policy. As outlined in *The Loss of Our Family*

Farms, a U.S. Farmer's Association booklet, a Committee for Economic Development (CED) was formed by corporate leaders and academic economists during World War II. The committee was set up to create policies designed to prevent economic chaos following the war.

Among their proposals was that of rapidly reducing the number of people on farms by cutting government price supports in the parity program. The move was justified by rhetorical concern about farmers' low incomes, which would be increased once there were fewer farmers. Getting rid of farmers was more in the interest of the corporations represented on the CED, however. Among the ways they stood to gain, Unity members say, was the creation of an agricultural sector more favorable to large capital investment and the depression of wages caused by the entrance of over two million farm people into the labor pool. With the virtual elimination of parity in the mid-'50s, the CED proposals became government practice, and millions began to leave the land.

To achieve parity, Unity hopes to create a political base among farmers, workers and consumers which will be powerful enough to influence legislation — and in time effect radical social change in the direction of democratic socialism. "The biggest obstacle to real change in this country, " says Tom Quinn, "is calm acceptance of hard times and inequities; what breaks that down is vision." Unity's vision draws much inspiration from American Populism, particularly as described by Lawrence Goodwyn in his book *The Populist Movement*.

Following the Civil War, Goodwyn claims, the manipulation of money by banking interests led to farm disasters. Prices dropped cruelly: corn sold for less than 10 cents a bushel, wheat for less than 30 cents. Where, say, 100 bushels of wheat had equalled a mortgage payment, 200 to 400 bushels were now required. And debts were being repaid in dollars much more costly than those borrowed. Interest rates also soared, forcing many farmers into forms of debt-peonage little different from slavery.

Conditions were worst in the South, where a crop-lien system required that farmers sign over future crops to local "furnishing merchants" in exchange for credit at the merchants' stores. These "advancing men" would charge up to 200 per cent interest, ensuring that whatever price a farmer's crop brought, and it was lower each year, it never would pay off the loan. Following years of debt, farmers eventually "paid out" by turning their land over to the merchants and then staying on as tenants. By World War II, over fifty per cent of land in the South and Southwest was tenant-farmed. The majority of those still owning land were also heavily indebted.

To combat the crop-lien system, a group of men founded a "Farmers Alliance" in Lampasas County, Texas, in 1877. Denouncing the railroads, trusts, capitalists and money power in general, the movement inspired others. By 1885, the Texas Alliance had 50,000 members. Alliance members established what Goodwyn calls the "world's first large-scale working-class cooperative" to sell their cotton and buy necessities wholesale. In its attempt to circumvent the merchant bankers and end the crop-lien system, the cooperative brought enormous hope to farmers. By 1890, 40,000 suballiances included more than a million members in the South, West and Midwest.

The Alliance cooperatives foundered, however, on the ever-present rock of credit. Wholesalers and bankers, natural antagonists of the Alliance, refused to deal with the co-ops. In response, C. W. McCune, an Alliance leader, created a "sub-treasury" plan. McCune proposed, essentially, to socialize American agriculture — and, by extension, the American financial system. In every county producing more than $500,000 of agricultural goods, a federal warehouse, or "subtreasury," would be built. Farmers would store their crops in these warehouses to await a favorable price. To tide them over, they could secure a government loan of up to 80 percent of the market value of their stored crops. This loan would be given in the form of certificates of deposit — "greenbacks" — which would be legal tender. When the farmer sold his crop, he would repay the loan with 2 per cent interest plus handling charges. The program thus would have allowed farmers to avoid having to sell their crops at harvest time, when prices were lowest. They could also sell to whomever they chose, instead of solely to the furnishing merchants. Private lenders, in fact, with their usuriously high rates, were to be replaced by the federal government, with low interest rates.

This "fundamental restructuring of the monetary system" would have ended the power that moneylenders had over individual farmers and organizations such as the Alliance, and because of the millions of greenbacks issued after each harvest, would also have ended the "hard money" currency contraction supported by bankers in favor of the soft "people's currency" advocated by farming and labor interests. In effect, the "subtreasury" system would have enabled the producing classes to gain control of their economic destiny.

Greeted with grateful approval by Alliance members, McCune's plan was ridiculed by the forces of finance. To bring the plan to legislative possibility, political action was needed. The Alliance had already been successful in electing numerous local, state and federal representatives. Some of this political work was carried out within the prevailing Democratic and Republican parties. When both parties refused to support the subtreasury plan, however, Alliance men created a "People's Party" with the objective of uniting all working class Americans against their common foe, the finance capitalists. For a number of reasons best read about in Goodwyn's book, the Party effort failed, and Populism faded into ignominious history.

Equally important with the economic considerations of McCune's plan were its social and political implications. The Alliance, members said, was a schoolroom. In it, vast numbers of oppressed people began to understand the source of their oppression and to find an exit from it in mutual aid. The Alliance cooperative, offering the possibility of an end to crop-liens, engaged farmers' energies and aspirations so completely as to take on religious significance.

Populist organizers, called "lecturers," were self-educated farmers with oratorical skills who spread the gospel of what came to be called the "Cooperative Commonwealth." Revivalistic encampments, lasting up to a week, held thousands of inspired people. The result, in a remarkably short time, was a subculture complete with its own worldview ("an industrial society in which generous social relations among masses of people might prevail") and the means — including lecturers, newspapers, social and political activists and cooperatives — of maintaining it against the forces of the dominant culture. That the Alliance culture survived the end of the cooperatives was attested to by Populist influence in subsequent successful organizing efforts, including the American Socialist Party and the Farmers Union, as well as numerous lesser forms of agrarian reform and revolt. Most importantly, the vision still holds promise.

A newspaper I receive recently featured a dairy farmer who, "vowing to fight rather go under," is milking his cows four times a day. The results of this effort to "increase production," the dairyman's mantra, probably will be disastrous for both the farmer and his cows. As it is, many dairy herds are overbred, overfed and overmilked by farmers who are severely overworked.

I respect and envy these men. Their level of skill and intelligence far surpasses most anything I've encountered. I also think they are crazy in a singleminded way that it is usefully wondrous for everyone to be on occasion but that as a way of life is simply no good. And their success, if you call it that, bodes ill for agriculture. Just like their supercows, these farmers are supermen. If everyone else has to be like them to survive in farming, and that is what is being advertised, hardly anyone (and we are dangerously close to that now) will be farming.

This new breed of farmer is above all a "good manager." The Unity farmers challenge the very notion of "managing" a farm. I agree with them. "Managing," as I see it, is done by "management," an overseer class in the business bureaucracy. To call farmers "managers" is to claim that farming is primarily a business, where profit must take precedence over the nurturance, husbandry and good work that is really farming. Farmers *should* turn a dollar, but they should get it *because*, and not in spite of, the care they lavish on soil, animals, their families and communities. Such care is contrary to the business ethic. "Manager" is agribusiness newspeak which seeks to convince farmers that they are members of the very class invading their domain. This is a tactic as old and obvious as imperialism, which seeks to create its own reflection in the faces of the colonized.

If increasing production and management are not the farmers' answers, then what is? The Unity people say "price." As I choose to understand them, "price" is a code word, a temporary rack on which to hang our seed caps. At the meeting, we find out that "price" means "parity" means the "subtreasury" means "populism" means "cooperative commonwealth" means "something better" in the way we relate to one another, to the land and, if you like, to God.

In order to offer "something better," several things have to be done. The foremost is education, which is part of Unity's effort. Whatever the narrow merits of raw-material economics, it is a good way of getting at important questions. Why do many Americans eat so carelessly, for example, remaining ignorant of and unconcerned with farming issues?

Observing a camp of African Bushmen by contrast, we would note the care taken by people as they distribute meat from a kill. The size, quality and order of giving each piece is of great significance, revealing much about the group's social order. In most such pre-state societies, food is the primary means of value, with matters of status, prestige, social responsibility and expression of humanity linked inextricably with the procurement and distribution of food.

The creation and control of food surpluses has everything to do with the formation of states and empires. Pomp, pyramids and the mystification of great numbers of people are largely impossible without granaries. In recent times, the noted political economist David Ricardo proposed a corn (wheat) theory of value which recognized the pivotal political and price-setting role of agriculture in the industrial world. Farms, he argued, are of singular importance in that they provide the one "input" — food — required by all other endeavors. In all of the excitement with high tech, we seem to have forgotten that you can grow corn without computers, but you can't grow computers without corn. Whoever controls the corn controls the country — and the city, a lesson we may have to relearn at the cost of our remaining freedoms.

Basic to any society is a system of distribution — who gets what, and why. Always a complicated matter, distribution and its effects are nonetheless fairly clear in small, face-to-face societies. Perhaps because things are so clear, much tension, frequent arguments and special care surround the movement of goods, say, on a small Pacific island. As human groups grow larger in size and systems of exchange more complicated, room appears for individuals and elites to claim special knowledge about distribution. Such claims can be and often are self-fulfilling in that as they are honored, the claimants gain control over the local economy. On the other hand, such claims are often not borne out by events. So they are in need of bolstering from all possible areas, including the religious, where gods are called in to explain the inexplicable and support the insupportable. Hence systems of distribution come to be seen as divinely ordained, or as part of the natural order.

Such is the situation in America today. The "economy," all-pervasive in our lives, is increasingly seen as a natural phenomenon governed by obscure laws which only the most perceptive can figure out. Millions of farmers are forced from their land, millions of workers are without work, and we are told that the "silent hand" of the marketplace (the god of economists) is nevertheless working toward good ends.

By exposing the activities of the Committee for Economic Development and similar enterprises, Farm Unity reminds us that the "silent hands," not surprisingly, are those of powerful, moneyed individuals and organizations whose interest is usually at our expense. Economies are created and controlled by human beings exercising social, political, religious and cultural influence. If we seek to end our participation in the culture of usury, we must exercise similar influence.

Parity removes farmers' financial destinies from the tender mercies of the market and places them in the hands of the government. So what? During Populist times the government was controlled by bankers, and now it is largely influenced by the corporate world. The only way that the government will be truly responsive to the people is if it is the people. Us. But in an age of "mass political alienation" when, as Goodwyn states, "sophisticated deference masks private resignation," how do people seriously begin to think of themselves as the government?

"Active democracy," says Tom Quinn, "has very little to do with voting but has a lot to do with connections that people have with each other, a feeling of community that this culture deprives people of, all those things that give people self respect and a sense that change is possible. So Unity's chief effort must be "to build the places where people see themselves practicing democracy." The meeting at Mondovi, and similar gatherings, are such places. Perhaps the only good thing about the small number of people still farming is that they should find it easier to define their mutual interest — and organize accordingly.

Ties must then be created with the vast urban citizenry, a problem the earlier Populists were unable to solve. To forge a new alliance of farm and city is, it seems to me, the major task facing all of us who live in the country and hope to see rural life flourish. For those in town, it is a major task for all of those who hope to eat. "To restore a proper balance between city and rural life is perhaps the greatest task in front of modern man," said E. F. Schumacher.

Unity members are working at this with something called a Credit Alliance. Its rationale is this: most of the money and most of the people are in the city. Most of the land and a great deal of the work, good work, is in the country. Unions, churches, and "socially conscious" folks together command vast sums. This money should be used to keep existing farmers farming, and to encourage lots of other people, now unemployed or poorly employed, to return to the land. Low-interest loans or long-tenure leases on Alliance-controlled land would entail, like parity programs, certain production limits and land stewardship requirements. Unity is talking to a number of people about such a program, and the response is enthusiastic.

Historian Goodwyn charges that most American radicals never get out of the kitchen, where they are busy theorizing, backbiting and nursing their imagined wounds. In becoming farmers, Adams, Saunders and Quinn are well out of the kitchen. Now, with their Populist vision of a cooperative commonwealth, they must get out of the barn. Once out, they will find that a lot of people know what the hell to do. The real work, then, is to get them together to do it.

Reflections on Mercury Vapor Light

By Paul Gilk

THERE ARE A NUMBER OF people here in southeastern Minnesota who are among the most creative and energetic of farm activists, yet who are also fundamentally opposed to many of the agricultural practices of the very farmers they support and defend. These activists are seeing more and more clearly that the absence of a positive rural vision on the part of pro-farm organizations reflects — not so much a lack of imagination on the part of farmers — but a hidden defense of the rural status quo. That is, the reason why save-the-family-farm organizations are not calling for an *increase* in the number of small farms is due to the farmers' inclination to protect their agribusiness turf.

One sees this trait as well in the startling absence of proposals for a less chemically-addictive farming, for less machine and fossil fuel dependence, and for reduction in the size of operations. Say what one will, farmers (with some significant exceptions) have bought into the macho productivist mentality.

A man I know, who is himself an organic commercial gardener and an actively concerned citizen, has chosen not to become involved with farm organizations. It's not that he doesn't understand that food is wildly underpriced and undervalued in the urban-industrial, capitalist economy — he knows that clearly and unmistakably at first hand. But he is so repulsed by the kind of farming he sees going on around him that he cannot, in good conscience, come to its defense.

Nor is this a lofty and abstract ideological "purity." These agribusiness addictions — chemical use, excessive mechanization, large-scale operations — are exactly what's wrong with American farming. Many activists are fighting for the family farm because they fear that the consequences of yet more auctions and foreclosures will only make an already awful situation worse — namely, that even larger agribusiness operation will be so totally dependent on chemicals and huge machines that grassroots protest would be utterly ineffective.

A decent price for farm products and debt relief for farmers bur-dened by outrageous interest rates are important issues. Important, yes, but not entirely adequate. The issue is not merely that farmers caught with expansion fantasies are being foreclosed on, nor even that prices for agricultural commodities make repayment, in some cases, impos-sible. The basic issue is one of social and ecological policy. And the policy in question is, simply stated, whether we shall encourage and promote an ecological reconstruction of rural culture or whether rural culture will be let go to the dogs.

For the most part, rural culture has already gone to the dogs. There are no small rural schools. Activities within the consolidated school system and noise over the commercial media constitute the heart of "folk culture" in the countryside. There are no barn raisings, no horses and buggies, no quilting bees, no barn dances, no folk songs, no coop-erative harvest crews, no neighborhood inns or hostels.

Several of us were returning from a potluck supper the other night, driving through the countryside on back roads. The woman who was at the wheel said, suddenly — "Why do all these farmers have mercu-ry vapor lights? Don't people *like* the darkness?"

This woman is a skilled homesteader who gardens well, cuts her own firewood, builds and repairs buildings, and tends her bees and poultry with care. She lives in an old farmhouse with a woodburning heater and a woodburning cookstove, and she wouldn't install a mer-cury vapor lamp if one were offered to her free. Her intent is to create and live out a household economy of simple abundance. She knows that her psychological and spiritual well-being come through doing what she does well — treating the soil and animals with respect, hav-ing time to walk in the woods, listen to music, read books and maga-zines, visit with friends. She is also one of the leading farm activists in the area, sometimes sick at heart over what she feels called upon to defend.

The tragic irony is that these activists, whose aid and support many beleaguered farmers need and appreciate, are only grudgingly listened to when they speak of deeper issues. Could it be that the lives of farm-ers are already so devoid of natural pleasures and cultural convivialities, so plugged into the Standard of Living, and its commercial opiates, that they are incapable of breaking out of their productivist and consumerist addictions?

In my opinion, the most immediate and critical farm issue is the use of agribusiness poisons. I say this because, important as decent prices, debt relief and reduction of scale are, the poisoning of the soil and water is the most sinister feature of current agricultural practice. Our excessive fossil-fuel consumption may well be robbing the future, but the use of chemicals is *poisoning* the future.

Without chemicals, it would he extremely difficult if not impossible to sustain present farm size. A chemical-free agriculture would, to some degree, reduce the quantity (but not the quality) of yields. This would serve to elevate commodity prices while reducing overhead. Organic practice on the farm, in the context of smaller scale, diversification and rotation, would result in the restoring of cultivation to its proper place, and therefore strengthen the bond of affection that good farmers must, instinctively, have for the life of the soil. Any person who does not respect the ecological integrity of the land has no right to disturb the land, much less to be engaged in farming.

All this said, it is probably unrealistic to expect farmers to adopt ecologicallv sound practices in the context of a larger society which, while paying lip service to conservation and "the environment," is unwilling to acknowledge the clear connection between the Standard of Living and ecological degradation, as well as the connection between Progress and cultural sterility. None of us wants a radioactive waste repository in our area, but that doesn't mean we are willing to let go the luxury — and it *is* luxury, not necessity — of amusing ourselves with electrical gadgets and appliances run off nuclear power plants. We refuse to look at the whole picture, and so our little piecemeal solutions only postpone dealing with the real problem, and the problem gets worse.

In other words, the contradictions in our cultural schizophrenia are becoming increasingly apparent; but to make do with less commercial affluence, to allow the fertile darkness of the rural night to embrace us, to renounce the greed and vanity of our productivist and consumerist fantasies in all their mercury vapor sterility, all this requires a major change (call it a transformation) of social and political consciousness. Yet virtually everyone wants more of the prevailing economic pie, not less.

These local activists have already settled for less, and their lives are richer for it. They are coming to the defense of farmers because they themselves need a cooperative and sensible rural culture to live in. For the most part, those whom the activists defend are unworthy of the passionate and citizenly support they are given free of charge. To earn this support, farmers need to repent of their agribusiness fantasies and practices, and begin to take seriously both the ecological integrity of the land and the cultural coherence of the rural community.

If the lives of these activists are indicative of what settling for less will do for the quality of life, then getting out of the mainstream is (or can be) a wonderful exercise in learning that small is beautiful. We've substituted technology for cooperation, economic abstractions for cultural vitality. "Saving the family farm" is only one aspect of what activists are about; their deeper purpose is the reconstruction of rural life and culture.

Who Owns "Organic"?

By Steven Schwen

THE ORGANIC GROWERS AND BUYERS Association (OGBA) was formed in the early 1970s to promote and legitimize the organic farm as a necessary alternative to commercial agriculture. The organization has always been short on funds and run by volunteers, depending on folks who are already pretty busy. Many of these people were young, idealistic "back-to-the-landers," bringing with them a spectrum of notions about the earth and human relationships. Some were traditional farmers who never liked the chemical onslaught in agriculture — or who saw the damage being done and re-evaluated their use of chemicals. (There were, and are, as many organic farmers who didn't join the organization and are content, independently, to let their lives be the statement of their convictions.)

There has been an attempt to include buyers of organic produce, and there are members who are consumers, wholesalers, and retailers, processors and suppliers of related goods and services.

The certification program has gone from farmers and buyers volunteering to certify other farmers who reimbursed them for mileage — to a lapse when the program didn't exist for a couple of years — to the present, where "professional" certifiers are hired (some of whom have never farmed organically). Fees are in the range of $80 a year or a little more.

Certification cost is becoming the take-off point for a controversy that is building currently. But the real issue is not limited to the cost of certification, or who certifies, or even whether or not certification is necessary. It really involves a clash of visions between idealists and economic pragmatists (economic opportunists?), between small and large, between spiritual and political, between grassroots democracy and bureaucratic dominance. The importance of this collision is that it represents a critical point in the stage-set for the next act of the Great American Agricultural Drama.

The organic farm movement has grown to where it has broad acceptance and support. It owes this growth to the farmers who struggled against the current, to the organizations and magazines, to earth-keeping spirituality, to the food co-ops, to the counter-culture, and to the chemical disasters affecting people and the land.

And now that politicians and bureaucrats are uncomfortably trying to explain themselves in the face of the current agricultural disaster, they are anxious to pick up on some new agricultural approaches that can avoid such disaster. And here we have "market potential," perhaps enough in the near future to support bureaucracies, agribusiness and the economic structure that the privileged American business class thrives in. They want to own "organic" so they can best control it and use it to "further the interests of the public." This has produced a marriage between one faction of the OBGA and the State of Minnesota. This faction has used the smaller growers and buyers over the years, talked them into the certification program, enticed them into membership, used them as statistics for funding and clout, and then excluded them from participation in "their own" organization.

But there is more than market potential here. "Organic" has been the property of those outside the mainstream, those dedicated to a vision of a new world without pollution, with economic justice, with more people on the land using appropriate technology, revitalizing rural America and developing a sense of community based on personal interaction and interdependence, as well as renewed faith in God (the spiritual), rather than in business and government.

The organic vision has given them viability both on the farm and in the alternative economy represented by the food co-ops and co-op restaurants, as well as other alternative businesses run by individuals devoted to a more wholistic vision. Organic food has allowed like-minded individuals to funnel their dollars into this alternative economy and buy more than chemically-free food. They have been buying a whole new world on the installment plan.

For many small growers, and for organic growers in general, this meant that they could develop a committed clientele that was willing to pay more for their produce. This has allowed wages for the farmers' labor to reach a level that makes economic survival possible.

Full Circle Organic Growers' Cooperative, which has a strong commitment to the ideals of appropriate technology, appropriate earth-people and people-people relationships, has used these ideals to promote and market organic produce through the alternative food system with great success. Full Circle, which represents six full-time farms and that many more part-time farms, operates by consensus and volunteerism and has in the past four years been one of the prime forces in getting a decent wage for organic farmers for the Twin Cities marketplace. This has happened because of commitment to ideals, hard work, good-quality food, and hand-in-hand cooperation and consciousness-raising efforts by farmers and produce workers in the alternative businesses. It occurred independently of whether the OGBA had its certification program in place or not.

In the past few years the OGBA has been headed by Yvonne Buckley, who is not a farmer but is dedicated to organic agriculture. Faced with constant lack of funds and a burgeoning workload in the office, she has pursued grants, donations and memberships to raise money for the office and staff. But it is finally to certification fees that she has turned, seeing this as the most reliable and realistic source of income. So the focus of the OGBA for the last few years has been almost entirely on certification, to the neglect of other important functions, and in some instances to their detriment.

A marriage with the state became necessary as part of the plan, which includes setting up a professional certifying organization, licensed and regulated by the state. In exchange, they "sell" organic to the state. The state defines and controls what is organic. This means that organic is no longer an alternative. It doesn't involve questions of scale, appropriate technology, or the sustainability of fossil-fuel-dependent export economics. The state decides who gets certified and by whom. The state sets user fees to pay the costs of the program. This makes organic mainstream.

This is not all bad. It may reduce chemical use on the land and get more chemically uncontaminated food on the shelves. The argument is that by making organic official, this will lend credibility to the product, so that the price will rise as more people buy organic because they now know that it is truly "organic" and not the product of some opportunist taking advantage of them. But this may also supplant the movement back to the land by small farmers — with a temporary revitalization of the "commercial" farm and the agribusiness industry that has destroyed rural America in the last four decades.

Geared toward distant markets, it will eventually backfire on the growers and put them in competition with other growers in Mexico or Guatemala or Idaho or California because none of the other values discussed — like scale or economic justice — will be considered. Farmers will be at the mercy of the traders and of distant markets, and the price eventually will go down. The fees for the bureaucracy, however, will remain the same or go up, and the red tape, paperwork, and legal hassles will increase exponentially. The well-to-do in Europe, Japan, or the Eastern U.S. will get the good food; our neighbors will not. There is also a question of whether high certification fees ($500 per year or more) will actually encourage more organic farming (or consuming).

These are issues that need to be discussed, now and intensely. And yet to achieve their agenda, Buckley and the executive committee have thwarted efforts to have this very discussion. Why the struggle? What is at stake? This: a salary of $30,000 to $40,000 a year for Buckley, $18 per hour for certification-committee work, $300 a day plus expenses for professional certifiers . . . and on the other side, the struggle to hang onto some hard-won turf by small alternative farmers. We could see the same legislative process, the same big-is-better bureaucratic solution, the same governmental-regulation-produces-clean-safe-food mentality that destroyed small dairy farmers and prevented people from selling home-baked bread, home-made maple syrup or apple cider, and destroyed the real alternative agriculture.

What can we do? The present approach is a bad one. We've seen it before. We need to reassess, look around some more. We could look at the cooperative, grower-oriented Maine Organic Farmers' and Gardeners' Association as an example and model. We could implement democracy and discussion in the OGBA and save it from worse evils than lack of funds. We could, all of us — farmers and consumers alike

— retain ownership of "organic" and let its power change the rural landscape the world over.

Father

Outside, in the dark, your grandson's
first winter is breaking another record.
The breakfast table's polished wood
warms us in its dome of light.
I think of a joke you could have said
and stick my smile into a mug of coffee.
It's cool spring, and I walk the plowed
earth with a lunch pail and coffee jar.
You stop the B John Deere, and I run
deep. You throttle back
to a slow gallop. The dark exhaust
curls up into the northern you eye.
You look all around before climbing
down to where I stare up to you.
We hunker down against the big yellow
wheel. As you eat you look to the trees
and the house beyond. I sit beside,
afraid to touch. Your cap's bill
is bent up on a plane with your face,
your eyes are red with the wind, tired
with the routine of plowing under last
year's alfalfa, its smell mixed
with the heaviness of new soil,
the sharpness of grease and gasoline,
the narcotic of coffee you drink
straight from its pint jar. The jagged
blaze of your World War Zippo
warms the day. I breathe all
the sweetness from your discarded
cigarette pack. The last swallow
of coffee hangs for a moment in the blue
wind before the turned earth claims it.

I crumple the empty pack in my hand,
the tinfoil resisting like the tiniest
bones, and lean back behind my desk.
Your grandson sleeps warm
on his belly under handmade quilts.
There's no moon tonight and snow's
expected. I lock the door against it,
and make my way back through the house,
extinguishing lights as I go.
I keep my home as well as I know.

—J. V. Brummels
(Anvil #47)

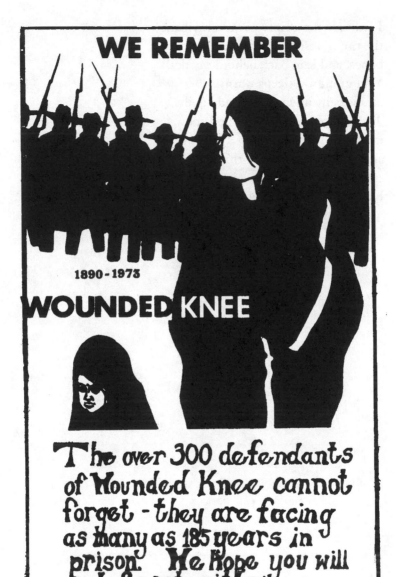

Wounded Knee and After

Few reflections on the black civil rights movement appeared in the Anvil. *The struggles of Indian people, however, were closer to home. The second "battle" of Wounded Knee, South Dakota, started in March, 1973. The* Anvil's *coverage of it was extensive and continued throughout the long aftermath of trials, legal maneuvering, and FBI harassment of Indian militants. Much of this was due to Paula Giese, who was in close touch with the events and the Indian participants. Another contributor was St. Paul attorney Kenneth Tilsen, who himself played a major role in the drama. Tilsen spent almost a week in Wounded Knee during the siege, and he returned to witness the surrender. Two of his reports appeared in numbers 5 and 6, during the spring and summer of 1973. Here they are condensed into a single article.*

The scene enacted in courtrooms and jails had a lasting counterpart in classrooms and libraries, where scholars, both Indian and white, began to attack the stereotypes, misrepresentations, and misunderstandings that had passed as American history for generations. This process was seen in an article by Bruce White, who reinterpreted an often-repeated story from Minnesota's bloody Dakota conflict of 1862. "A Mouthful of Grass" was published in Anvil *number 43 (1983).*

In the first issue of the Anvil *(1972), Gerald Vizenor had reflected on the name — and hence the identity — of his own people. They were, he wrote, "Not 'Chippewa,' not ' Ojibway' . . . Anishinabe." As years passed the question of "who is an Indian?" continued to provoke discussion, especially when tribal leaders and treaty rights activists found themselves making common cause with others who were asserting the sacredness of the natural environment and demanding alternatives to the industrial society that was destroying it. Walt Bresette, a member of the Red Cliff Band of Lake Superior Chippewa, was also a founder of the Green movement in northern Wisconsin. His "Cultural Confessions" appeared in number 51 (1985–86).*

Dennis Banks

Russell Means

Struggle at Wounded Knee

By Kenneth E. Tilsen

FROM EARLY MARCH, 1973, THE people of Wounded Knee were encircled by a military blockade aided by armed vehicles, helicopters and electronic devices. Without any effort to justify the siege by presidential proclamation and acts — as is required by law — an entire community was arrested, and an effort was made to systematically starve them out. Their homes and buildings were burned; electricity and water were shut off. Food and medicine in nearby communities and Rapid City were seized under search warrants issued by the South Dakota Federal Court. In spite of this, the people of Wounded Knee did not surrender. Instead, their support on the Pine Ridge Reservation grew.

I and several other Twin Cities lawyers went to Rapid City on March 22 to represent some 150 Sioux charged with various offenses stemming from the struggle of the Independent Oglala Nation (ION). We were there as part of a defense effort organized by the Center for Constitutional Rights, of New York. We have now formed a Minnesota Lawyers Committee for Justice at Wounded Knee; some of its members are Bob Metcalfe, Dick Oakes, Doug Hall, Ken Enkel, Larry Leventhal, and Don Heffernan.

The best analogy to the political situation on the Pine Ridge Reservation is South Vietnam. There is a corrupt and brutal puppet government of "natives," who are set up, armed, supplied, financed, propagandized for, and maintained in power by the U.S. government. Richard Wilson, whom the government and the press repeatedly style "the elected leader of the Pine Ridge Reservation people," plays a role like that of Thieu and Ky in South Vietnam — ruling and repressing the people of Pine Ridge in the interest of a foreign power.

This role of Wilson and his recruits is obvious to anyone who is in the area for any length of time. More evidence is provided by the following facts: At a public meeting in Rapid City on March 28, the highest government official in the area, U.S. Interior Department Solicitor-Nominee Kent Frizzell, openly admitted that an agreement had been made with Wilson not to arrest his vigilantes for their law violations and violence.

The agreement allowed them to set up an illegal roadblock, allowed them to violate court orders requiring passage of food and medicine, and allowed them to continue firing from surrounding positions into the streets and houses of the town. Frizzell said the agreement was that Wilson should "try to get the vigilantes under control," because their crossfire from between and outside the federal lines was "endangering the lives of FBI men and federal marshals."

Frizzell and other government officials have also admitted both publicly and privately that the Wilson regime is not really "legitimate" in the sense of having been fairly elected. There was ballot stealing and other irregularities. Officials publicly admit the need for a new election — something members of the tribe have been demanding for some time. They also declare openly that under the present and recent past conditions of repression and terrorism imposed by Wilson's "reservation police," there is no prospect of a "free" or fair election. They speak vaguely of the need for such special precautions as were taken in the recent United Mine Workers Union election, where, for years, a corrupt and repressive leadership used force, fraud and murder to maintain its power against the interests of UMW members.

The Wounded Knee-Pine Ridge situation really came to a crisis because of government complicity with the actions of Wilson and other government-supported "tribal leaders." During the months immediately before the takeover of Wounded Knee, reservation Indians filed at least 150 separate written complaints of civil rights violations, many involving physical violence and threats of it, against Wilson and his "reservation police." Not one of these legal complaints was responded to by the federal government — they were simply buried.

Wilson has now considerably expanded the number of vigilantes he commands. Local white ranchers — who have advantageous arrangements to lease tribal lands, arrangements made with the present "tribal leadership" — have been recruited. Notices were posted in bars for hundreds of miles around, offering the "job" of "cleaning the communists out of Wounded Knee." Sometimes Wilson deputizes his barroom recruits as "reservation police," sometimes not, depending on whether it is more expedient to present their actions to the public as "Indian" or to be able to disavow the actions. Arms, ammunition, supplies, and government trucks have been supplied to these vigilante squads by the U.S. government — we could see the equipment they were using with our own eyes.

The press has given the impression that a few "outside agitators" — AIM leaders from the Twin Cities — are the cause of the situation. This is not true. The basic cause is intolerable living conditions for the reservation's 13,000 Sioux, conditions made worse by the corruption and brutality of an "Indian" regime which has no real power to redress political and economic injustices inflicted on the Indians by the U.S., or to alter conditions for the better. The only opportunities are for graft and patronage. The regime's real function is to serve as an intermediary which legitimizes actions and policies that favor white economic interests.

The land problem is very serious. Pine Ridge Reservation's lands have been cut from 9,000,000 acres to 3,000,000 — and the land they were left with is dry, hilly, rocky, untillable badlands, some of the worst, most barren in the world. That part which could be used for grazing (much of it now under lease to white ranchers), is so poor that it takes 25 acres to graze one steer. A government agronomist estimated that if the 3,000,000 acres were evenly divided and distributed, the usable portions could support only 300 families. This is the land on which 13,000 Sioux try to eke out a miserable living.

This economic background has to be kept in mind when we consider what the Independent Oglala Nation want. They want freedom to determine their own destinies and lives as a sovereign people, a freedom they were supposedly guaranteed under a host of broken treaties. The U.S. government does not understand — or does not want to understand — this desire, and what it means, and the press has not transmitted what the struggle is really about.

You feel this when you are in the liberated territory — Wounded Knee. The town is under almost constant fire. There was one day and night when you couldn't leave any building you happened to be in, because the gunfire from the hills around the town was so heavy. Even though food is very short, and living conditions are poor, the feeling you get in Wounded Knee is that you are in a free place. It is one small spot of ground, surrounded and besieged, where people have created their own government, where they run their affairs in the traditions of a culture which is their own.

An indication of the high level of local support for the Independent Oglala Nation and the defenders of Wounded Knee is the help the people living on the reservation have given them. This is another analogy to Vietnam — the defenders of Wounded Knee have been able to move freely through the Oglala Sioux territory, visiting villages many miles away, calling public meetings attended by hundreds, raising money, food, and supplies. They are very much "fish swimming in a friendly sea," the classic description of guerrillas who have wide and strong support from their people. If that were not the case, the occupation of Wounded Knee, now entering its second month, would long ago have collapsed under the siege of the U.S. government.

While I was there, the Independent Oglala Nation leaders drew up seven negotiating points that I later carried out through the lines. These are preliminaries to talks, setting conditions under which they are to be held, with whom, and where. Tuesday, the government announced that some "Indian civil rights leaders" were going to sign an agreement on Wednesday in Rapid City, settling the problem and ending the occupation. They also told the press — which docilely repeated it — that Dennis Banks and Russell Means (two AIM leaders) had "slipped away from Wounded Knee under cover of darkness," presumably to escape arrest, and that most of the "outside agitators" had left with them, leaving Wounded Knee occupied only by a handful of "hard core militants." All this was false. So Tuesday night, using small videotape equipment that is in the town, the defenders made a videotape of the people still in Wounded Knee with Banks and Means — and the seven points were read.

Very few people understand the depth of commitment of the defenders of Wounded Knee. It is not rhetoric when they say they are willing to die for their people's independence. A part of their culture, a part which is quite different from ours, is an emphasis on a "good death" as a measure of a man's life and worth. "What is 'impractical' about spending my life for my people?" was often the response to my lawyerly cautions. The young men defending Wounded Knee are militarily skilled and trained. Almost all are Vietnam veterans, and most of these were in the Special Forces — the Green Berets. In Southeast Asia they learned about guerrilla warfare, courtesy of the U.S. government, and now they're using what they learned for their own people.

We should understand the political significance of their struggle and support it. They are confronting the U.S. government's complete unwillingness to take seriously their claim to be recognized as a free and sovereign people — a claim guaranteed by numerous treaties whose violation is a continuing shame to us all. In part, the Independent Oglala Nation is trying to go back to the freedom and sovereignty they had before they were conquered and robbed. They were then a people of free nations. This is what they want, rather than a paper recognition of "sovereignty" that has the self-contradictory characteristics of many of the treaty agreements which robbed them of lands that could support a meaningful independence. In part, it is something new they are trying to build — a free society like they had before, in which they can live by the beliefs and values of their culture and also survive in the 20th century. Whether they can win this will depend on their own determination and on mass support.

❖ ❖ ❖

A turning point came when an elder chief and medicine man, Fools Crow, who lives near Kyle on the reservation about 15 miles from Wounded Knee, issued an invitation to all traditional chiefs and headmen from the seven tribes of the Teton Sioux Nation to gather for four days of conference. More than fifty chiefs came.

Resolutions were passed supporting the right of Morning Star Clearwater to bury her martyred husband, Frank Clearwater, in Wounded Knee; supporting the original April 5th demand for a presidential treaty commission; calling for the removal of the corrupt puppet BIA-sponsored government, and the firing of the officials who installed this regime; and generally commending the American Indian Movement (AIM) for their efforts to protect the people on the reservation. It was evident that the support for Wounded Knee had expanded to almost every reservation in South Dakota. A final agreement to end the confrontation was signed on May 5 by the traditional chiefs and accepted by the people of Wounded Knee as the act of respected leaders.

The government had made it clear that it has the power and intent to kill all the people. Larry Lamont, a local Oglala Sioux, had been killed. Five or six others inside Wounded Knee were wounded by the government forces, which riddled all the buildings with thousands of rounds of heavy ammunition. The perimeter around the village had been tightened and the armored personnel carriers had been moved in to the "demilitarized zone" in violation of specific agreements. Large quantities of gas and devices enough to blanket the village had been openly displayed, ready for immediate use.

Government deception, lying and two-faced dishonesty is nothing new for American Indians; but it was still difficult to be fully prepared for the scope of that dishonesty at Wounded Knee. Dennis Banks said it best in negotiations when asked to trust the government: "I trust the United States Government completely. I trust them to lie and cheat. I trust them to starve my people. I trust them to kill me and my people at their earliest opportunity. I have absolute trust that the government is a criminal murderer."

I traveled to South Dakota to help when the agreement became effective. At 5:45 a.m. I arrived at the BIA office in Pine Ridge. The stand-down was to take place at 7 a.m. Hundreds of U.S. marshals and FBI agents, armed in military fashion, bustled about and took off for Wounded Knee. About an hour later, three more volunteer attorneys arrived, and we drove to the designated government roadblock on the Big Foot Trail leading into Wounded Knee. The FBI and U.S. marshals told us to wait in the cars.

The agreement of May 5 provided that attorneys would enter the village and accompany the people to a collection point. Attorneys were to be present during the searching of the individuals, their questioning and their booking where they were arrested. Attorneys were to accompany the marshal on a "quick sweep" of the village to see if it was safe. The residents were to be permitted in their homes and attorneys were to be present during any search of a person's home and belongings.

We waited in our car for over an hour and a half, making repeated demands that the agreement be honored. Surrounded by FBI agents and U.S. marshals, we watched the movement of armored carriers and military personnel. We were starting to see the scope of the betrayal by the U.S. government of the latest agreement.

Finally, one of the experienced persons in the village surrendered. He said that the people would not come out until the attorneys were allowed in. So the government was forced to let us in to the designated collection point for arrests. After a bitter argument with the government officials, they agreed that one attorney could go in to explain the new government procedures. I was selected to go in.

While in the village I got specific information about five persons who had cars they wanted to drive out. The cars were in perfect operating condition. One of them was the property of Black Elk, elder medicine man and religious leader. In the car was his sacred peace pipe and other important religious articles, as well as the property of Crow Dog, who was then in jail in Rapid City. The sacred articles of Black Elk and Crow Dog were irreplaceable.

I received a specific promise that Black Elk would be permitted back to get his car as soon as he was processed. I confirmed the promise with the head of the Community Relations Service and with the non-lawyer Justice Department officials who served as liaison people. I reconfirmed it at least three times before I left Wounded Knee.

I was the last non-government person to leave the village. When I got to the collection point, the people had been searched before they had a chance to see the other attorneys. In the meantime, the government sweep took place without attorneys. Our demands to go into the village were ignored. The government's promise to withdraw the armored personnel carriers was ignored. The promise that the traditional chiefs would be in the bunkers to observe the agreement was "met" — they were all placed at a roadblock three miles away from the collection point. The specific agreement that Wilson's local police would not enter the village was ignored as their cars sped by us into Wounded Knee.

Later that afternoon, other attorneys drove through the village. It was a shambles. The cars were physically wrecked. Black Elk's and Crow Dog's sacred articles were strewn about the area. Black Elk's peacepipe had been deliberately broken. He has not been permitted — nor have any of the others — to go back into Wounded Knee to get their possessions. And in the meantime, every scavenger, reporter, Indian thug cop or quasi-cop, had gone through the village. By May 8, when the end came, most of the residents of Wounded Knee had already been forced or tricked out of their homes. The 40 persons who remained were treated in an especially brutal manner. Their homes were literally torn apart by repeated search parties.

The facts have been twisted and distorted by dishonest government officials, aided by press and media which, for the most part, are only too anxious to print the daily government press releases as their only news coverage. No reporters had been permitted in Wounded Knee for over six weeks. Those few who went in, like the people, by infiltrating through the government lines, were arrested when they left.

A dedicated group of people from Unicorn News Service worked from beginning to end. Kevin McKiernan of KSJN, St. Paul, and Jeff Williams of CBS tried to get the real story out. They were arrested for being in Wounded Knee when the government moved in on May 8. Only those who received clearance from the government information officer got into the village afterward.

The result was the predictably slanted stories about the destruction by the "occupiers" — written by those who had no possible means of knowing who had destroyed what property.

Even worse was the dishonest selection of persons to be interviewed. The whites, the trading post operator, the white ranchers and the Indian sellouts were prominently displayed on TV and in news releases. But not one interview was held with the fantastic Indian women of Wounded Knee who were the heart and backbone of the Independent Nation during the entire siege.

In March and April, 1973, between 250 and 350 persons were illegally arrested and held at Pine Ridge jail under the worst possible physical conditions. The charges against them can never be tried and the "court" in Pine Ridge complains that if it had to try these cases, it could not do so. The Indian bureaucrats in Pine Ridge (who are called "judges") and their friends have collected close to $10,000 in bail. Government civil rights attorneys acknowledge that almost every arrest and charge has been illegal, but they are still investigating, they say.

In Rapid City a court-authorized reign of terror is in progress. Search warrants have been issued for food and medicine. A search warrant was issued for the records of the Wounded Knee Communications Center in Rapid City and records were seized. We have new crimes in South Dakota: eating, healing the sick, or maintaining records that aid in the defense of hundreds of persons facing federal criminal charges. There is not the slightest possibility of a fair trial in South Dakota.

There have been more than 250 arrests by federal officials and at the present time more than 100 federal indictments. Most of the alleged leaders face close to 100 years in prison. Almost all of them face charges of interfering with a U.S. marshal in the course of a civil disorder in violation of the civil obedience act of 1968. Many face charges of crossing state lines to participate in a civil disorder (the Rap Brown act). There are a number of conspiracy counts. People have been arrested around the country for trying to bring food and medicine to Wounded Knee. Every available dollar has gone into bail needs. As of this writing, AIM leader Russell Means is still in jail in lieu of $125,000 bail. Pedro Bissonnette is held on $100,000, Stan Holder, $55,000, Al Cooper, $25,000, Gene Heavy Runner, Jr., $25,000.

In Watergate and again in the Pentagon cases the federal judiciary has shown remarkable courage and independence. Not so in Rapid City. Most importantly, the question concerning the entire illegality of the military siege was ignored, although it is the untold legal story of Wounded Knee.

"Little Crow" watercolor by T.W. Wood (1860)

MINNESOTA HISTORICAL SOCIETY

A Mouthful of Grass

By Bruce M. White

FOR GENERATIONS, MINNESOTA SCHOOLCHILDREN HEARD about Andrew J. Myrick when they learned about the history of their state. It was Myrick the Indian trader who, according to the stories, helped bring about the Sioux Uprising of 1862 — that unsuccessful attempt by some of Minnesota's Dakota Indians finally to cut off the flow of white people into the state. It was Myrick who, when the Dakota were hungry, refused them food from his storehouse. In words reminiscent of Marie Antoinette, he told them to eat grass if they were hungry. A few days later the first killings of white settlers took place that began the uprising. Myrick was one of the first victims, found dead, according to some stories, with his mouth full of grass. According to others, he had the blade of a scythe through his body.

A story like this, so clearly fitting the folklorist's motif of "Punishment fitted to crime," is just the sort of thing that historians long to discredit. Such an attitude is one that one might expect from Gary Clayton Anderson's article "Myrick's Insult: A Fresh Look at Myth and Reality, " in the Spring 1983 issue of *Minnesota History*.

It turns out, however, that Anderson has little quarrel with the story. Despite his best efforts, he (like historian William Watts Folwell) could find nothing to prove that the incident did not take place or that Myrick did not say what he was reported to have said. Instead, Anderson shows simply that the incident may not have taken place when or where it was traditionally supposed to have taken place. As such it could hardly have been a major cause of the uprising. It was not because of sudden anger over Myrick's words, Anderson says, that the Dakota fought their war. Instead, there were deeper causes: the war cannot be blamed on the rash words of one trader.

Of course, except for a few general works and schoolbooks, few people ever actually suggested that Myrick was the direct cause of the Sioux Uprising. But the story of Myrick is significant. It and other stories like it can teach a great deal about relations between whites and Indians in Minnesota in those years. From this point of view the textbooks were not wrong in writing of Myrick. What they never gave, however, was a good understanding of what was behind the incident. What was the story of Andrew Myrick really about?

One good way to approach the story's meaning is to consider other stories of the kind. In a footnote to Anderson's article, we learn that a few years before the uprising, Johann Georg Kohl, a German ethnographer, visited Minnesota and recorded an incident that had taken place along the frontier between the Dakota Indians and the settlers. As a result of one altercation, some Dakota "stuffed a white man through the mouth with soil . . . snarling: "Eat dirt, you land-thief!" The incident resembles the Myrick story in that the Indians in both cases were able to wreak a fitting revenge for what they might have considered a crime. In another sense it is a manifestation of Indian frustration over white people's imposition of a foreign cultural system on the Minnesota landscape.

As the anthropologist A. Irving Hallowell suggested in his essay on "The Nature and Function of Property as a Social Institution," groups like the Indians had a concept of property appreciably different from that of Europeans. For whites property is usually a physical thing, an object over which the owner has exclusive use and which he can cut off from others by lock, key, door and fence. For Indians, property was rather a certain number of rights and duties that a person had over objects and intangible things. There was little sense of exclusivity in the Indian view of things, especially in relation to land.

Hence, the way in which the oncoming settlers sought to own the land must have seemed very strange to the Dakota. The fact that the settlers sought to close off the land from others must have made it appear as though they were trying to use it up, and in a sense, consume it. This must have seemed as monstrous as eating dirt.

It is remarkable how philosophically similar this symbolic statement about land-use is to the attitudes expressed by Henry David Thoreau in his book *Walden*. Throughout the book Thoreau refers to farmers and their slavery to the land they cultivate. Especially striking is his statement early in the book: "I see young men, my townsmen, whose misfortune it is to have inherited farms, houses, barns, cattle and farming tools; for these are more easily acquired than got rid of. Better if they had been born in the open pasture and suckled by a wolf, that they might have seen with clearer eyes what field they were called to labor in. Who made them serfs of the soil? Why should they eat their sixty acres, when man is condemned to eat only his peck of dirt?"

Clearly to Thoreau and the Dakota, both of whom had a strong antipathy to farming as a way of life, there were alternative ways for human beings to deal with the earth on which they lived. Thoreau and the Dakota were hunters and gatherers. Land use for them did not have to mean dividing up the earth. To own land was as much to be possessed by it as it was to possess it, just as much of European technology possessed human beings who sought to make use of it.

It is not surprising that the ideas of the settlers, rather than those of the Dakota or Thoreau, should have permeated much of the historical writing about the Europeanizing of North America. Reading the works of many frontier historians who are imbued both with the idea of progress and a belief in the superiority of European technology, one is left with the inescapable conclusion that it was only by means of such technology that white people managed to assert their well-known moral superiority over the American Indian.

Reading the work of Thoreau and seriously considering the culture of American Indians can thus provide a valuable corrective for the theory behind many of the more blatant historical accounts of the "settling" of places like Minnesota — the belief that somehow the technology of white people was synonymous with civilization and without such technology civilization was not possible.

The dirt-in-mouth story is a good corrective in another sense. Though a story like this is often ignored in favor of statistical and institutional accounts of peoples and places, such anecdotes have an important quality missed in other kinds of history. They often summarize the essence of historical situations and arrive at a human truth that is never otherwise approached. Another statement of Thoreau's should probably be required reading for historians in their formative years: To some extent, he said in his *Week on the Concord and Merrimac Rivers*, "mytholology is only the most ancient history and biography. So far from being false or fabulous in the common sense, it contains only enduring and essential truth, the I and you, the here and there, the now and then, being omitted ."

The story of Andrew Myrick, too, contains a great deal of enduring truth, though a truth perhaps never dreamed of by those who have repeated it for years. Paradoxically, to get at something of this human truth, it is necessary to consider the historical and cultural context of the incident, not so much to find out whether Myrick "caused" the Sioux Uprising of 1862, but rather to get at the symbolic vocabulary in which the incident was acted out.

Documentation of the events leading up to the uprising records the reason for which Myrick made his famous remark. Myrick, like other traders in the area, had been looking forward to the annuity payments scheduled that summer of 1862 with as much expectation as the Dakota. These traders were hoping that, as had been done with many other annuity payments, some of the money set aside by the government for payment to Indians would be given to the traders for past debts incurred by the Dakota. Some of the Dakota, who were annoyed at the fact that often too much of their annuity and treaty money had gone to the traders directly, had decided to request that the practice be stopped. Debts owed to traders would be paid directly by individual Indians.

The traders, including Myrick, were not at all happy with this proposition, which would make their profits more uncertain. By way of retaliation, when some Indians came to their trading posts to ask for food (they were waiting for the payment and did not want to leave to go hunting), the traders refused. Myrick, in particular, told them: "You will be sorry for what you have done. . . . After a while you will come to me and beg for meat and flour to keep you and your wives and children from starving and I will not let you have a thing. You and your wives and children may starve, or eat grass, or your own filth."

For hundreds of years, the credit system — that means by which fur traders advanced merchandise and equipment to the Indians in the fall, to be repaid with furs and other things in the winter and spring — had been part of the fur trade. It was one of the most important means by which fur traders and Indians showed their trust for each other. The credit system, like the gifts that Indians and traders often gave each other, was a way by which the Indian kinship-based economy could be incorporated into a system of European capitalism.

In earlier years this system worked. Traders had a trusting relationship with the Indians. They understood enough about the Indians to know how to ensure that most of the time when goods were advanced, repayment could be expected. Traders and Indians began the trade year by giving ceremonial presents back and forth, presents that demonstrated their common regard. Sometimes it was hard to tell at what point gift-giving left off and barter began.

Food, especially, was an important symbolic gift. In the early years of the trade, in fact, it was more often the Indians who fed the trader than the other way around. In so doing the Indians were showing by symbolic means their willingness to have the trader in their midst. By giving food certain symbolic values Indians had a lot in common with other groups. As ethnographer A. I. Richards writes: "Food is the source of [man's] most intense emotions, provides the basis for some of his most abstract ideas and the metaphors of his religious life. . . . To the primitive man it may come to symbolize some of his highest spiritual experiences and express his most significant social ties."

Claude Levi-Strauss, who quotes Richards' words in one of his own books, quite rightly points out that such feelings are not limited to "Primitive" man. Fundamentally we are all affected by such beliefs, as such concepts as "the milk of human kindness" and the wine that becomes "the Blood of Christ" would indicate.

For many people, food is a symbol of solidarity, of community, a way of showing concern for other people in ways that make possible the extension of the relationship to other levels of intimacy. It has been suggested, for example, that the term "company," now used primarily in an economic sense, had its origins in reference to a group of people, usually members of the same family, who broke bread together, and so had reason to trust each other. Even in modern companies, non-institutionalized networks exist on the basis of who eats with whom, and it is through such networks that much important communication takes place.

But of course in capitalist societies, as in most companies, such non-institutionalized relations have been covered over by another level of metaphor that people seem to think is more important. These are the economic metaphors — the market place and the free-enterprise system — that are so basic to the world-view of people like Ronald Reagan. Such people believe that we should deal with each other purely in terms of economic gain. Though they profess to believe strongly in the family, they refuse to extend the metaphor of the family beyond the walls of the home. Society should allow the acquisitive mentality free rein — and all will ultimately benefit in the process.

Clearly many fur traders shared such beliefs. They were in business to make money out of their dealings with the Indians. But they had sense enough to know that they could not deal with the Indians as though they were Europeans. They knew the importance of kinship, of hospitality and of sharing, for the Indian and so took these things into account in gift-giving and credit. This is not to say that they did not build the costs of hospitality into their profit margins. But more than anything the traders knew that words could never substitute for actions and that if they wished to win the commercial loyalty of Indians they must manifest their words in ceremonial hospitality.

One of the most important means by which traders made their words tangible was by giving Indians rum and other forms of alcohol. For all the damaging things one can say about such beverages in the trade, they were seldom given in order to make the Indians drunk and then to cheat them. They were beverages demanded by Indians, beverages that the Ojibway and Dakota of Minnesota referred to in ceremonial terms as milk — a fact which demonstrates the role of alcohol in cementing bonds between whites and Indians in the trade. As such — with this reference to the relationship between mother and child — the term seems to echo Karl Marx's description of primitive society as being one in which man had not yet severed the umbilical cord linking him to his fellows. In other words, in giving Indians rum, traders demonstrated their willingness to participate in this kinship-based economy, to carry on the discourse of trade in terminology that was familiar to the Indians.

By the 1820s, this multicultural, kinship-capitalist system known as the fur trade had begun to break down. American settlers were coming into the Great Lakes area, pressing for Indian lands and helping to put pressure on the ecosystem, making it less and less possible for traders and Indians to operate. The U.S. government, responding to the needs and demands of its white people, began to make treaties that whittled away — in purely legal ways, of course — at Indian homelands. In return for these lands the government promised, though it did not ensure, that Indians would have smaller sections of ground within their former homelands. The Indians also were given annuities of money, tools, household goods, and food.

Sometimes in the treaties of the early 1820s, the Indians requested that the government give a certain amount of treaty money to the Indians' fur traders — men who had spent all their lives among the Indians and whose credits to the Indians they had, occasionally, because of bad hunting or wars, been unable to pay. These debts the government was happy to pay and it appeared that the Indians and the traders were content.

But such a new feature of Indian-white treaty-making had a great potential for abuse. Soon other whites who had never been in the fur trade at all began to see the potential for a lucrative business. It was a business that would have surer returns than furs, since furs were subject to market fluctuations and could meet with accidents on the trip from the Midwest to the East Coast. Knowing that the government would soon be making treaties with various tribes, these new traders would pack up a load of merchandise and enter the area shortly before the treaty. They would advance goods to the Indians. The prices they charged the Indians for these goods were high; but then, these traders did not really expect to be repaid by their customers. The point of it all, like many another exercise in "free" enterprise, was the government payment. All in all, it was a very effective alchemy. It has been estimated that several million dollars were paid out in this fashion in the

1830s and 1840s. Some of it went to veteran fur traders, who, one may argue, were entitled to it. But a large amount of it went to people who were not traders at all. They were practitioners of what one historian has called the "Indian business."

It is thus in the context of this centuries-old system of trade and its 19th-century permutations that the events involving Andrew Myrick should be seen. Myrick and other traders were people who knew well that the fur trade — that is, the trade involving Indians as major producers — was ending. It would fall victim to the Indians' lack of an adequate land base. For Myrick, the trick in making a living was to profit from the Indians' passing. In a sense Myrick needed the Indians' acquiescence in this. And so when the Dakota threatened that they would no longer permit it, no longer allow their money to be sidetracked, Myrick fought back. What he did in threatening to refuse credit was contrary to what one could have expected of a trader from an earlier day. Myrick's position was based on the fact that he was no longer interested in a long-term relationship with the Indians. His payoff was from the government. His refusing food to the Indians was perhaps entirely consistent with the standards of a market economy, yet it was certainly out of keeping with the system of peaceful trade that had existed for hundreds of years.

We should consider how the Indians interpreted Myrick's words. It must have been clear that Myrick was not dealing with them as one human being would deal with another. He was not manifesting the kind of sharing attitude that they would show each other. Instead he was holding food hostage for economic benefit, something that earlier traders would never have been foolish enough to do explicitly. Implicit in Myrick's words is something that must have been increasingly prevalent on the frontier in those days — a definition of Indians as subhuman. What human eats his own waste? What human eats grass? These are the actions of pigs and cattle. What more damning way could Myrick have picked for saying to the Indians: You are not human.

But in speaking in this way, Myrick not only condemned the Indians, he condemned himself. The Indians after all knew that they were human beings. A statement such as Myrick's must have made them wonder about the trader. Was he a human being or a monster? What human being would refuse food to his starving neighbors, and in the process call them pigs and cattle? So Myrick, in denying the Indians' humanity, also denies his own. In this sense what happened to him afterwards — whatever it was — does not seem surprising.

The Myrick story summarizes a great deal of Midwestern history in a few sentences. It describes succinctly the end of the fur trade and the beginning of the wars on the plains. It is a sorrowful epitaph for an older system of peaceful trade. It is unfortunate that Myrick's words have come to symbolize the actions of all traders who preceded him. Just so, the killing of Myrick represented, for many white settlers of that time and since, what it was to be an Indian. If the story is told again, perhaps those who tell it will take the time to reconsider what the story really means.

Not "Chippewa," not "Ojibway" ... Anishinabe

By Gerald Vizenor

THE *ANISHINABE* ARE THE HUMAN BEINGS and the people of the woodland in the language of those who have been known for more than a century in the dominant society as the *chippewa* and *ojibway*. The tribal names *chippewa* and *ojibway* are spoken in the language of the dominant society and not in the language of the *anishinabe* people (the plural form is *anishinabeg*).

This is a modest proposal to relume the tribal identity of the woodland people by changing the tribal name to *anishinabe*. The dominant society has perpetuated the invented names and has not assumed the responsibility to correct the inaccurate homogenized history of the *chippewa indian*. The *chippewa indians* exist in the mind of the dominant society. The *anishinabe* exist in the hearts of the woodland people. The myths of the *american indian* and the *minnesota chippewa indian* should be left to the cultural hobbyist in the dominant society.

The Kiowa novelist and teacher N. Scott Momaday, who won the Pulitzer Prize for his novel *House Made of Dawn*, told me in an interview that "the Indian has been for a long time generalized in the imagination of the white man. Denied the acknowledgement of individuality and change, he has been made to become in theory what he could not become in fact, a synthesis of himself . . . the relationship between the white man and the red was in a sense doomed from the onset by a conflict of attitudes and the disposition of intolerance . . . the persistent attempt to generalize the *indian* has resulted in a delusion and a nomenclature of half truths. . ."

This proposal means that the tribal name should be changed to the *anishinabe* in all references — educational, religious, social, political, and legal — and the homogenized historical name *indian* should be dropped from usage. The collective invented name *indian* homogenizes our identity and denies the *anishinabe* and other tribal families their unique identity and cultural diversity. The Minnesota Chippewa Tribe should be changed to the *anishinabe* tribe, and other organizations of the people should begin using the name *anishinabe* in the language of the people. The public media — newspapers, magazines, radio and television — should also begin referring to the people of the woodland as the *anishinabe* and not the *chippewa* or *ojibway* except in quotations and in references originating in the dominant society.

In the original tales of the people the sacred *migis* shell of the *anishinabe* spirit — a shell resembling the cowrie, which is still used to decorate ceremonial vestments — arose from the eastern sea and moved along the inland waters guiding the people through the sleeping sun of the woodland to *bawitig* — the long rapids in the river. The *anishinabe* — the people of the woodland — were given wisdom and life color from the reflection of the sun on the sacred *migis* shell during this long migration. Five hundred years ago the sacred shell appeared in the sun for the last time at *moningwunakauning* in *anishinabe kitchigami* — Madeline Island in Lake Superior — the great sea of the *anishinabe*.

The *anishinabe* community at *moningwunakauning* was established about five hundred years ago. More than a century ago the *anishinabe* historian and legislator William Warren described in his *History of the Ojibways* a copper plate with incised marks showing three *anishinabe* generations living on the island before the voyageurs arrived and established fur trading posts. Warren wrote that he viewed the copper historical record of the people in the middle of the 19th century when it had eight incised marks — each mark an estimated forty-year generation.

The fur trade interposed an economic anomaly between the intuitive rhythm of woodland life and the equipoise of the *anishinabe* spirit. While the people were reluming the human unity of tribal life, thousands of white settlers procured the land with new laws and enslaved the *anishinabe* in the fury of discovery.

The rhythm of the woodland was broken by the marching cadence of Christian patriotism. The *anishinabe* orators of the *mang odem* —

the loon family, the legions of the *makwa odem* — the bear family, and the people of the *amik odem* — the beaver family, were colonized and mythologized and alienated from their woodland life and religion while the voices of the conquering crusaders of the new world rang with freedom. The woodland identity of the people was homogenized in patent histories and the religious songs of the *anishinabe* were latinized by nervy missionaries. The *anishinabe* lost their land and were renamed in nine treaties with the federal government.

More than a century ago Henry Rowe Schoolcraft, a student of geology and mineralogy, named the *anishinabe* the *ojibwa*. The meaning of the invented name is not clear in the *anishinabe* language, but Schoolcraft reasoned that the root meaning of the word *ojibwa* described the peculiar nasal sound of the *anishinabe* voice. The story is told that the word *ojibwa* was misunderstood by a traveling federal bureaucrat who heard *chippewa* for *ojibwa*. Once recorded in the treaties between the *anishinabe* and the federal government the invented name was a matter of law.

The *anishinabe* must still wear the invented names. The tragedy is that today many young people of the tribe do not know the difference between the names. Some believe they are the *chippewa*, or the *ojibway*, and others know they are the *anishinabe*. But the people named the *odjibwa*, *otchipwe*, *ojibway*, *chippewa*, *chippeway* and *indian* still speak of themselves in the language of their religion as the *anishinabe*.

Only two generations ago the *anishinabe* were systematically forbidden to speak their language and practice their religion. Now the people are summoned to be proud of their invented *indian* and *chippewa* heritage. Their cultural and political histories were written in the language of those who invented the *indian*, renamed the tribes, allotted the land, divided ancestry by geometric degrees — the federal government identifies the *anishinabe* by degrees of *indian* blood — and categorized identity by the geography of colonial reservations.

Drawing by Randall W. Scholes

Cultural Confessions

By Walt Bresette

INDIANS, LIKE ENVIRONMENTALISTS, SUFFER FROM severe misconception. We're feared, romanticized, and often underestimated. Despite both of our ecological legacies, many of us are often ignored in high-tech environments and fast-paced policy decisions.

And regardless of our assured self-importance, we are often frustrated, even fearful, of a world decaying or of others practicing ecological euthanasia. As I write, ecological damage is reported widely through mass media; huge ecological systems are being threatened on the planet. Perhaps this latest recognition of ecological disasters will spawn a partnership between us.

However, in order for a coalition to occur, we must see through and discard many of the misconceptions we have of each other. Furthermore, success will only occur if our goals and actions are inspirational, measurable and attainable. Because I'm also an Indian, I'll focus primarily on Indian misperceptions.

In order to understand where Indians fit into ecological movements, an understanding of *who Indians are* is essential. Out of self-survival and personal exploration I've identified three general categories: Political, Cultural and Racial. If you ask me which is most important (which obviously you have), my answer is political. Let me explain.

By using my tribe (Lake Superior Chippewa, Red Cliff Reservation) and our history, I've concluded that we are primarily political beings, rather than racial or cultural critters. After a decade of searching, I've found that race and culture (including spirituality) are important, but only within a political context. In the past, these two factors were the primary indicators; however, I think history has changed our identities.

In looking back at recorded history, I can pinpoint events which have shaped our current political identity. In my case, I point to the

1825 Prairie du Chien Treaty. It is at this instant in time that I believe my tribe adopted a new identity, one that has been with us since.

My tribe is once more embroiled in controversy over treaty rights. Although any decent ninth-grade civics or history class would stem the non-Indian backlash, there are additional lessons to be learned from these treaty rights cases. Today, in an attempt to have a "meaningful exercise" of treaty rights we cite the terms of the treaties of 1825, 1837, 1842 and 1854.

In addition to the treaties withstanding the scrutiny of U.S. courts, being recognized as deeds to property, they also speak to the myths and misperceptions we often hold dear. Essentially what history has recorded and what today's tribal leaders are arguing is that in 1825 we acknowledged that we owned pieces of Mother Earth and in 1837, 1842, and 1854, we sold those pieces.

The 1825 treaty also names for the first time a group called the "Lake Superior Chippewa." Prior to this historic moment we were Anishinabe or Gitchigummi-ininni. Thereafter, in treaty and in relations with other political groups, we became and are the Lake Superior Chippewa. Also changing with our name was, as a group, our culture and our racial purity. These changes began in 1825 and continue today.

My tribe has been undergoing a long-term shift in identity, originally through contact with other tribes and then with colonial powers. When the U.S. government gained the balance of power, our full complement of sovereign powers were subsumed, leaving us, as the U.S. courts have said, "semi-sovereign domestic dependent nations."

By consenting to define our territory in 1825 and subsequently selling this land, we accepted our role in the contemporary political world. Despite this identity and political shift, we learned how to play the new game. How this political identity can help prevent ecological disaster is what I'll deal with at the conclusion of this essay. First though, I'll deal with the other Indian identities and also present a model on how political tribes can work together and effect change,

Although a political identity runs counter to those who insist that race is the most important criterion, the racial argument points out its own contradictions. Of the many questions tied to race, the most important is: What is acceptable purity and who determines the standards?

Some traditionalists and many half-breed neo-traditionalists opt for racial purity — yet won't define the standards. If successful, they will either join the short-lived Shaker movement or line up with the aberrant behavior of white South Africans. Using racial purity as a primary identity is unnecessary, it excludes important resources and ultimately it will be self-defeating. In addition to racial purity there have been and are other race formulas for determining "Indianness." The Bureau of Indian Affairs and other U.S. agencies use arbitrary blood quantum measurements. Some tribal governments have adopted this latter formula with some modifications.

So, today, if you seek enrollment in any "federally recognized tribe," you must meet some racial — or at least lineal — descendent criteria. Many fix their membership at ¼ blood or more, an arbitrary but nonetheless effective way to control membership. The concept of membership criteria is entrenched in each federally recognized tribe's constitution.

Although some traditional leaders and medicine people insist on this identity, at least they practice what they preach. Many others, neo-traditionalists and born again Indians, simply adopt the outward appearances for PR, personal or political reasons. While the facade of traditionalism is loudly worn on many people's sleeves, traditional spirituality, culture, lifestyles and values are quietly continuing.

Many neo-traditionalists were influenced by the revolutionary period begun by students, blacks and women in the '60s and '70s. Some, recognizing the revolutionary current, effectively began organizing Indians and Indian supporters. Hair length grew and, like jeans and sandals and song, spiritual Indianness became a marketable commodity. The most successful organizers were those who formed the American Indian Movement.

AIM, an urban-based subculture, captured America's attention, garnered moral and financial support and gave inspiration to many young Indians. Through effective organizing tactics, keen use of PR techniques, and protests, and through an alliance with traditional spir-

RINGING IN THE WILDERNESS

itual leaders, they provided ways for spiritual empowerment. (Ronald Reagan, even more adept at these techniques, has shown the world the power of this formula.) AIM has done a great but limited service to America and to Indian country.

AIM forced other Indians, tribal councils, national organizations and the public to remember that Indian "power" is still around. Simultaneously, groups concerned about environmental ethics became more visible, using many of the same tactics. Environmental law was evolving, meanwhile, and the two groups began running along the same track. According to one policy analyst, the greening of Indian law occurred about the same time and on similar issues as the latest environmental movement.

Analyst Dave Siegler suggests that concerns for ecological damage caused by hydropower in the Pacific Northwest also involved Indians, particularly as these power systems affected the fishery and habitat protected by treaties, Although laws and concern predate this volatile period, it is like the 1825 Prairie du Chien treaty, a discernable turning point in history.

Now, back to my tribe and the thesis of political identity.

For the past two decades the debate over who is an Indian has been raging. Fingers point like shotguns: "You're not an Indian because . . . your hair's too short, you speak the wrong language, you drive the wrong kind of car, you sleep with the wrong kind of people, your skin's too light," ad infinitum. Serving my young adulthood during these times offered excitement — and tremendous self-doubt.

The crux of the finger-pointing is best illustrated perhaps by looking at the culturally correct American Indian Movement and the slow, often plodding, actions of reservation tribal councils. AIM, often at odds with elected tribal councils, usually referred to them as puppets of the BIA. Tribal councils, faced with delivery of services, often viewed AIM members as having been off the reservation too long. One council member said, "They may have a corner on the peace pipes but they're using the wrong tobacco." Some have reduced this internecine battle to a finger-pointing fight between "traditional" and "progressive" forces.

As mentioned earlier, I've concluded that Indian is a political identity. I'll say, too, that this political tribe also needs traditional values, racial distinctions and other tools to relate to other progressive political groups. There is no either/or solution here. In searching for an Indian identity, I also found a model for coalition.

I used Wisconsin as my geopolitical lab. I first stepped across the Mississippi and (scientifically) yelled: "Hey Indian!" When someone responded, I put an X on their back. Interestingly those who responded looked like Jesse Jackson's rainbow.

Racially pure full-bloods, half-breeds and descendants of great-grandmother Cherokee princesses responded. Blacks, Hispanics, Asians, Jews and other racial groups responded. Leftists, feminists and conservative lovers of the U.S. Constitution responded. Politicians, educators and even some liberals responded. White planners, attorneys and other tribal employees responded. Indians of all stripes, traditionalists and progressives, responded.

Due to the wide spectrum of response I concluded that "Indianness" crossed racial lines and also defied any narrow cultural, spiritual or lifestyle definition. The next step then was to find out what this motley rainbow had in common. I then tested the political goals of survival. I asked each if they believed in tribal sovereignty. Most said yes, although a few were more interested in racial purity or cultural correctness. Interestingly, some who looked like Indians wanted no part of tribal sovereignty.

I concluded that we are supporters or Indians because of inherited history and our political beliefs. That decided, the next step was to stop the finger-pointing and crank up this coalition. I redrew the borders of Wisconsin to represent the body politic and the political goal of tribal sovereignty. The new community is modeled after the natural phenomena of a circle, the human brain and gravity.

The circle contains only those who believe in the political goal. The left side, like the brain, represents the clinical, empirical , pragmatic, logical, scientific parts of our community. The right side is the spiritual, dogmatic, poetic and sensual parts of our community. The east and west tangents represent the extremes or opposite skills of the community members (Progressives vs. Traditionals). Between these extremes is a continuum or spectrum: a place where every individual — regardless of race, lifestyle, religion, skill or inheritance — can fit and actively participate in the common political goal.

The key to making this political community work is that all individuals choose for themselves where they fit on the continuum. Finger-pointing, like disregard for the political goal, is simply not tolerated. Once people choose their space and skill, their efforts, like the force of gravity, move inward where representatives of all the people can make decisions. Everyone, from lawyer to bookkeeper to parent to child to medicine man to Christian Pastor, fits — as long as she or he remains committed in action to the political goal. Diversity is a strength rather than a sin.

Fullbloods, traditionalists, linguists, storytellers, musicians, poets . . . all have an important role in a healthy community . Lawyers, planners, secretaries, economists and journalists have equally important roles, especially in relating to other political communities.

As long as other political communities exist it is essential that we have a full complement of left and right-side resources. If the economy fails, war resumes or the environment dies, all the technicians in the world won't be as important as a single medicine man or a singer of sacred song.

Outside of this political context it is nearly impossible to determine where Indians fit in an ecological movement. You will get divergent responses and finger-pointing. Within it, you gain access to "semi-sovereign" people with treaty and aboriginal property rights. These rights should be viewed as another environmental-protection device: an additional tool to help stop further degradation.

Equally important, then, is to find out who belongs to the political tribe known as environmentalists. One way to find this out is to find a common political goal. Perhaps one of you could step off the earth and yell: "Hey environmentalist! " All who turn around get an X on their backs. Most importantly, even more than lifestyle or looks, ask them if they believe and will work for the political goal. If you're able to do this, then I guarantee that you will also find many political Indians concerned about the environment.

In the meantime, without this political goal, you're taking a chance that whoever responds is only looking into the past and not at today's realities or tomorrow's dream. I suggest the Green movement seek visionaries of all stripes, and not just reporters such as myself, or reluctant but revisionist historians such as Russell Means.

from Handful of Thunder

The White Bubble

1

This vastness of grassland   gone
to corn and beans   is a tiny thing
under the nighttime leaping prairie fire
of galaxies. Yes, the entire universe
is involved,   everything
beaming good influence through
everything else. The mind receiving
becomes calm
enough to begin:

for ten thousand years
these prairies had been living
balance,   hovering,   sensitive as
a white bubble over black water
under ice. A balance,
the grasses rising even
as that last glacier sank back, retreated
to its pole, and the buffalo
followed the grass, the wolves
and red men and women, living deep
in the balance, followed the buffalo,
and the great flights
of swans and geese and cranes
followed the seasons. . . .

Finer and finer: sunlight, trace element,
microbe, mist, nematode, mole. . . . O,
the eyes, even of red men, cannot
follow the claw marks of electrons,

atoms, ions, starlight, all
radiations and migrations infinitely seeking,
reaching   balance.

3

Buffalo hunters stank, they say,
so that, down wind your gorge grew
to a filthy fist   in your throat.
The stink of carcasses, those years
must have been   buzzard heaven.
Buzzards must have fallen
drunk from the skies.

That was the last,
that great maggot squirm, that glut
(we're talking, now, only a bit
more than one long lifetime back)
was the end, the buzzard feast
which sent the white bubble leaping —

*"Well, how in hell you gonna string a fence
with sixty million buffalo"*
thundering on the balance.
*"How in hell
you gonna run a railroad
with sixty million buffalo"*
thundering on a balance
which has so little to do
with the market.

And the land has to be cross-hatched
and plotted   for white men
to sleep easy on it.
White men can't sleep on land uncut

by fences, fields, roads,
power lines, phone lines, gas lines, water mains. . . .
They trick him
into a sort of ease,
are the mesh on which his mattress swings.

No room, then, for immense
migrations of matted and hooved tons.
Buffalo guns, heavy-barreled Sharps —
on rest sticks, from train windows —
boomed a somber dirge, and each
single buffalo coughed bright blood
into the light, sank to its knees
and down   into grass. The great
herds receded like glaciers. Great
innocent carcasses sank back in
to roots   like melting ice.

—Joe Paddock
(Anvil #42)

Drawing by Chuck Trapkus

Voices of Women

The writings of radical women held a prominent place in the Anvil *from its beginning, but the magazine was slow to recognize the new feminism of the 1970s. Gradually, nevertheless, pieces of prose and poetry by women sounded a more consciously feminist tone, and experiences unique to women — old, young, mothers, lovers, activists, breadwinners, and victims — were celebrated in their own right. One of the earliest of these was an angry, poignant "Letter from a Welfare Mother" by Neala J. Schleuning, published in number 17 (1976). Evelyn Roehl played many roles in producing the* Anvil *and contributed a number of articles on food and the economics of the food industry, but in "Encounter," which appeared in number 24 (1977), she spoke wholly as a woman. Linda Hasselstrom's story "Grandma Is Dancing," in number 38 (1982) portrayed an aged homesteader whose grit and humor were equal to the loneliness of the South Dakota plains.*

The coming of the 1980s saw women playing new and distinctive roles in protest politics and social change movements. In number 41 (1982) Alice Tripp recalled the leadership of a "North Country Woman in Action" during the power line struggle, and in number 47 (1984) Madge Micheels-Cyrus described "The Women's Peace Presence" in northern Wisconsin and elsewhere.

Photos by Cheryl Walsh

Letter From a Welfare Mother

By N. J. Schleuning

I CAN'T TELL YOU HOW much I enjoy my reading of the *Anvil*. I just picked up the latest issue (I guess my subscription ran out, because I didn't get it at home) and sat down and read it from cover to cover, my mind and my soul comfortably balancing between "down home" alternative-living-in-the-country folks and the cool intellectual arguments of the city-educated folks who contribute their erudite observations.

But there was something missing. And I guess I felt it just after I laid down the paper and thought about my own reality. What was missing was something about the people I know. The poor people. And I mean the really poor people, the folks living on public welfare, the majority of whom are single women like myself who are struggling to raise children in an incredibly hostile environment.

And I guess I am angry. Angry because we're not in your paper, we don't have a voice, often we don't have an articulated ideology, and we certainly don't have any advice to give the world, other than how to survive as a human being on next to nothing. You see, we can't move to the country and grow our own food (by god how many times hasn't that dream and fantasy crossed my mind as I looked out on the many concrete strips surrounding me).

Most of us aren't educated, so we can't get a good job for a couple of years, continue raising a family, and save enough money to buy everything with cash to avoid paying high interest rates. Most of the time we're even one of the "good" guys — we don't drive cars and use up resources and pollute the environment, because we can't afford them; we save food by eating simply (too simply — the government doesn't give us enough food stamps to feed our families well). We can't buy all the expensive paper articles (it's hard, some months, even to afford toilet paper, and these new "environmental" paper products called Generation are so high priced that only liberals can afford them). We recycle all our clothing, because the welfare gives us only $7 per month for clothing. (Ever try to buy boots, jackets, gloves, caps, scarves, etc. for two teen-aged boys on that kind of money?)

Often, we can't even afford Goodwill any more. And so we have a wonderful sub-capitalistic, even sub-counterculture community. We share with each other the meagre joys of whatever we have. Every guest is invited for dinner. Those of us who have cars buy food stamps for the rest who have no way of getting to the centers except in a 4-hour bus ride.

We've even got good politics. We know who's got and who ain't. And we know about economic exploitation, because we have the welfare department forcing us into low-paying jobs just to get us "working" — meaning that our work of raising the next generation is not "constructive" or "productive." And so we get jobs that won't support our families, but will give us a little extra every month and keep the WIN (formerly WIP) program off our asses.

But we're *the people* too. And we never hear that from anyone. Everyone complains. The radicals say welfare should be abolished and everyone should work in a job to satisfy his basic needs. The right wing wants us just to go to work (but they forget that unemployment is at 8.5 per cent). The feminists want us to go to work, to compete in the capitalistic world, to be successful hard-driving woman executives, or exploited secretaries. But nobody wants us to be mothers. Nobody wants to raise the children, I guess. We send them off to government-(!) run daycare centers, where the attendants are angry welfare mothers forced to work at subsistance wages or get thrown off welfare.

We're also forced into lots of strange situations. We have men who we sell our bodies to, to make up the difference between what the welfare thinks we need for rent, and what we actually need. And then we live in fear, lest we be "found out." Some of us cheat, some of us steal, some of us shoplift — or prostitute our bodies — to keep our families alive.

We don't like to lie, cheat, steal or fill out nosy forms for the welfare department. (Each form comes with a short statement at the end, saying that if you don't give the information requested, you won't get your check.) But we sometimes need to do these things to live. And we tell our kids it's neat to wear pants with holes in them, even tho none of the other kids in school do. And they believe us, because they are strong and beautiful people. And they know already about poverty. And they remember my radical friends who trashed me because I wouldn't get arrested, I wouldn't "stand up on the line" for what I believed in, when all I could believe in at the time, besides the glorious revolution which will come, was that I couldn't get arrested because I had to make dinner for the kids that night.

So my angry question is, I guess, "whatcha gonna do about us?" We can't be a vanguard when we have kids to feed, so we're pretty loose about our politics. A few of us get educated, so we can speak out. The women's movement occasionally tosses out a few comments, but nothing about the welfare program being the greatest oppressor of women in the culture. Why, they've even written lots of sociological books about us, how we live, how we starve, how we live our sex lives — even all kinds of intellectual explanations as to why things are the way they are. Why, we're not even the proletariat! We're not the working class! Most of us don't vote, so we're at least together in agreeing that the system is not for us. But what is? Can we all move out to the country? Will someone give us 40 acres and a mule so we can support outselves?

I realize that these are hard questions. And I guess we already know a lot about struggling, so we don't need anyone to tell us how to do that. But we need to know that others know we're here. Many of us, while praying for the revolution, and committing our lives to it, often, in the dark of night, hope and pray that it doesn't stop the welfare checks, because things are rough enough, and what the fuck are we going to do if there's no food stamps? We're conservatives in many ways, because we have others, totally dependent on us for their very lives. But we're radicals in a way, too, because *anything* has got to be better than what we've got now. But, as we look to the economic conditions in Germany before World War II, what *kind* of radicals we are is pretty important, and the Left ought to look at this. They might recall that Hitler fed the people. He got them jobs, and then he gave them back their dignity as people.

You see, we're important too. So maybe someone could write an article about us. About how we're people, and how we think politically all the time, because that's just a part of living. We know where Reagan is at. We knew where Nixon was at. And we're not going to be turned on by all this class analysis shit. Because we're all classes, we're all colors, we're all just plain poor. And most of us are women. And even on the left, that's still not too popular a sex to be.

I guess I'm pretty angry and I guess I'm pretty sad tonight. And if you've gotten this far, I thank you for listening. I guess I love all the poor people I know so much, and I wish that everyone could know these wonderful, strong women who have survived god knows what kinds of horrors. And I guess I love their beautiful children who, in spite of everything, grow up to be beautiful human beings.

And I don't know any answers either, I guess. I couldn't stand a motherfucking liberal hanging around my door wanting to help me. It would remind me of the social workers I have to avoid with all my dealings with the welfare department. And I guess I'm not ready to take to the streets, either, because, like I said, I gotta make dinner tonight. But I'm here, we're all here, and I guess the people we'll support in a revolution are those folks who speak out for loving children, loving the land, and loving each other.

I wish you well in all your ventures. Your lovely words have kept me alive on many lonely, cold nights, when I wondered how to pay the rent. Somebody out there knows about people. But I hope they don't forget us.

Encounter

By Evelyn Roehl

I'M NOT USUALLY ONE WHO takes things too seriously at first when it comes to male-female sexual-type interactions. These dealings tend to grow in significance after a few days, weeks, or months of more concentrated thinking about the relationships. So at this point, three days after a quite bizarre episode, I can still chuckle over the craziness of what I know should not be taken lightly. Anyway, the following occurred on Sunday, July 31, about 1:30 p.m. It is as accurate as my memory.

Sunday is typically a day I set aside to do tasks for myself — wash clothes, clean my room, defrost the refrigerator. . . — and last Sunday I decided to get done some weeding and harvesting in my plot in the community garden. Figuring it would probably get warmer, I set out midmorning with a swimsuit top on under a workshirt and cutoffs, and filled a jar full of water. As usual, I rode my bike out to the site, which is about two miles from my apartment, and kickstooded it on the gravel road where it would be visible from my plot if I looked up. No lampposts or parking meters out there, ya know; just some skinny bushes and fat trees that can't take a chain lock around them are in the ditches. I trucked on down the path through the falling cornstalks, sprawling squash vines, and five- to six-foot-tall weeds growing on unkempt spaces, carrying a nifty cardboard box in which to put the gathered goodies, which fits perfectly on my bicycle rack. But first, the milkweeds and swampgrass need to be pulled from the tomatoes, celery, and cabbage sections. . . .

People frequent their plots rather sporadically. Seldom can one see neighbors working in their gardens. So it's relatively quiet and peaceful out there in a big field of 170-some 40-by-40-foot plots with one to yourself. A space I do take notice of and have exchanges with is cared for by a Vietnamese family of about ten children, with various members coming at various times, most often the father and three ten- to twelve-year-old boys. After a short period of no noise, Chai (dad) and the gang came, made a lot of verbal sounds, picked some food, and left again. They are "good peepoh," as they like to say. I like 'em.

It had rained the night before; actually the clouds were moving in again. The ground was muddy and my hands got pretty grimy from the weed pulling. It had warmed up, too — probably due more to the physical actions — so I periodically stopped to take a drink of water from my jar. I also removed my workshirt to stay a little cooler. The Energy Gardens, sponsored by the Winona Park and Recreation Department, come "furnished" with hand pumps for water to feed plants in time of soil dehydration. Undrinkable, smelly stuff, but good for washing hands. A barrel under the spout serves as a basin.

With all the weeds I felt like pulling for the day uprooted, I traipsed on over to the pump barrel — one plot space away — and washed my hands. Just as I planned to walk down the short path, a white van stopped on the road and somebody bopped out. So while I washed off the mud from my fingernails, a guy carrying a white five-gallon pail walked by. I said "Hi!" and he replied similarly, continuing past. I went back to my plot, began the harvesting aspect, and once in a while looked up to make sure my Batavus was still up there on the road or to watch a vehicle go by.

I picked purple, green, and yellow beans, okra, cucumbers, navy beans, Swedish brown beans, and sweet corn, (ate some of the sweet corn raw), then I pulled up the stalks and laid them as mulch amid the tomato bushes and on open ground. I noticed the now all cloudy sky and felt the wind, put on my shirt again, and moved on to the peas. I had planted two double rows of peas about 30 feet long, so I had quite a bit to pick over. After taking the last of the pods, I'd yank out the plants and any weeds that had snarled in the vines.

Mildly lamenting the end of part of the gardening season, my mind was concentrating upon many internal happenings. It was only a strong gust of wind or a loud semi truck on the nearby highway that broke my inward attention.

In the midst of the pea picking, a sudden clasp of a hand over my mouth and lunging force on my back by another body brought on a new wave of thoughts. My shocked throat let out a muffled protest.

"Don't scream!" a male voice said. I tried to talk, but was blocked, so vocals came out again as a muffled noise.

"Don't scream, baby, or I'll cut your throat!"

"I won't scream!" I screamed, not loudly.

Well, I perceived, he obviously wasn't someone I knew who might be trying to surprise me from the rear. He was too big to be one of two kids whom I had met the Sunday before out here. And he most likely, I figured, wasn't after money or my veggies. Run!!

I tried to throw him off my back. No good — at a total disadvantage — I was flattened out on the ground.

"Knock it off baby, or I'll break your neck!" he threatened. I squirmed some more, then he clapped my head and twisted it.

"You wanna get hurt?" he asked.

"No."

"Well, then knock it off."

Okay. Another thought flash: Where would I run anyway? What would I do with the food I picked? (Of all the dumb things to worry about at a time like this. . .)

"Put your hands behind your back," a gruff tough voice spoke.

"I can't!" I pleaded.

"Put 'em behind your back, baby — I'll cut your throat!"

"I can't!" I yelled again, realistically. "Your leg is in the way."

He moved his leg, grabbed my right arm, and whipped it on top of my vertebrae. "Now if you'll just cooperate," he warned, as my left arm joined my right, "no one's gonna get hurt." He then proceeded to tie my wrists with some tape.

Some time during this insidiousness, with minor glimpses of the person on top of me, I deduced that he was the dude with the white bucket . . . only he had approached from the opposite corner. Hmmm . . . Anyway, by now it became apparent that I was to be sexually assaulted. Rape in a community garden, geez — after all the hitchhiking I've done. Forced intercourse on muddy ground, on top of my pea patch? Forced intercourse, period!? I revealed my anguish:

"You want sex, right?" I questioned. He replied affirmative, as the final tape was ripped from the roll. Well, "It'd be a lot more enjoyable if it was done the regular way," I said, or something to that effect.

"But you won't do it," came the response. He probably figured I'd run if he got off me, I reasoned. Yeah, I probably would. Though I doubt it — not in this predicament.

"I would too."

"No you wouldn't."

"I would, too!" I repeated caustically, realizing I didn't have much of a choice over the matter. (What would you rather do: have sex or get raped?) I broke the tape from my arms (cheap tape), saw a pea pod in front of my nose, opened it and popped the peas into my mouth. Chewed the peas. Swallowed.

"Okay, but I gotta do one thing," I heard simultaneously with the rip of some more tape.

"What?" I queried.

"Cover up your eyes."

"What for?"

" 'Cuz you're a beautiful woman and I don't want you to see me."

"Why?" I puzzled, as he slapped the tape over my eyes.

" 'Cuz I'm ugly," his self-image expressed.

"You're not ugly," I assured him.

"Yes I am," he reassured himself.

"No, you're not. I saw you before." I tore the tape from my face.

"Look," I stated, something to the likes of "I'll have a lot better feeling afterwards mentally if we did it normally. You don't have to get so violent about it."

He said, some time shortly after, "This is the first time I did this." His fantasy play was turning out all wrong!

The weight on my back got off, and for a relieving second I laid there and then finally got up. He rapidly rose, and confessed, "I can't do it. . . . I never did this before. . . . God, I feel terrible. I'm sorry!"

Slightly amazed, I went, or must have looked, "Huh?" He wandered away, carrying his roll of white tape, and iterated, "I'm really sorry," and hung his head in shame.

I watched for a while as he walked down the path to the road. Then I went to the pump to wash my mud-covered legs and arms. I looked toward the road and discovered his van was gone but I didn't hear it drive away. He was nowhere in sight. I finished picking the peas, thinned some carrots, pulled up a fat beet, and went home.

❖ ❖ ❖

Who was this creature, anyway? Well, he looked to be about 25 years old, 5 feet, 9 inches tall, 172 or so pounds, had shoulder-length brownish-blonde hair, a reddish scruffy beard growing mostly under his chin, beer gut and round-shaped face and legs. (Wearing a turquoise blue tank top and maize colored cutoffs. . .) He wasn't ugly, but certainly not outstanding — very typical looking. He looked like the type, categorically speaking, who listens to country-western or country-rock music, got a C-minus average in school, works in a factory at a shit job, and hadn't had a lay for a while. Seeing a female body in summer clothes in an open garden with no other people present, possibly watching through the weeds from his plot (or one he could have been stealing from?), and going back to his van, since a fairly long time elapsed between the pump sight, veggie harvesting, and attack, he apparently built up some strange energy, got the white four-inch plastic tape from the van, and snuck down a different path. The negative self-image, possible working class expoitation, and male horniness seem to be plausible *modus operandi* for trying to exert strength over the "weaker sex." He must be thoroughly baffled by the end result.

And if I ever see him again in the garden, or on the street or at a bar, I'll go up to him and ask what his trip was.

I doubt that he would try to pull this stunt again with another woman, since his "first try" was an utter failure.

Meanwhile, the scraps of tape are crumpled on the floor under some boards with back issues of the *Anvil* on them.

Grandma is Dancing

By Linda M. Hasselstrom

I NEVER LEARNED MUCH ABOUT Grandma, not even her name, so I'll have to invent all that when I write the story. But I've taken notes on it off and on through the years, and now is as good a time as any to collect them and see what I have.

Of course, she wasn't my Grandma — or anybody's, so far as I know. Everyone called her that. But for all their familiarity, they knew little about her.

She came to the U.S. from Finland when she was about twenty, according to my notes.

(Perhaps she told me that.) I see her as a tiny, slim-waisted girl. She married; whether in Finland or New York, I don't know. They came west and for some reason filed on a claim near Camp Crook, South Dakota — a place of rolling prairie, rough buttes and few trees, in the northwest corner of the state. That must have been around 1910, and as desolate as Camp Crook is today, it must have been worse then. Perhaps I can do some research, find some old pictures. Now it has a grocery store and a gravel road, sixty-five miles to the nearest town. Then, the road must have been a wagon trail, and the only grocery sixty-five miles away in Belle Fourche. I suppose it was quite a town then, as a shipping terminal for cattle and wheat — one of the few towns in that wide expanse of prairie.

Anyway, Grandma's husband went back to New York after the first snow. Who could blame him? I've seen it snow up there: thirty-five-foot drifts, mile after mile, with winds sixty, seventy miles an hour, burying cows, even antelope. In the spring, with snowmelt , every gully floods; the corpses of winter — killed animals pile up against brush piles, and the roads closed by snow all winter are torn out by flood. Even today the people there may spend four months isolated in winter, and several weeks in spring.

Grandma stayed two years, proved up the claim, and then went back to New York and her husband. I see her, nearly thirty by then, wind- and sun-burned, riding the train back east with the slip of paper saying they owned their 160 acres tucked safely in her purse. There would be no fear in eyes that had seen a South Dakota winter, alone, probably in a sod house. But there must have been a softness and joy in those blue eyes, too, for she had also seen the green creep over the hills, and thousands of wildflowers blooming.

She stayed in New York until her husband died; no one I've talked to is sure how long that was, or what they did. Perhaps I can make something up. But she buried him there, had a tombstone put up, bought the plot beside him for herself, and took the train back to Camp Crook. She may have been sixty then. Perhaps that's when she became Grandma and lost her name.

Somehow her land disappeared; perhaps she'd sold it years ago — but then why come back to Camp Crook at all? Unless it was the only other place in the world she knew of where she felt comfortable. Perhaps she had enough money to go to Camp Crook, but not back to Finland. Perhaps she was wise enough to know that after living her life in New York, she wouldn't be happy in Finland.

However it happened, she returned to Camp Crook, and soon went to work for a priest who bought a small ranch on the river and took in homeless boys. The ranch grew; the priest named it Sky Ranch and began to get sizable contributions from liquor dealers across the nation — guilt money, perhaps. He built dormitories, hired counselors. Grandma cooked all the meals and did the laundry until she was ninety-two. Then she retired from cooking and just did laundry for a few years.

That's when I caught up with her, briefly: I came to the ranch once a year to help the homeless boys — who by then were more often full-fledged juvenile delinquents — write poetry. The boys were of various types; some rapists, robbers, car thieves; some abandoned; some just tough-mouthed children whose parents were too tired or too bored or too lazy to take care of them. They teased Grandma, and followed me around making indecent suggestions until they found out I was over thirty ("Why, that's older than my MOTHER!") And they wrote wonderful poetry.

Once while I was there, one of them, running on an icy sidewalk, slammed into Grandma and knocked her down. She scrambled to her feet and stood tall, which brought her eyes level with the boy's third shirt button, and cussed him in what may have been Finnish. He was a big black kid with an Afro and a mean look, but Grandma shook her finger in his face and cussed him in some strange language, and he hung his head and mumbled, "I'm sorry, Grandma, I'm sorry. I won't do it again, honest."

Another time I was eating lunch with Grandma and the cook, an attractive wench from one of the ranches in the area. The boys were confined to the ranch: the neighbors alternately feared and hated them, there were no women counselors. The only women they ever saw were Grandma, the cook, and me — once a year for a week. Some of them were men, for all practical purposes, and they made propositions logical under the circumstances.

One sauntered over to our table during lunch and implied that only he possessed the key to the cook's happiness, which she could find by lowering his zipper. Grandma poked the cook and me in the ribs, held her thumb and forefinger two inches apart, looked him straight in the eye, and giggled. The cook and I tried not to laugh, but we couldn't help it, and the boy went back to his own table, blushing.

When she was ninety-three or four, she retired; she and a dozen "poosycats" and a scrub brush gathered in an old white house in town, four miles from Sky Ranch. I always heard news of her when I visited the ranch, and stopped by to see her when I could. She heated the house to eighty degrees, scrubbed it daily with Lysol, and covered the walls with pictures of Jesus, heart pierced and flaming. From every available surface — walls, dresser, bathroom shelves — he looked down. The cats had their kittens in the bathtub, and whenever I came she'd lead me in to see the latest batch, kneeling by the tub and crooning to them, "Poosycats, poosycats."

Finally the ranch hired an unusual nun as a counselor — she could cuss the boys in their own language if necessary, since she'd worked in the barrios in Los Angeles and knew all about tough kids. They loved her. At least twice a week she visited Grandma, to give her communion.

Though I didn't participate, I always went along for another glimpse of the old lady. Even then I was thinking of a story about her.

Liz, the nun, told me that for perhaps forty years Grandma had been slipping up to the back door of the saloon once a week for her blackberry brandy. Everyone in town knew it, and thought no less of her for it, but in her code it was impossible to go in the front way.

I remember one incident I'll be sure to use in the story: I was sitting in the kitchen with a cup of strong black coffee, choking on the Lysol smell. Grandma knelt piously on the living room rug beside the praying Sister Liz, surrounded by pictures of Jesus of the flaming heart. Suddenly, mid-prayer, Grandma looked up and said, "You sure got nice teeth, honey. Are they all yours?"

Liz paused, giggled, said, "Yes," and went on praying.

A few cold March Sundays later, in church, Grandma told Liz that she was going back to New York to scrub her husband's tombstone. Liz took her to the station, and she rode the bus two days. I don't know if she took her Lysol and her scrub brush with her. Her only relative in New York (this was news to the town) was ill, and he wanted to wait a few days until he felt well enough to drive her to the cemetery. She didn't have time to waste, she said, so she stayed with him one night, got back on the bus and two days later was back in Camp Crook.

No one believed she'd gone. The parishioners in the little church were stern. They did not smile when she told her story. They told her she ought to go to a nice home where she'd be taken care of. She stared at them, then dashed down the church steps to a wide pool of ice in the parking lot, and slid out onto it, laughing like a girl. None of them pursued her, but they shouted at her from the outskirts of her pond. They were firm. They insisted that she visit the doctor, and deputized Liz to take her the next week.

Liz will make a good sympathetic character too, though I'll have to be careful not to stereotype her either as Pious Nun or Rebellious Nun. She was simply a very intelligent, very religious woman — who didn't let religion interfere with intelligence, or vice versa.

Anyway, Liz took her to the doctor, and on the way they stopped for lunch at a restaurant in the nearby town. Liz took Grandma's arm to guide her across another icy spot. She jerked away, shot out onto the ice, and announced, "Grandma is dancing. Look, Grandma is dancing on the ice." She slipped once, and even the passersby looked stern. Liz caught her, finally, by skating out on the ice herself, and dragged her inside for a good lunch, trying not to giggle.

In the parking lot of the doctor's office she did it again, holding her long skirts above her ankles, "Grandma is dancing. Grandma doesn't need a doctor."

The doctor pronounced her healthy as a horse, but undernourished; she had been cutting back on her groceries to buy cat food. Liz took her back to Camp Crook and asked some of the stern parishioners to help out with groceries. An order had to be passed to the grocery store to keep her from trading the groceries that were delivered weekly for cat food.

Every time she caught one of the parishioners watching her on her way to the back door of the saloon, she would hunt up a patch of ice, or just dance in the middle of the street, and laugh: "Grandma is dancing. See, Grandma can dance on ice."

A party was deputized to slip into the old shed behind her house at night and remove twenty or thirty cats, on the theory that she wouldn't notice, since she had almost as many in the house. She did, and her tongue got sharper. She stopped going to church, and Liz went oftener to her house with communion. She asked Liz, again and again, to make sure her body was sent back to New York, so she could be buried beside her husband. But she couldn't tell exactly where that was.

The story doesn't end right, but perhaps I should arrange that. I'd like to see her skating right off into a heaven full of poosycats, blackberry brandy and a smiling Jesus with a scrub brush and Lysol in one hand, the other held out to welcome her. But she lived on into summer, the poosycats disappeared. They buried her in Camp Crook, as she must have suspected they would. Liz moved somewhere else. I presume she remembers. She will in my story.

American Agriculture Meeting, 1978. left to right : Peter Kallenberg,
Harvey Johnson, Ann Kanten, Wayne Riseth.
Photo by Ken Meter.

North Country Woman in Action

By Alice Tripp

I HAVE ALWAYS QUESTIONED AUTHORITY and resented following irrelevant or unfair rules, but I never expected to go to jail. When I was arrested and hauled off to the squad car, I did not feel evil or criminal or guilty of wrongdoing.

I was in jail for three days and three nights. After the weekend, they decided it was not smart to have an old lady in jail, so they released me. It was a test of endurance for me. I wrote letters, read every book they found for me, took frequent showers and exercised to keep my circulation going. I did not weep. I was angry. Sometimes during those three days I wondered if I was being foolish or even exhibitionist. But mostly, I was so mad — I felt the weight of big business coming down on me, and I knew my government was helping them instead of me. Indeed, even the courts were taking the side of the utilities and issuing injunctions which were used by the utilities as tools to arrest us, so they could proceed with their project. I was in jail for talking to an electrical construction worker. I was charged with "obstructing legal process."

I was one of a group of farmers who were defending our land. We were fighting the network of electric cooperatives (ostensibly the Rural Electrification Administration) which was erecting on our West-Central Minnesota farms the world's biggest powerline — untested technology, unnecessary and uneconomic. Since the powerline has been up and operating, we have been proved to be right. The power plant produces excess power which they must sell outside our system cheaper than we can buy it, and our power bills have doubled twice to pay for the project. In addition, people and animals under the line are experiencing adverse health effects.

In the course of our resistance, we discovered that the state government and even the courts operated in favor of established business. Keeping the wheels turning — no matter what the consequences to individuals — is important to our legal system. In St. Paul and in Washington, the pressure of the business establishment has more influence than the voice of the people. So when we resisted and opposed first the utilities then the law, we were not ashamed. There were over one hundred arrests in the winter of 1978 — people who had never broken even traffic laws. People who had paid their taxes and their bills all their lives, who felt they had used every legal channel and had received no help from their own government, were defying the court's injunctions.

Because we saw our rights being trampled, we became more sensitive to others who are being ignored, disenfranchised and mistreated. The farmers in our area have supported the Indians, have gone to their meetings and even helped supply food for these meetings. In addition to trying to help Indians, we farmers (traditionally inimical to unions) supported coal miners in their strike, verbally and with food. During the 1978 gubernatorial campaign, some auto workers from Minneapolis offered us their support, and we have made lasting friendships with those and other union people. A few of us have had conversations with Blacks who have been fighting oppression in Mississippi. As Arnett Lews of Mississippi said, "Those of us who are down have got to talk together." We are still sending information all over the country and travelling to help inspire people to speak up for their rights.

Women were important in this movement, as they have been in many protests past and present. The current organization resisting the powerline, General Assembly to Stop the Powerline (GASP), never had a formal structure with elected officers. Each meeting — and we met every day for awhile — was like a town meeting. Whoever wanted to could chair the meeting for the day. Women often took to the podium.

Many women pulled on their snowmobile suits and came out day after day in the cold winter of '78. Gloria Woida, a striking blond who spoke up and spoke well, was a favorite of the media. Debbie Pick, now in Brussels, Belgium, is a precocious young person who moved to Lowry and helped to run the office and edit our paper *Hold That Line*. White-haired Esther Hedlin, who farms with her brother, has a sharp intellect and is well-read — she often brought us background material.

Henrietta McCrory, a widow who is fiercely protective of her farm, embroidered slogans on shirts and jackets and wrote rousing songs about politicians and corporate managers. Phyllis and Sharon, the two young Pederson wives joined their mother-in-law Irene and gave many hours to help with fundraisers, publicity affairs and actual picketing. I remember one morning when Sharon got up at 2:00 a.m. to help with milking so she could be part of a TV panel. We marched; we spoke; we telephoned; we even made coffee and sandwiches. The list could go on and on — brave women, thinking and responsive, willing to give their time and themselves to a cause they know is important.

We are not alone. The problem of large, unneeded power plants and powerlines is arousing protest all around the world. Our small group in Minnesota has become one center for disseminating information as far away as France and Scotland. Ordinary people everywhere are resisting bigger-is-better technology.

My growing concern for a government which could, in the crunch, vote on the side of the corporation, led me into active politicking. Four people in Pope County asked me to run for governor in 1978 in the Democratic primary. We campaigned from the back of a pickup with little financial backing and no big political machine behind us. The candidate for lieutenant-governor, Mike Casper, is a human dynamo and he actually put the campaign together. We had help from the Farmer Labor Association and several young people: singer Patty Kakac; Russ Packard who wrote a song for us; Dick Hanson who shared his experience in politics; and my husband. We were astonished to get 100,000 votes in the primary election against a "populist" governor, and we were really impressed with the wide and rising level of dissatisfaction this vote represented.

Two years later the Farmer Labor Association managed to get some time on the platform of the National Democratic Convention in New York. I was chosen to nominate Ron Dellums who was concerned (as we were) that the convention was not addressing vital issues: farm problems, peace, human rights, and the downsliding economy. It was an exciting moment for me and my family and a real triumph for the Farmer Labor Association.

The FLA consists of liberal activists who work within the Democratic Party to force the party to face the real issues of our time instead of constantly compromising to get votes. I have been very active in the FLA; I think they are the smartest, most honest politicians in town.

I do not expect to run for public office again. I am stubborn about some of my principles to the point where I alienate some people. I guess I am a radical. I am not a socialist; farmers are capitalists and my father was a small business man. I believe in individual enterprise and I have seen so much bungling by the bureaucracy that I cannot have faith in the ability of the government to run anything. But I am a radical in the sense that I think we need drastic changes, both in our government and in our economic system. I do not like the way the class system is developing in this country. I also think the collusion between government and big business is a greater threat to our democracy than Communism. It is alarming to see that this threat was perceived in 1865 by none other than Abraham Lincoln who said: "I see in the future a crisis that causes me to tremble for the safety of my country. . . . Corporations have been enthroned."

We borrow wisdom from great thinkers. Courage comes from our convictions. There comes a time when love of our land and our community convinces us that legal reprimand and the disgrace of arrest cannot hurt us as much as compromise.

I will continue to confront authority when I think authority is wrong. I have joined the fight against underground hazardous waste dumps. I have played a small part in the anti-nuclear arms movement. My concern for the loss of small family farms demands more than lip service — I want real action. I will continue to contribute in my small way because I do feel we cannot sit back. As Frederick Douglass said, "Power concedes nothing without a demand. It never has and it never will."

Women's Peace Presence

By Madge Micheels-Cyrus

WOMEN'S PEACE ENCAMPMENTS ARE SPRINGING up all over the world. Greenham Common, Seneca Falls, Sperry Univac, and now the Women's Peace Presence to Stop Project ELF [Extremely Low Frequency — a U.S. Navy communications installation in northern Wisconsin]. It is a response to women's concern for the continuity of life. It not only encircles the globe but it comes down to us from women of many generations and through the centuries. "Lysistrata," the story of Greek women who refused sex to men until they gave up war, is one of the earliest references to this concern. Today, the impetus for these gatherings is reinforced by two other factors. One is that women are getting together to help each other take over their own lives. The other is the finalness of nuclear war. Women understand there will not be another chance for peace. We must achieve this goal before the button is pushed.

I am one of the women planning the Peace Presence. There are frustrations as we struggle with our differences to find a common bond to save the earth. There is also a very refreshing, satisfying relationship that encompasses these meetings. I come away from them impressed with the strength of individual women and moved by our deep, intuitive understanding that change is not merely possible; it is absolutely necessary for our survival.

There is no doubt in my mind that the world is in the mess it is today because of masculine, macho thinking. Men have been fed a line for centuries that manhood means being Number One, on top, the power, in control. They talk of pushing buttons, deterrence, first-strike, and of "showing them we won't be pushed around." They play war games and talk about our losses in hundreds of millions. They use their brains and their money to develop weapons of destruction, some too complicated for our own military to operate. They raise their sons to be soldiers to die in their games. They offer treaties that would put the other nation in an inferior position and call them war-mongers for not accepting the terms. They see people's struggles for food, health and education as communist conspiracies. They see women as sex symbols to be conquered.

But they are not monsters. Some of them are even women. They are people who have put their trust in the wrong things. They are frightened and have been taught the wrong moves to become secure. Some of them have learned to be oppressors because they too have been oppressed. Some of them have suffered psychological distress because of their conflict between the image of manhood and their concern for life — people, creatures of the earth and the very earth itself.

The qualities that are identified mostly with women are what are necessary to bring about a change for survival. In order to turn this mess around it is imperative that we look at the human mind and heart and pull together despite our differences; to accept conflict without destroying those we disagree with; to set an example that will lead the world to creative solutions; to build bridges, not walls; to recognize the sameness in people; to appeal to the spirit of love in everyone.

Since this is my goal, I have a grave concern for the trend toward women's peace groups, in that they leave out the many men and older male children who know we are right and want to strengthen their nurturing skills. Some women say that all-women groups have a special quality to them. They do. So do all-men groups and all-children groups, and there are places and times for these. Many women desperately need these encounters to develop their own sense of worth and strength. But there must be a time to leave and join the real world and test their new-found skills.

I hear many women say they like a women's-only action because there is less chance for violence and they feel safer. What are we saying here? Do we want to avoid conflict? When I marched in Chicago in the open-housing struggle we discovered that a lot of the violence — spitting and throwing of bricks and bottles — was directed at the white marchers. It was difficult for those who hated blacks to understand our participation. They were not as threatened by blacks marching as they were by their white supporters. Perhaps the reason there is less violence in women-only groups is that the male police forces and male military forces are letting us have our day because we do not threaten them — we are only women. If men join us, that questions their manhood. In the South, in the '60s, and in India, it was necessary to surface the feelings and deal with them in order for healing to take place. Maybe for change to happen, their violence needs to be faced, while we keep our nonviolence firm.

In dealing with cruise missiles, military contractors and ELF, we are dealing with men. In dealing with Congress, the president and the Pentagon, we are dealing mainly with men. How can we then reject them as part of the solution, when they are overwhelmingly the problem? They must be dealt with. They must be talked to. They must be challenged. They are the ones that must change. We are the ones who must deal with them, talk to them, challenge them. How much easier that task will be if, when we are successful they can join us — person by person — instead of being excluded from our success because of their gender. There is a tendency for people who want change to reject everything that has gone before. Do we throw out the words of Jefferson, Thoreau, Gandhi, King, because they are men? Do we reject our fathers, our brothers, our sons? Or do we sift through their truths, recognize their fallibilities and their strengths and build on the good that came before?

Our goal is to allow men to cry, to feel, to rejoin the human race. To be able to dream of a world where differences are allowed. To redefine their manhood in ways that are creative and not destructive to the earth and its people. To feel part of a group, people have to belong to it. To dream with us, they must be allowed into the vision.

I do not want a woman-only world. I want a world where the qualities described as masculine are in harmony with the person, within the nation, within the world. To reach that kind of an end, men must be part of the means. For peace is an inclusive, not exclusive, quality. It is the one place where no one should be kept out.

Pam McAllister, in the introduction to *Reweaving the Web of Life*, said: "The fabric of the new society will be made of nothing more or less than the threads woven in today's interactions." Those threads must be both masculine and feminine for the cloth of peace to be strong. So, while I cheer all efforts for peace, I only hope that forms like the women's peace groups (which have made a powerful statement) grow into people's peace groups, so we can move swiftly toward our goal.

She Grows Older

for Meridel Le Sueur

Spring is too painful for her now. The
tight buds' aching pressure like babies' fists
clasping nothing; daffodils spraying up
brilliant as headaches to her; lilacs cloying,
coating the inside of her throat
with a crackling asthmatic sheen. It is

roses she loves — the full bunches climbing
in the window, shedding bloodlight; the
heavy-headed bushes lolling
fat in the sun, each cluster of petals a
pink coliseum for bees or a
red bedroom, clean & rich
as her summer woman's body, clean & rich
as the sun. The trees

all reach out to her; eucalyptus
rising, straight & fragrant with oil
in the heat; the elm,
a vivid green fountain; the oak
squatting before her in his age to
advise & do her honor, his branches
bending to touch the earth. We all

lift up our hands
to the medallion of her face, we all
grow moist & fat even in the dark for her. We all
grow toward her tomorrow's heat, gypsies
gliding around the fire in our swirling shirts, our

bodies full of her hot, black bread; oranges, limes
& tequila; our heads

full of her sun, lingering
in the rich, purple dusk.

—Wendy Knox
(Anvil #40)

Mammogram

I have these breasts
in between A and B cups
which is to say, not big enough
for the movies, too big for high fashion.
My husband fancies them.
They have suckled three robust children,
but do not quite fill a god's hands.
The technician has me
position each in turn
on the cardboard.
They have to be just so.
The room is cold, my breasts
clinging to me for shelter.
I think of women friends
who are breastless now,
but bought time by the knife.
Little hills, your spurting is over.
Still I need you for my sense
of off-balance symmetry,
as referent for my mothering time.
Let me hear those old milky ballads,
inviting suck!
Soft weapon that thinks
it can conquer by succoring,
twins who grew up in the same house,
without a mother —
you adopted me
but dream of leaving.
Don't go yet.
Stay to lead me forward
into my own arms.

—Florence Dacey
(Anvil #40)

Life in Portcullis County

I.   The Cook Book

She wrote the poem after breakfast, before the dishes were washed. It was short, like all the others:

We Three

> He, with the barn broom
> I, with the pitchfork
> Maneuvered the bull
> Into his pen
> Tonight. . .
> An improbable trio:
> One tall thin gentle man
> A short fat me,
> And the beast of fabled ferocity.

Then she filed it away, with all the others, in the notebook labeled "Cook Book."

II.   Apple Pickers

They gather the windfall apples every afternoon in the shadow of the unleafing branches. None may be left in the grass for gleaning mice or honey bees. This wheelbarrow for us, he says, that wheelbarrow for pigs, and he examines each apple with sincere deliberation before choosing a wheelbarrow. Safe under the brim of her hat, she smiles and picks by iambic pentameter: us pigs pigs, us pigs pigs. . . and throws in a sapphic or an alexandrine just as a joke, knowing the diversion isn't necessary.

III. Delivery

One afternoon a man knocked at the kitchen door and said he was delivering the semen her man had ordered. Maybe if she had noticed the dairy breeder's sign on the truck or maybe if she hadn't been reading one of her old story books, she wouldn't have laughed and laughed and laughed and cried.

IV. Going After the New Hens

He turned north after the six miles, following these as any instructions with patient literalness. The empty chicken crates in back shifted, sounded hollow behind them, as the pick-up dipped off the highway onto the weedy path. "This must be it. They said six miles," he explained and the path that couldn't get narrower got deeper in snow-tufted weeds. She swung her foot in all the warm places under the dashboard and smiled at the hills where there were no farmhouse lights. "What if we got stuck out here all night," he said, frowning into the darkness. "Oh, my yes! What if . . . ," she said, dreaming into the dark.

V. The Gift

In, after evening chores, he held out to her on his palm an acorn. She blinked and saw in his hand a snow leopard on its misty ledge, saw the crazy king's castle glittering above the river, saw a child with a yoyo and a peanut butter sandwich. "It's only an acorn from the lane," he said. And she said "I know."

—Myra Sullivan
(Anvil #45)

Old Woman

And I sit here drinking tea
and rum, and smoking,
the kids watching TV
in the other room,
my lover almost an ex —
only not quite,
and I with no rules
to tell me what to do now
                         or next.

What is this life I'm leading?
I don't recognize it,
or the things that happen in it,
as mine. I'm always amazed
and bewildered that things
just continue to happen.

If someone were to write
my biography
they'd find no theme,
only a disconnected
collection of events
with a vague pattern.

I have a horror
of that old woman I'll be
someday — sitting propped up
on pillows in a lonely bed,
regarding her life
and finding everything —
my now, my past, my future —
without structure or meaning.
She drives me to excesses.

I search for a symbol
to repel her,
to break her hold on me:
the cairns explorers left
to mark their way across
the wasteland,
or navigators on unknown
                            seas.

I will sing them to her,
and me, in myths
that say leave chart making
to the landbound and surveyors.
Whatever journey's made
is made only once.

I could ask again,
What now? What next?
Hindsight and guesses
don't plot a course
and rules cannot answer.
Those who know the most
                            are dead,
are the dead, and do not
speak our language.

Old woman, I raise my cup
to you — a pledge:
I'll not give up my seeking,
if you won't regret
what I never found.

                            —J. Yarrow
                            (Anvil #49)

Listening to the Land

The sacred link between the land and its people rivaled life styles as an underlying theme in the hearts of those for whom the Anvil *spoke. It was implicit in most of the magazine's discussions of agriculture and Native Americans, and it appeared time after time in both prose and poetry that celebrated nature, animals, and the distinctive character of the north country. As awareness of the environmental crisis sharpened in the '80s, preservation of the earth and its waters became a more explicit cause.*

Revival of the Mississippi River was the subject of two articles by Sandra Gue that appeared in numbers 39 (1982) and 47 (1984). Here they are condensed into a single piece. Richard Broderick examined the spiritual tie between humans and wilderness in the story "Brother Wolf," published in number 42 (1983), and the Greens as a political and cultural movement were heralded in the Midwest during the winter of 1985-86 by Anvil *number 51. This special issue included a variety of perspectives on the ecological vision. Among them, poet Joe Paddock affirmed the organic tie between land and the life that arises from it, while Maynard Kaufman, a professor of religion and farmer from Michigan, pondered the cultural and political implications for American society.*

NORTH COUNTRY

ANVIL

No. 47

$2.00

A Nicaraguan Farm

Wisconsin Women's Peace Presence

The Mississippi

Mississippi River Revival : Headwaters of a Movement

By Sandra Gue

> Floating down the Mississippi River
> Turning gold up and down her shores,
> Can you hear the voices of the river?
> She'll be clean once more.
> — Larry Long, 1981

ONCE IN A WHILE A SKEPTIC comes up to Larry Long and wants to know, "What can a bunch of folk singers do to clean up the river?" Far from taking offense, the man who dreamed up the Mississippi River Revival and remains its main organizer welcomes the chance to explain the place of music in organizing.

"Music is a spiritual thing," Larry says. "When people hear my song 'Blue Highway' it gives them comfort and hope. It's a positive symbol. People need hope — that's the major thing this movement has given them. That alone makes the Revival a success."

In the 1970s Larry traveled around the country as a folk singer, doing odd jobs, singing in bars, writing songs for people. He also found himself becoming a community organizer, helping start a marketing co-op for farmers in Tennessee and helping farmers fight a powerline in Minnesota. Back in his home town of St. Cloud, Minnesota, he organized a Home Festival, a series of celebrations that involved old people, young people and many ethnic groups.

It was from another folk singer, Pete Seeger, that Larry got the idea of a Mississippi River Revival, modeled on Seeger's campaign for the Hudson River in New York. Some people tried to discourage him by pointing out that the Hudson is "only 160 miles and three newspapers long," while the Mississippi is over 2,500 miles in length. Long, however, has that peculiar brand of innocence that doesn't admit things *can't* be done just because they *haven't* been done. He views the river as an important part of the cultural heritage of the people in the ten states along its reaches, and he insists that a healthy river is essential for the survival of its people. After 150 years of turning their backs to the river, they now must turn around to face it again.

The most visible part of the revival is an annual festival designed to bring together all those who have an interest in the river. Recreation users, musicians, biologists, poets, nature lovers, people who fish — everyone. The first festival was held in 1981 under the partial sponsorship of the Farmer Labor Education Committee of Minnesota. On a rainy October Sunday over 1,200 persons attended the gathering on Nicollet Island in Minneapolis to celebrate their ties to the river and the efforts being made to clean it up.

The annual festival, however, is only one part of the overall Mississippi River Revival. Plans were also made for a boatcade from the Twin Cities down to New Orleans. Thus it was that in the summer of 1983 I was one of nine canoeists who paddled across a northern Minnesota lake and debarked at the outlet of a small stream. There we joined a group of tourists around a large sign which said: "Lake Itasca . . . headwaters of the Mississippi River . . . 2552 miles to the Gulf of Mexico."

We weren't going that far, but, as the first flotilla of the Mississippi River Revival, we would cover 700 miles during the next nine weeks, and nearly a hundred people would go with us part of the way. At a dozen places along the way Revival chapters had set up festivals to coincide with the arrival of our flotilla.

Each of us was familiar with only a small part of the river, and for the first two weeks, all of us were in new territory. We found first that the river begins as a knee-deep stream so narrow you can touch the dogwood bushes on the other side. Fallen trees and beaver dams sometimes block the way. It grows not only from the tributaries that pour in from the sides but from underground springs. The main channel twists lazily through the marshes, often stretching two aerial miles into ten aquatic miles.

We saw beds of wild rice and wild iris, and tamarack trees that stain the river brown. We saw evening skies roiling with clouds of gray, purple, gold and pink. We heard the call of loons and the racket of heron rookeries. But "seeing" the river was not automatic. It is not easy to appreciate otter runs when you are exhausted from long paddling against the wind, when the sun is setting and when several miles of marsh lie ahead.

The seemingly gentle current turned fierce when we had to paddle upstream because of a missed turn or a forgotten dog. Heavy winds blew us into mud banks. Swarms of mosquitoes covered our arms like gray angora when we paddled too close to shore. Near-freezing temperatures numbed our rain-soaked bodies, forcing us to seek shelter under a bridge or to rig a tarpaulin between trees. We were into the second week before we set up a dry tent.

All was not ordeal, however. The Anishinabe (Ojibway) Indians in our party taught us new ways to show respect for Mother Earth. Never did we take anything from the land or water without first making an offering. After a fruitless week of fishing, we caught our first only after making a tobacco offering. Before each meal we said prayers of thanks in the Anishinabe language.

The river has its own time frame, its own rhythm; it cares nothing for our human schedule. An adverse wind lengthened a lake crossing. . . Good fishing kept us in one place. . . A strong current on a sunny day invited drifting, watching the birds overhead. We usually ended up cooking in the dark. Only after converting to "river time" were we able to alter our artificial sense of time and give ourselves over to the discovery of an eagle's nest, to waiting out a thunderstorm, to the earned relaxation of drifting after a hard paddle. We learned to measure time by the angle of the sun in the sky, to use as maps the underwater grasses flowing in the direction of the main current. The flow of the river marked the flow of our days.

Keeping the river clean — and cleaning up after others — became integral to our flotilla activity. In the upper stretches we found no more than an occasional pop or beer can every other mile; but in other places we often spent an hour picking up broken glass and styrofoam litter from campsites by roads. At snags on bends in the river we found quantities of floating debris. We also joined community cleanups organized by Revival chapters.

Bemidji was the site of the first Revival festival. Backed by an orange-and-white striped parachute on stage, area musicians, poets and story-tellers drew a large audience. To the side was a children's tent, alive with stories and activities. Around the grassy field were booths of many groups with displays of their concerns for the river: Girl Scouts showing projects that had earned "Gift of Water" merit badges, Minnesota COACT (the citizens' advocate) presenting statistics on the dumping of toxic chemicals and the Audubon Society displaying books with outstanding photos of Mississippi River wildlife.

One of the festival-goers was Winona LaDuke, an Anishinabe woman who works for native rights and serves as an advisor to the North American Water Office. LaDuke believes that community people can play a large role in halting toxic waste dumping. Since discharge permits are required for a municipality or industry dumping poisons, the required data can be used to organize cleanup campaigns. In addition, the 1972 Clean Water Act sets "zero discharge" as its 1985 priority. Among groups using this information, according to LaDuke, is "the massive organizing drive initiated by the North American Water Office to combat water pollution along the entire Mississippi River. Environmentalists plan to move from pipe to pipe and drain to drain, investigating the permitting process, the legality of those permits, and the extent to which zero discharge is being sought at each stop."

As we paddled south of Grand Rapids, we kept expecting the wilderness character of the river to change. Instead, we passed occasional farms, with sand banks dropping sharply to the river, and deciduous forests, but there was little evidence of human activity. In part, riverbank development has been kept to a minimum because of people whose memories go back to the 1950s, when terrible flooding — including the disaster at Jacobson — altered the course of the river. Riverbank development also is controlled through the joint-powers agreement signed by the eight counties along the upper 466 miles of the river. The so-named Mississippi Headwaters Board is set up to preserve the scenic and recreational aspects of the river. It does this by preventing uncontrolled and unplanned development through strong local zoning ordinances and through a recreation plan for the river and nearby public lands.

In Aitkin, Mayor Carol Norris said that until recently no organizations were working to protect the river. "That's why we have a sewage treatment plant on the river," she said, referring to a plant built some years before. "That could not happen today, not with the Headwaters Board." While it is too late to site the plant properly, the same environmental awareness that gave rise to the board has made it possible for the city to get money to make the plant's outflow less polluting.

As we paddled downstream, the river became wider and muddier. Occasional power dams — where once natural falls had blocked passage of steamboats — now blocked the river for us, and we had to portage. South of Brainerd we encountered a large deer population in an unlikely setting: the Camp Ripley Military Reservation, where automatic weapons were firing in the background and National Guard troops with tanks were at mess on the river's edge. Several miles north of St. Cloud we found one of the few places with obvious evidence of poor agricultural practices. Corn had been planted from the edge of the river straight up a hill.

At the Monticello nuclear power plant, a huge complex rising from the riverbank, we had our first encounter with the potential source of an even more deadly pollutant: radioactivity in waste water and steam. There we planted grain and wild flower seeds just outside the fence and offered prayers for the return of the land to its proper use — growing food. We did the same at nuclear plants near Red Wing, Minnesota, and Genoa, Wisconsin.

From Anoka to Minneapolis, 15 miles to the south, the river took on a new character. Houses hunched close to the banks, and lawns swept down to the water's edge. Multi-lane bridges criss-crossed the river. Rock-filled sites supported storage yards, junk yards, loading docks and silos. Barges — some rusting, some filled — lay anchored to the shore.

But what loomed most ominously were the huge pipes poking out of hillsides. What caused those rusty-red, or those bluish-green drip marks? What was that noxious smell? What was that gray vapor? We could only hope that the "pipe-to-pipe, drain-to-drain" project of the North American Water Office might eventually answer these questions.

The 14 miles of river through the Twin Cities were a study in dramatic contrasts. Steep, tree-lined bluffs — so high they almost blocked the sky — gave way suddenly to storage yards and rusting barges, some long-neglected and listing. Pristine wilderness streams entered a choppy, cloudy river dominated by cabin cruisers, excursion boats, and multitow barges. These contrasts were part of the backdrop for other stories: conflicts over use of the river that were being argued in courtrooms and committee rooms.

In St. Paul, Revival member Kiki Sonnen had a story to tell. "We have here a little chunk of wilderness in the city limits," she said, "and the largest heron rookery in the Upper Midwest." Sonnen was describing 200 acres of river land a company wants to use for parking barges. The U.S. Army Corps of Engineers is the one agency that must give approval, in this case to the St. Paul Port Authority. Forty groups are part of the Pig's Eye Coalition, which wants the area added to adjacent city land for park and open space. After five years of preparing documents, raising funds and testifying, the Coalition recently received word that the Port Authority has withdrawn its request for the fleeting-area permit. But the barge company is suing the state and city, saying they were illegally involved in the site decision. The issue is a broad and important one: Do state and local agencies have the right to a say in how the river is used — or does this power belong only to the Corps of Engineers?

The Pig's Eye name attaches also to another environmental group, but we wouldn't encounter it until we reached Pepin, Wisconsin, 66 miles downstream. There, at the lower end of Lake Pepin, we met Dorothy Hill, founder and president of Citizens for a Clean Mississippi. "The biggest processing plant for rough fish on the Mississippi is on Lake Pepin," she said. "A hundred local fishermen used to bring their catch here. But now, all the fish come from the other side of the state."

What changed everything was the Interstate Commerce Commission's finding in the mid-1970s that polychlorinated biphenyls (PCBs) contaminate the flesh of Lake Pepin fish. This industrial chemical, found in everything from TV sets to transformers, from paint to copy paper, is highly toxic and very slow to break down. Lake Pepin, where the Mississippi widens and its current slows, has become a natural settling basin for pollutants carried by the river.

Where was this pollution coming from? It turned out to be a long-standing problem — and one the Minnesota Pollution Control Agency had done nothing about. Most of the pollutants in Lake Pepin — not only PCBs, but dioxin, heavy metals, and organic wastes — come from the Pig's Eye sewage plant, where Twin Cities wastes are treated — or, when there is a heavy rain, *not* treated. This is because the storm and sanitary sewer systems are combined, and when rainwater pours into the system, it often backs up. The overflow then is dumped, untreated, into the Mississippi.

Tired of dealing with other people's wastes, Citizens for a Clean Mississippi took the government to court. It succeeded in forcing pollution control agencies to comply with their own regulations. As a result, sludge now is deposited on land, permits are issued, public hearings held and the impact of sewer extensions considered.

"If we want to save our environment for our grandchildren," Hill said, "we have to work now." While we were seated in her kitchen that July afternoon, she looked out to where her own grandchildren were swimming in Lake Pepin. "I used to be able to walk out only 25 feet from shore before I'd be up to my neck in water," she said. "Now I have to go out 200 feet." Contaminants may be threatening the health of organisms that live in the river, but sediment is killing the river itself. Hill knows where that sediment is coming from. She cites Soil Conservation Service figures showing that some farms above Lake Pepin lose as much as 20 tons of topsoil per acre per year — five times the rate of natural loss. More graphically, she has seen each year where the topsoil gets thinner on the tops of knolls and where roots of trees are more exposed .

Downriver at Winona, we met Wayne Hammer, coordinator of the Winona chapter of the Revival, who is concerned about what soil erosion is doing to the backwaters of the Mississippi. "The backwaters are the lifeblood of the river," he said as he met the flotilla on an island campsite south of Lake Pepin. He showed us the quiet areas where vegetation and small animals flourish and serve as food for the larger fish and wildlife. The backwaters, not the main channel, are the spawning and feeding grounds.

Hammer is half the age of Dorothy Hill, but he too has seen changes in the river he has lived with all his life. "It used to be that four boats abreast could go through these side channels," he told us, "now you have to pull a boat through some of them. The river isn't getting lower — the bottom is coming up." As Hill had put it earlier, "River issues are land issues and land issues are river issues."

Threats to the river seldom are visible directly, and their solutions, when they are known at all, may take years. For these reasons it was therapeutic — both for ourselves and for the river — to get involved in an all-day cleanup of river islands around Winona. The project involved 60 volunteers, who collected 12 barrels of cans and glass for recycling, 500 pounds of scrap metal and 140 fifty-five-gallon drums. The river was visibly cleaner for our efforts.

Another kind of cleanup has been going on in the Mississippi River for most of this century. Each year tons of sediment are dredged from the bottom of the river to keep open a nine-foot-deep channel. Since 1909 the U.S. Army Corps of Engineers has been charged by Congress with keeping the river open for the shipment of grain, fertilizers, chemicals, fuel oil, coal and other bulk commodities. This commercial waterway is now maintained by dams, dredging, and dikes.

Where once the river flowed over rapids and flushed its sediments in an unbroken stream down to the Gulf of Mexico, now it is a "staircase of water." A series of 29 locks and dams have created the same number of pools on the Upper Mississippi River. This major public works project, carried out in the 1930s, utterly changed the character of the river. New backwater areas were formed as the water spread out behind the dams, and at the same time these areas began to fill in as the dams trapped sediment. As the tows push their barges upstream, their turbulence resuspends the sediment — sometimes as much as one ton per mile — spreading silt even farther into the backwaters. Already one-fourth of the backwaters created by the dams have been converted by sedimentation into marsh and dry land.

Because sediment could not move downstream, dredging was begun. Dredge spoil usually was deposited as close as possible to the dredge site. In some areas islands were created, to the delight of recreational boaters who stopped at sandy beaches. In other areas, productive backwaters were filled and destroyed, to the disgust of biologists and people who hunt and fish. The backwaters contain valued feeding areas for the Mississippi Flyway, the route traveled by three-quarters of U.S. migratory waterfowl. So the Corps, by implementing one Congressional mandate, was interfering with another; for since 1924 the river and adjacent wetlands of the Upper Mississippi have been under the management of the U.S. Fish and Wildlife Service as a refuge. The Corps had a healthy budget for its work. Fish and Wildlife didn't. So it was that one set of values took precedence over another.

The conflict among competing uses of the river continued unresolved until 1973, when the State of Wisconsin filed suit to stop all dredging operations until an environmental impact statement was filed to show their effects. But not much information was available on the effects. The following year a project was set up to find out more about what was happening on the river and how some of the conflicts could be resolved. Called the Great River Environmental Action Team (GREAT), it was a partnership among the Corps of Engineers, the Fish and Wildlife Service, the Coast Guard, the Soil Conservation Service and the environmental protection agencies of the federal government and the states of Minnesota, Wisconsin and Iowa. GREAT's goal was to recommend ways to manage the river as a multi-purpose resource, taking into account the competing demands. Funded by the Corps, the members worked for six years with scientists, recreation users, shippers and the public to develop a channel-maintenance plan and other proposals. The results have been published and portions of the plan now are being put into effect.

When the Revival flotilla arrived in La Crosse, Wisconsin, we found one of the festival organizers to be Dave Kennedy, who works for the Wisconsin Department of Natural Resources. "The Corps was our worst enemy for years," Kennedy said. "Now they're much more cooperative." He sees a willingness by the Corps to fund projects they would have rejected before, such as their rehabilitation of a 200-acre backwater above Fountain City, Wisconsin. Another improvement is the disposal of dredged material in specific sites outside the floodplain, where it is available for fill, road sanding, and concrete aggregate. "None of this would be taking place without the GREAT study," Kennedy said.

Implementation of the GREAT study is being carried out by the Channel Maintenance Forum, made up of representatives of the state and federal agencies which cooperated on the study. Detailed plans for channel work, such as specific dredge cuts, are drawn up by the Corps. These plans are reviewed by the forum. During development of the GREAT recommendations, an extensive effort was made to involve people with interests in the river. When the report was published in 1980, there was no further provision for citizen input, but Corps projects do require public hearings.

By coincidence, our flotilla arrived in Lansing, Iowa the day the Corps was holding a hearing on their plans to place six wing dams — three on each side of the main channel — above Lansing. An area where much dredging has been required, it was expected that the dams would speed the current and thus sweep bottom material farther downstream. Sediment would settle out gradually and not need to be dredged. Dave Kennedy testified in favor of the project. But Gus Kerndt, a lifelong resident of the area and the local Revival chapter coordinator, testified against it. Kerndt argued that one particular dike would block a small channel through a backwater, causing oxygen to be cut off and the area to silt in. After the hearing a decision was made to put in equipment to monitor the oxygen level.

Kerndt's involvement goes far beyond the Lansing backwater. For several years he served as coordinator of River Country Voices, a group formed out of concern that increases in commercial navigation and development pressures would seriously deteriorate the Upper Mississippi. In 1978 Congress approved a replacement Lock and Dam 26 at Alton, Illinois, that would double the capacity of the old one. Because of questions raised about increased traffic, funding was included for development of a master plan that would consider the effects of commercial navigation on the river and its associated lands. The study was undertaken by the Upper Mississippi Basin Commission, whose members include those of the GREAT study and the additional states of Missouri and Illinois.

River Country Voices soon became convinced that the master plan was going to be too limited. They saw the Basin Commission continuing the Corps' favor of shipping interests at the expense of river conservation, recreation and environmental concerns. To redress this imbalance, the group prepared "A Citizens Plan for the Upper Mississippi River." Among its recommendations were that shippers be charged user fees; that railroad capacity be considered in estimating future bulk shipment; that the duplicate Lock 26 not be built; that future levels of barge traffic be set to protect river life, recreation, shorelines and river communities, and that winter navigation be prohibited.

While having no paid staff, River Country Voices receives Washington news through member groups such as the Sierra Club and Audubon Society. "We then let our group members know so they can contact their representatives," says Steve Hiniker, executive director. "The Basin Commission sees the second lock (at Alton) as inevitable. We don't." What River Country Voices *does* see — and fear — is the potential for construction of more duplicate locks on up the river and for the dredging of a 12-foot channel (from the present nine feet), both of which a Corps report has recommended.

At Lansing, the last stop for this first flotilla, the main channel takes a sharp turn and brings barges loaded with grain and coal right past the town's waterfront. Pleasure boats and fishing boats come and go from the marinas. But between the Iowa and Wisconsin bluffs lie three miles of beautiful backwaters, where we followed narrow channels past islands towering with elms and maples and over shallow waters carpeted with bright yellow lotus blossoms. Here the river is very different from the tiny stream at Lake Itasca, but the awesome beauty and power of the natural world is the same. Having seen the river in its many configurations, we knew that only the efforts of people in the communities along the way would ensure the beauty, health and vitality of the Mississippi for the seventh generation, and beyond.

She'll be clean once more. She'll be clean once more.
Floating up and down along the Mississippi shore,
Can you hear the voices of the river?
She'll be clean once more.

—Larry Long, 1981

Brother Wolf

By Richard Broderick

"LISTEN!"

The sound returned to the three men ranged around the camp — a long keening howl that wavered harmonically on the wind. Henry waited for the last echo to die in the dark.

"You hear that?" He cocked his ear toward the snow-covered timber, shining ghostly in the moonlight, and raised an index finger to hold Steve's attention.

Steve shivered. "Yeah — I hear it." In the distance, the pack cried again.

"You try it."

Mimicking Henry, Steve cupped his hand against his mouth and raised a throaty cry. Within a few moments the howl was picked up by the pack, which by now had moved in a northward arc that brought it closer to the camp.

"You think that's the same pack whose tracks we saw?"

Henry stamped his feet against the intense cold. "Could be. It's impossible to tell. Lots of packs probably use those old logging roads in the winter. It's easier for them." He blew on his hands and then licked the ice beads that had formed on his ginger-colored moustache. Steve howled again. "That's better," Henry encouraged. "Less inhibited."

"How many do you think there are?" Steve asked, a trace of anxiety in his voice.

"Sounds like a fair-sized pack. Half a dozen adults at least."

"They close by?"

Henry bunched his lips thoughtfully. "Well the wind is light but we can still hear them pretty clearly. I'd say they're maybe a mile or so away." Laughing, he gave Steve a friendly slap on the back. "Don't worry though. All that stuff about wolves attacking people . . . a lot of old wives tales. They want to steer clear of us just as much as we want to steer clear of them."

On the far side of the clearing they'd made for the campfire and the Coleman stove, Jack sat on a log waiting for a pan of water to boil. He was looking forward to this cup of tea. They'd skied continuously all day, pausing only to gulp down a quick lunch of sausage, cheese and bread. Henry said they were at Fall Lake now, a dog-leg clearing buried beneath a couple feet of snow; Jack would have to take Henry's word for it. He'd never been in the Boundary Waters during winter before.

"It's too bad wolves have gotten such a bad rap," Henry was telling Steve. "They're really not so bad. They help to hold down the deer population up here. And for the most part they leave the livestock alone. They aren't even that terribly violent with each other. About the only time they'll fight — I mean fight so somebody gets hurt — is when a lone wolf wanders into a pack's territory and won't leave."

"Oh yeah?" Steve said, his words coming out in clouds of vapor.

"Good parents too," Henry observed with a wry laugh. "Very loyal. All the things we like about dogs come from wolves. Their devotion to a master is a carry-over from a wolf's devotion to the pack's alpha male. They share quite a few traits with human beings, too. Gregariousness, group coordination, a certain emotional neediness. In fact," Henry chuckled, "wolves are a lot like people — only better."

In the dark, Jack smiled to himself at the old gibe, repeated by Henry dozens of times. Henry Dodd, tall, thin, pedantic, with a trim beard, wire-rimmed glasses and vaguely ascetic manner, was their resident expert on wolves, a graduate student in wildlife biology who'd studied with Mech and spent two winters on Isle Royale. Jack knew him from undergraduate days at the U. Henry was a sort of mentor, an older brother without an older brother's ties of memory and shared associations. In the past year or so, with Henry busy teaching or on field expeditions they'd grown apart, their friendship comfortable but a little remote, revolving around a mutual enthusiasm for the outdoors. As for Steve Bass, Jack knew him only slightly — Henry had invited him along — and he had to admit to an irrational impulse of jealousy. Agreeable enough companions, though, even if Jack was feeling a little distant from them.

Steve looked around. "God, it's pretty up here. So still." His sibilants drifted off, getting lost in the sound of the wind blowing through the pine trees. "You ever been up here before, Jack?" he threw over his shoulder.

"Oh, yeah. Lots of times. Never in the winter though."

Gazing into the Coleman's blue crown of flames, Jack thought of the last time he'd been in the Boundary Waters. Three years had reduced the pain to a dull ache.

He and his older brother Phil had come up for a canoe trip with a couple of their buddies. Neither of the other two guys had done much canoeing so he and Phil split up, Phil going with Ron Christiansen, Jack with Mark Owens. The route they mapped out was strenuous — four days, 100 miles in a circuit that took them up into Quetico Park, then back down to Moose Lake Landing outside of Ely. On the last two days out, they ran into heavy weather. A gale came up as they were making a run down Alice Lake, a sliver of water set between a crack of high granite ridges. The ridges acted as a wind tunnel, setting up a chop that came over the gunnels. At the portage, Ron Christiansen — sitting up in the prow — suddenly brought the boat around broadside to the wind. Jack was on the shore when they went over, Phil, Ron and all their equipment. Already wet from the spray, Jack and Mark offered to come down and help. Phil waved them off.

"Go on ahead. We'll take care of this."

"You sure?" Jack asked dubiously.

"No problem. It's more important that you guys get there to meet the van. We'll catch up." The outfitter had agreed to meet them at Moose Lake around 3 p.m. that afternoon.

"Okay."

He knew even at the time that he should have stayed, and if he hadn't been so tired and hungry and cold and dreading the 20 miles of open water that lay between them and Moose Lake, he would have. But he left.

It was the last time he ever saw Phil.

Henry's voice came out of the shadows, quiet and spooky. "I've heard stories about adults allowing themselves to be killed by hunters, sacrificing themselves for the pack. It's pretty amazing."

Jack stared at the pan of water its surface beginning to pucker. The trip between the outfitter's lodge and Moose Lake got longer and longer each time Jack and Chuck Beecham bumped over it in the van. Beecham was a round, cheerful guy who wore a red beret with a pheasant feather cresting along its side — a real Northwoods character. Initially, he thought Phil and Ron's chances were pretty good — "They'll show up in a few hours," he assured Jack. "Probably just stopped to build a fire, dry off" — but by the end of the second day, even his cheer was waning. That night, Jack camped on the gravelly shore of Moose Lake. The next morning, he hitched into Ely and called the Forest Service.

Henry had the pack in full cry now; he and Steve took turns keeping it going.

"Come on," Henry yelled cheerfully. "Give it a try, Jack!"

"That's okay. You guys seem to be doing pretty well without me."

There was a time when he wouldn't have hung back. Smiling sadly, he thought of how he and Phil had called to each other from their canoes, yodelling like loons over the open water. If Phil were up here now, he'd be howling at the wolves too. No question about it. But he wasn't, and now there were a lot of things Jack wouldn't do either, a lot of chances he wouldn't take, roads he wouldn't follow. Phil's disappearance — that had changed everything. Turned the whole world into a wilderness. No place felt safe. No place felt familiar.

"I saw a kill once," Henry said quietly.

"Oh yeah?"

"Yeah. Up in the Quetico, oh, late one November. I was there with one of my profs. We hiked down into a ravine and came to a spot where a pack had just brought down a white-tail doe. The kill was so fresh that there was still blood sprinkled on the ground. It was pretty gruesome. Her nose was torn off and then they'd finished her by ripping open her stomach. She had her entrails wrapped around her back legs so I guess she must have run a ways like that."

"Shit!" Steve intoned. "Did you see any of them?"

"No," replied Henry. He laughed suddenly. "I guess we scared them off. We saw plenty of tracks though. They were probably up in the timber keeping an eye on us."

The water, melted down from snow, finally rolled to a boil. Pouring some into a folding cup with a tea bag in it, Jack walked stiffly toward his two companions while blowing on the steaming liquid. The pack had moved off and the only sound now, besides the murmur of Henry's voice, was the noise of the wind sighing through the black spruce behind the tent. Jack took a balanced stance and glanced up at the moonless sky, flinching slightly at the sight of millions of brilliant, unexpected stars rushing down out of the disc of the Milky Way. The Babylonians, or whoever, would have had a hard time tracing constellations on a night like this. He watched a satellite's pinprick of light drift across the sky like a second hand sweeping a clock face.

"I guess they're gone," Henry breathed. "We can look for their tracks tomorrow."

The cold, the quiet — it was making Jack's insides shrink. Even the hair inside his nose was stiff, ice crystals turning it brittle. If only Phil hadn't disappeared, he thought despairingly. If he'd been mauled by a bear, or fallen off a ridge and cracked his skull, or drowned in three feet of water on a clear day — anything, anything so long as there was some trace of him, some visible proof that he was gone, dead, over with. But no. There was nothing. Nothing! That was the spooky part. No clothes, no canoe, no equipment. It's as if he never existed except in my head, Jack thought with a stab of fear and anger. Phil — vanished. Sucked up by the wilderness like the fucking sound of the proverbial tree falling in the forest. And me left with this feeling, this pervasive sense that he might be out there somewhere, even now, hurt but alive and waiting for me to come back to rescue him.

Oh Christ, why did I even come, he wondered, stamping his feet hard.

"You guys want some tea?" he asked quietly. Steve jumped a little, as if he'd been expecting a wolf to sneak up out of the darkness.

"Sounds good!" Henry chirped. "I could use something to warm me up. Must be ten below already. It's going to be a cold one."

"Yeah," Jack said into his teacup. "Sure is."

A rustling outside the tent. Something or someone brushing up against the nylon shell, dropping a brief, shocking snowstorm of condensation. Sleeping lightly, Jack started out of a dream in which he was skiing across an endless snowfield, trying to catch up with some shadowy figure in the distance. The radium dials on his watch read 2:40. It was cold inside the tent. It would be even colder outside. A drop of water rolled into his eyes and there was another sound, something snuffling in the snow near the foot of the tent.

He lay still, trying hard to listen. Beside him, the steady draw of Henry and Steve breathing. He rested his arm across his chest, waited. Again, the noise, only this time it was accompanied by a low-throated growl, a playful noise like a puppy playing with a rubber bone.

"Henry?"

No answer. He fumbled around in the pack beneath his head and retrieved a flashlight, switching it on. Henry was burrowed deep in his royal blue mummy bag, face turned to the far wall. Steve slept with his head back and his mouth open, like a child.

Jack turned the flashlight off, sat up and felt around for his boots. When he poked his head outside, his eyes took a few moments to adjust. The clear, blue-black night had given way to a silvery glow. It was the cloud cover, low and milky, rolling in as they slept. Some sea change had occurred; the air was now warmer — much warmer than before. Standing, Jack poked the trembling flashlight ahead of him like a knife and stabbed a glimpse of something large and grey and hairy retreating just beyond the range of the beam. Whatever it was was too big for a hare, the wrong color for a deer. It was, he realized with an odd sense of inevitability, a wolf.

Boots squeaking on the hardpack snow around the campsite, his breath coming in short puffs of steam, he stepped to the far side of the tent and switched the light off. Another low growl, this time from the edge of the lake about 30 yards away. A doglike shadow loped from there to a ridge that descended the shoreline, stopped, returned to the lake with a hopping, prancing step — something festive in its attitude. He's waiting for me, Jack realized with dull amazement.

He'd seen wolves before, up in Idaho with Phil. A pack came down to investigate their camp one cold moonlit night. That was before he met Henry and had learned of the wolf's relatively benign ways, yet he still hadn't been afraid; Phil was with him and Phil, however irrational it might have been, always made him feel safe.

But Phil wasn't here now, and even with Henry and Steve sleeping a few feet away, he felt alone and vulnerable — alone and vulnerable and not at all sure why he was walking back to the place where the skis were stuck in a drift, determined to put them on and follow this wolf.

What will Henry think, he wondered as he locked his boots into the bindings. He'll think it's stupid. Jack felt a surge of rebellion. Fuck Henry. Fuck his careful, contrived, deliberate way of going about things — the scientific cast of mind applied to everything. Trembling with cold and excitement, he started off in the direction where he'd last seen the shadow.

He came upon the tracks at the shoreline. They looked the same as the ones they'd seen earlier in the day along the logging road, except fresher. Only one set, too. A lone wolf? Did all the virtues Henry ascribed to wolfdom apply to the creature alone? And if not? He shook his head irritably. What the hell are you afraid of, he asked himself. A grown man armed with steel tip poles and sharp wooden slats — what's the problem? The dark?

For Christ sake, you can't even get lost. All you have to do is follow the tracks back into camp. And even if you do get lost, what the hell difference does it make?

None, he said to himself. He looked back at the tent, its sides still, his friends sleeping inside. A howl came from behind the ridge, as if to hurry him on. Putting his head down, he pushed off on the poles, following the tracks over the slope and down into a timbered ravine.

At first it was tough going, the skiing difficult, his breathing labored. Climbing the hills was easy, going down harder. He started to fear he'd lose the wolf. Deep in the forest, the snow so dry the skis scraped across it like sand, the air grew colder, burning deep at the root of his throat. He stopped to scrape off the kick wax and apply a thin coat of Arctic, low temperature wax along the length of his skis. It had begun to snow, a powdery ash that fell straight to earth with a light hiss. He had no idea how far he'd come — a couple miles or more. At all events, the snow was too light to cover his tracks. At least not yet. He took off again, coming out into a low lying area of tamarack and black spruce which was probably a swamp in the summer. At its edge, he ascended a clear-cut slope and came upon a logging road that might have been the same one they'd followed earlier in the day. It, too, was rutted with wolf tracks. The tracks crossed the road and passed a drift whose face had been hollowed out by packs using it as a scent post. A trace of steam rose from its yellowed interior — his wolf had stopped to raise his leg. It could only be a few hundred yards ahead.

Jack wiped his nose and skied down toward a line of timber. With a starless sky, it was impossible to tell in which direction he was headed. I'll be okay, he thought, so long as the weather doesn't get much worse. He entered a forest of white pine and cedar, the snowy air sharp with the smell of pitch, the long needles scraping against the shell of his parka, his skis rasping through the snow. He began to ease his stride, to feel it, arms and legs pumping in a tireless rhythm, his mind absorbed in the tracks. He quickened his pace, hoping to catch up with the wolf before he got much further from camp. The snow was coming harder — a worry — but, lost now in the skiing, he didn't care. Tucked into an eggshell position, he glided down a hard-packed section of trail. The simple meditative pleasure of physical exertion, dreamlike, lovely — how he'd like to get lost in it! How he'd like to be drawn out of himself.

He jogged up a steep hill, then swooped down the far side in a straight quick run, telemarking sharply to his left onto a frozen streambed. He kept on, driving himself, his breath deepening, expanding, taking in snow on every inhalation until, coming to a spot where the streambed narrowed under a low overhang, he stopped abruptly. The hair on the back of his neck stood upright. The thick snowfall blurred the overhang, turning it into a shadowy outline. A number of "ifs" crowded to mind. If the wolf were playing him along, if it were not as benign as Henry liked to make the animals out to be, if it were playing by its own rules, planning to attack a human being, planning to ambush him, this would be the perfect place for it.

Jack remained still, his lungs burning with fatigue, wondering what to do. If he turned back now he could probably make it to camp before the snow covered his tracks. Nobody would be any the wiser, nobody would criticize him for being imprudent. This was the Northwoods, buddy, in the dead of winter. You didn't screw around up here. Even when you weren't taking chances, the wilderness could come down on you like a steel trap.

He looked back up the trail and debated with himself. He knew he shouldn't go on, but the thought of retreating now, before he'd completed whatever it was he'd set out to do, filled him with a weariness that went far beyond physical fatigue. Filled him with a weariness that bordered on self-loathing. He plunged ahead, steeling himself as he came below the overhang, holding himself to a steady pace, fighting panic — like sharks, wolves might be attracted to panic, to the creature that flails. There's something in that, he thought, something deeper to chew on. But not now. The rock ledge loomed on his right. He passed under it, cringing as it drew parallel. There was a beat, then another, as he waited half-expectantly for the attack.

There was none. Nothing leaped out of the shadows. No wolf. No sharks. Atop the overhang the ragged jackpine hid nothing but snow beneath its boughs. He went on a little farther, then paused to allow his pulse to return to normal and his breathing to slow.

At the top of a long, slippery rise, he stopped, bent over and took in air with deep painful gulps. The snow was falling wet and heavy in fist-sized flakes, defeating all attempts to get traction, his skis sliding backward on each stride. By the time he reached the crest of a second slope, bright spots swam before his eyes and his legs and back ached. He knew he should stop and put on softer wax. But he was too tired — too tired to fight it. I'll never catch up, he thought, suddenly frightened again. Before him a gentle slope fell away, the snow coming so thick now that he could barely see the bottom. Resting, about to turn back at last, he heard a series of short muffled barks, followed by another series of barks a few moments later. The wolf, egging him on. What the hell's going on, Jack wondered.

A damned wolf daring him to go on, the way Phil used to dare him, running ahead into some dubious activity, calling over his shoulder "Come on, Jack — don't be a chicken!" Jack always gave in, his stomach jumping with excitement. Something about Phil made his challenges impossible to resist. Slowly, reluctantly, he proceeded down the hill, knowing even as he did that he probably didn't have the energy to make it back up. His mind had dulled. At the edge of yet another lake, he caught sight of the wolf, standing motionless, waiting for him. This is crazy, he thought with a fatigued detachment. I've got to turn around before it's too late. Even as the words crossed his mind, he knew it was already too late. He was already lost. All that was left was the compulsion to catch up with the wolf. After that, he wasn't sure what would happen.

He skied out onto the lake and within minutes was enveloped by a featureless grey world with no up, no down, lake and sky blended together in a seamless cloud. He clung to the tracks desperately, like a man hanging over an abyss. If he lost sight of them, if the snow covered them before they took him to the far shore, he'd be out there all night, skiing in circles, skiing until he ran out of steam, until he collapsed in the snow, until he fell into a sleep from which he'd never wake up. It would be so easy to die out here, he thought. So easy to lie down in the deep, soft snow, cold and numbing, fall asleep, allow all traces of self to be drifted over, obliterated. So easy. . .

He summoned up what seemed like his last strength and gave a tremendous kick, driving himself over the tips of his skis, never taking his eyes off the tracks. Something nameless, something beyond himself, took over, pushing him on. He would not stop.

The crossing seemed to take forever. As he neared the far shore, the snow began to let up. Underfoot, the surface was getting drier, easier to manage, the skiing less laborious. A hill ran parallel to the shoreline and he could see the wolf tracks there, clear and fresh, as they climbed over a hummock of snow and then reappeared a little way up the slope. He clambered over snow-covered rocks, the snow stopping completely and stars beginning to show through the overcast. Halfway up the hill, he stopped abruptly as if commanded by some inner voice and raised his eyes.

It was a wolf, a big grey standing in his path no more than 30 feet ahead. Jack was close enough to see the gold gleam of the eyes, the thick ruff of the shoulders, the intelligence in the animal's gaze. He returned the wolf's gaze, without fear. He took a step forward then stopped — something told him he was to come no closer. The two of them — animal and man — stood looking at each other. A spark of half-formed, unverbalized thought seemed to jump the gap between them. Yes, Jack thought. Yes. I understand. He raised a gloved hand in greeting and farewell. The wolf pawed the snow. In his head, Jack heard — or did not so much hear as sense — a shout of affirmation as wild, as rapturous as the sound of a pack baying at the moon. The great wolf turned and took a few steps up the hill. Stopping, he gave Jack a final look before loping off with a curious sideways gait into the black line of timber at the crest of the hill. Jack understood he was not to follow. Not tonight.

He was surprised at how quickly he made the return trip to camp. Surprised at how easy it was. He hadn't gone far at all.

Henry was waiting for him when he arrived, crouched beside a small fire, poking twigs into the flame whose beacon Jack had followed for the last half-mile home. Henry rose to watch Jack cover the final fifty yards.

"Where have you been?" he asked quietly.

Jack waited to catch his breath before replying, "Out doing a little skiing."

"At four in the morning?"

"Great time for it. No traffic." Henry looked at him silently. "I was following a wolf. It came into camp."

"I know. I saw the tracks."

"Well," Jack explained a little defensively, "that's where I was."

"Did you see him?"

Jack almost blurted out the truth, then thought better of it.

"No, never got close enough."

"Too bad. Maybe we'll see more signs tomorrow."

They stood and looked at each other over the fire, which by now had begun to flicker and die out.

"Skiing in the middle of the night," Henry reproached. "Not a very smart idea."

"Neither is winter camping," Jack returned cheerfully.

"No, I guess it would be a little hard to defend on strictly utilitarian grounds."

"My point exactly."

"Well," Henry said with a sudden change in tone. "We should try to get some sleep. You're going to be wiped out tomorrow."

"I'm okay."

Henry started for the tent, then stopped to face Jack. "You could have gotten lost," he said, peering into Jack's face.

Jack shrugged and smiled. "Well, I didn't."

Inside the tent he listened as Henry's breathing deepened into a steady rhythm. He was exhausted, played out from the physical exertion, and from something else — the release of something clenched for a long time. You could have gotten lost, he thought. Lost. He turned the word over and over in his mind like a smooth round stone until it began to separate from its meaning. Lost, he repeated, hefting the stone, knowing that in some way it no longer applied to him, no longer weighed him down. Closing his eyes and stretching out in his sleeping bag, he dropped the stone into the black well opening up beneath him.

Rising From the Earth

By Joe Paddock

IN THE UNITED STATES THE Green Movement is not yet well defined. This essay, this entire issue of the *Anvil*, is part of an on-going effort to achieve some definition. It is my belief, however, that, rather than insisting on bringing the movement into sharp focus, forcing out what does not fit, we should accept its amorphous nature as a strength. In fact, it would be extremely naive, I think, to assume that there exists some single or linear solution to the complex, interconnected problems which now confront us.

Many thinkers who might be described as Green believe that a new paradigm or intellectual framework through which humanity relates to the world is now emerging. The model for the old paradigm was the machine or factory. The model for the new is the interconnected ecosystem. In the old, the social and natural environments were seen as made up of isolated parts, often in competition one with the other. In the new, both are seen as living, entirely interconnected systems in which competition must be understood as occurring within a larger context of cooperation. For instance, on the rather obvious level of predation among species, it is clear that the wolf is good health to the deer. Without an "external" force to control the deer herd's population, it would soon destroy the habitat which sustains it.

For human beings, with our highly developed sense of individuality, this system of things, which seems mainly concerned with species survival, is at the heart of the tragedy of life. In the twentieth century, enormous human energy has gone into hiding the "painful" facts of the life and death cycle. Hospitals, nursing homes, birthing wards, slaughterhouses, supermarkets . . . part of the work of each of these institutions is to insulate us, in our daily lives, from what is perhaps the deepest of all truths: that we, too, rise up from the earth for a little time, then die back to nourish new life. Some thinkers have described civilization itself as a flight from death: thus cut off from the truth of things, our lives become increasingly weak, empty, and neurotic.

In my mind, the interconnected ecosystem (the model for the new paradigm) is synonymous with the land organism. The land and the life which rises from it do in fact make up a single living organism. As with the individual organs within, say, the human body, there is a continual exchange among the various parts or organs of this greater body. If the greater organism is to remain in good health, there must remain a harmonious or homeostatic balance among these parts. It can be tough to grasp this larger picture. I have tried to give a sense of it in a poem I call "Black Energy":

Life is seething in this soil
which has been millions of years
in the making.
It has been forever
in the making.

A mingling of everything
which ever whistled here, leaped
or waved in the wind.
Plants and animals,
grasses of this prairie,
buffalo and antelope grazing down
into roots and back again
into the sun.
Birds and insects, their wings still hum
in this soil.

And this swarm drinks
sunlight and rain,
and rises again and again
into corn and beans
and flesh and bone.

The quick bodies of animals and men

risen
from this black energy.

In the final lines of this poem, we have emerged, in continuity with the whole. The old paradigm did not place us within the whole. From that perspective, the natural environment was seen as something different from human civilization. The environment was to be used and, occasionally, to be protected. That was an anthropocentric world; we were at the center, calling (or trying to call) the tune. That paradigm began in a time when the natural world was still largely perceived as a threat. Tooth and claw, wind and weather, insect hordes . . . made life uncertain for our ancestors. The emphasis then, in Western consciousness, was on our competition with these factors. But now we are the threat, and the emphasis must shift.

It is deeply important that we realize that even our cities are in continuum with the ecosystem. The materials from which they are built — the lumber, the stone, the steel and the plastic — flow, as ever, from the natural world. So, too, with the energy which brought it all together and which circulates our activities. Even the original creative vision from which cities arose came from the intuitive depths, the wilderness, of the natural mind. Complex "ant hill" though it may have become, our "civilized" world does not exist outside the natural one. It *is* in continuum, a tighter curl in the spiral of things.

Since mid-century, human population on our planet has doubled, and as the planet has become more and more crowded, feed-back on our actions has become proportionately swift. Things have gotten very constricted within the seamless web: roads and housing developments now destroy the farmland which must feed us in the future, and it is clear that there no longer exists an acceptable place to dump our toxic and radioactive waste.

Within this tightening situation it has become clear, at least for those with "Green consciousness," that the ethical and practical are one: we must care for the whole, because in so doing, we are caring for ourselves. "Win or lose" attitudes and approaches, in this new context, must shift to "win-win." This does not, of course, mean that we do not have a right to wrest from the earth what we need to survive. It *does* mean that we now know, if we carelessly damage those portions of the system which sustain us, our lives, our being here, will be diminished, perhaps cut short.

As mentioned earlier, any species which becomes too successful, too abundant, eventually undermines the habitat which sustains it. For the time being at least, we have gained the upper hand over those forces which once controlled human populations. A species without restraints takes more from its environment than it returns. This is parasitism. Should such an imbalance get seriously out of hand, this species then becomes a disease of its host, the ecosystem. As that old Wintu Indian woman said long before environmental problems had gotten as serious as they now are, our earth is sore all over. It seems clear that humanity has, in fact, become a disease of this planet — an "Immense Disease":

> Our planet, its wondrous webbings
> of energy, is a single living creature,
> now diseased. As the tissues of a human
> are invaded by bacteria, virus, malignant
> tumor (the new colony digging in, wanting
> only a place to be and swell)
> and the human begins to ache and overall
> wane (the eyes dull, the forehead burning),
> so humanity has dug in on this planet,
> not benign as all else is that feeds
> and sings at sunset. This recent culture,
> bacterial swarm, sucks at life and structure
> everywhere, a slurp and munch, heard
> round all the cosmic rings, continues
> by day, continues by night, everywhere
> the teeth severing roots, links, veins
> till the planet aches and its streams
> stink and flame with strange waste:
> what flows through the human swarm

comes out wrong for all else here —
salamander, hawk, trout, slender bluestem
prairie grass, all living nerves
of the planet, now burning in vicious streams.
Even humanity,
even the human swarm, having outgrown
its host, is now drowning in its own
sewer: a strange healing.

Health, the Green future, is dependent on our achieving a harmonious balance with all other elements of the ecosystem. *Decision-making in such a time will always recognize the larger context within which we are imbedded, which, finally, is not other than us.* The gains, and I feel they are very great, of opening up to our larger self, the Universe, will not be achieved without our coming to terms with our individual selfishness. As individuals we will have to sacrifice for the well-being of the species and the overall ecosystem. It is unlikely, for instance, that each of us in a Green future could expect to have a private automobile continually at hand. Nor could affluent nations continue to receive specialty foods and forest products from Third World countries at the expense of the people and the land of those countries. Increasingly we will have to learn to live within the resources of our given bioregion, our given community. We will be less specialized, more whole.

It is probably true that, at rudimentary levels, most of the life-support systems necessary for a Green future have already been designed or at least imagined. Those who are likely to read this essay are already familiar with them: various forms of solar technology, food production (perennial and polycultural) based on natural systems, and architectural and community designs which bring the whole into a harmony. These systems would be, at one and the same time, *both modeled after the ecosystem and extensions of the ecosystem.* Such approaches, coupled with a simple, natural life style, could, I believe, lead us back into planetary health. And they are already with us. The problem, of course, is how to achieve that shift in consciousness which precedes change. We must hope that disaster is not the only motivator available to us. It must be admitted, however, that it is the pain, the disease, we are already experiencing which has led many of us to plan for a different sort of future, if not, in fact, to change our lives.

It is at the threshold of the unconscious that we human beings recognize, actually *experience*, our oneness with the greater whole. For this reason, I believe it is important to have the arts represented in this collective discussion of what a Green future might be. For a long time I have been fond of saying that prose implies a problem for which poetry (art) is the answer. The images, tones, rhythms . . . of art and myth are the *whole* language through which we can grasp the whole vision, the ecological vision. Prose, of course, can become art, too, but to the extent that it remains rational and linear, to that extent will the writer/reader remain fragmented and alienated, outside the wholeness of Green. Caught within the linear or left-brain mode, it is very difficult for us to break from the deep ruts of the old paradigm. We intuit, we yearn, but we do not experience deeply the wholeness of life. The creative evolution of self (and environment) which is art may also be at the heart of what we will *do* with ourselves in a more harmonious time.

We *are* in community with the land; and, as Aldo Leopold has taught us, when we are truly in community with others we must share an ethic with those others, be they human beings, songbirds or plant species. And, surely, a clear, strong land ethic has become one of the most pressing needs of our time. It would seem, however, that if ever the Green future fully matures, we will have evolved beyond the "thou shalt not" ethical relationship to the world around us. Living within a deep and full awareness of our oneness with the universe, our hunger for its richness, beyond true need, will, it would seem, diminish. We will no longer, like once-deprived children, punish ourselves with multifarious forms of neurotic gluttony. We will shift our role in the ecosystem from that of the child, involved almost entirely with its own hunger and growth, to that of the parent, the nurturant, caring adult, And we will *know* . . . that we already have, have always had . . . all that we need, . . . everything.

Emerging Green Culture

By Maynard Kaufman

TO CONSIDER THE POSSIBILITY OF Green Politics is to assume that the process of cultural transformation now occurring on a deep level in the United States will emerge into political reality.

Life in American society is increasingly stressful, and stresses are exacerbated by rising expectations for consumer goods and services in a time of growing unemployment. We are indeed at the point of "cultural distortion" which the anthropologist Anthony F. C. Wallace has identified as the stage in a culture which precedes either revitalization or disintegration. This cultural crisis is manifest in what Wallace called "psychodynamically regressive innovations," which are showing up as high rates of crime, substance abuse, passivity and indolence, intragroup violence, disregard of kinship and sexual mores, and irresponsibility among public officials. And this cultural crisis is reflected in the degradation of the natural environment. We advert to these conditions not to wring our hands in despair or to call for reform but to interpret them as symptoms of our cultural sickness. The movement toward Green Politics is a promising path to revitalization.

In contrast to the single-issue political movements so common today, Green Politics must be understood as a holistic vision which includes emphases on ecology, as suggested by the word "green," and also social responsibility, grassroots democracy and nonviolence. These concerns are, according to the book by Fritjof Capra and Charlene Spretnak, *Green Politics*, the four pillars of *die Grunen* in West Germany.

The ecological emphasis implies the restructuring of our industrial economy. Social responsibility expresses a concern for the well-being of people and especially that the poor should not get hurt by the ecological restructuring of the economy. It also includes the concern for social justice, an emphasis which grew out of the civil rights movement in America and now includes the feminist critique of a patriarchal society. Grassroots democracy implies decentralized political activism on a local level as in, for example, the emergence of nuclear-free zones in the United States. Nonviolence is the integrating ethical basis of social ecology or of an ecological society. It is implied by the goal of living in harmony with nature no less than in the concern for social justice. Given the military-industrial complex, nonviolence is also implicit in the ecological restructuring of the industrial economy.

Green politics will gain increasingly wide support and its emergence as a major political party will be the outcome of the process of cultural transformation on a deep level which is now occurring in most industrialized nations. This will be more obvious as we give these terms the clarification they require.

Cultural tranformation on a deep level implies change on a level of religious depth, a process which precedes political expression and implementation on a practical level. The fact that this transformation does not happen first in, or through, political activity has been expressed by Petra Kelly of the West German Greens:

The spiritual content of Green politics — which unfortunately is not expressed, and is almost opposed, in the party structure — means understanding how everything is connected and understanding your relationship with planet Earth in daily life. We've become so divorced from our ties with the Earth that most people don't even understand what the Greens are fighting for. With the holistic sense of spirituality, one's personal life is truly political and one's political life is truly personal. Anyone who does not comprehend within himself or herself this essential unity cannot achieve political change on a deep level and cannot strive for the true ideals of the Greens.

In this quotation, Petra Kelly expresses the frustration of one who lives and works by a spiritual vision which has not yet achieved a cultural consensus and cannot, therefore, be expressed on a political level. She does mention "political change on a deep level" and the authors of *Green Politics* go on to comment that "this consciousness of deep ecology and its exemplary expression in Native American spirituality was mentioned by Kelly and many other Greens." Is this emphasis on religious depth mere wishful thinking? What basis is there for this expectation of religious revitalization in our secular society?

We can begin answering these questions by considering the recent revolution in our attitude toward nature. For over three hundred years, since the beginning of the Scientific Revolution, nature has been seen as the adversary to be dominated and controlled. The main item on our cultural agenda has been the conquest of nature. Politics and technology thus evolved to protect us from nature, including human nature. But now that politics and technology constitute the artificial environment in our urban-industrial society, we sense our dependence on them and we are afraid.

The real threats we confront — nuclear annihilation and ecological disruption — are created by politics and technology. These tools which evolved to protect us from nature now confront us as the alien environment. And nature, which had been the adversary, is now embraced as our long-lost friend. It is this comprehensive transformation in our basic attitudes which underlies the counter-culture of the 1960s, the environmental movement, and the back-to-the-land movement of the 1970s. The new value we place on nature is expressed in each of these no less than in our desire for natural foods.

On the other hand, our anxiety over politics and technology is mounting to apocalyptic intensity. While secular people fear the end of the world in nuclear destruction, premillennialist Christians see such fearful events in the context of Christ's Second Coming. Hal Lindsey, whose book *The Late Great Planet Earth* was a best seller during the 1970s, argues that the end of the world will occur in our generation and that nuclear war may be a part of this end-time scenario. We are literally living through a time of apocalyptic turmoil. But because we are surrounded by trees, we do not see the forest.

To see where we are we need some historical perspective, and for this we turn to a recent book by William G. McLoughlin, a professor of history at Brown University. McLoughlin is a student of religious revivals, and in *Revivals, Awakenings and Reform* (1978) he interprets religious revivals as part of what anthropologists call "revitalization movements." He argues that we are now in the midst of our Fourth Great Awakening, which began during the 1960s and is, like those that preceded it, the result of social and ecological changes which have seriously disrupted our self-understanding.

A revitalization movement tends to occur in a culture under stress, as when day-to-day behavior has deviated from traditional beliefs. Or, the disjunction in self-understanding may emerge when cultural values and beliefs are challenged by new external circumstances. Thus, our cultural commitment to economic growth is challenged by our growing awareness of limits to natural resources. Sometimes these external constraints to industrial and economic growth coincide with internal constraints, as when our day-to-day behavior deviates from traditional norms and ideals because of the way social and economic practices have evolved.

In our urban-industrial society, for example, we experience tensions like those described by Daniel Bell in his *Cultural Contraditions of Capitalism*. The traditional emphasis on "personal fulfillment" or "self-realization" or "the whole person" is contradicted by the functional view of the person as a cog in the techno-economic production process. Productivity may become more important than the development of personhood. Nowhere is this more obvious than in agricultural policy, where a single-minded focus on productivity disregards both environmental and social consequences. No official consideration is given to farming as a way of life and the mid-size family farms are threatened with extinction.

Some people may adjust to this econo-centric orientation by internalizing it as they live to make money instead of making money to live. But since this strategy is not rooted in deeper cultural values, it is a pathological condition. And in every revitalization movement there are others, especially in the earlier phases of the movement, who refuse any adjustment of ideals to reality and urge a return to "the good old days" or to the "faith of our fathers." In our time this option is represented by those on the New Right, politically and religiously. But in the long run neither of these strategies works. It is not enough to give in to the new or to hold on to the old. In fact, such strategies, by postponing the needed adjustments, increase the pressure for change in the culture as a whole.

A revitalization movement can thus be compared to an earthquake: gradual shifts create stresses and strains which are eventually released with cataclysmic force. According to McLoughlin, "a religious revival or great awakening begins when accumulated pressures for change produce such acute personal and social stress that the whole culture must break the crust of custom, crash through the blocks in the mazeways, and find socially structured avenues along which the members of society may pursue their course in mutual harmony with one another." The revival or revitalization is successful only if the culture as a whole is reintegrated so that mutual harmony can occur.

We can now review the relevance of McLoughlin's Fourth Great Awakening to the emergence of Green Politics. This can been seen quite clearly as McLoughlin describes the outcome of the current revitalization movement:

At some point in the future, early in the 1990s at best, a consensus will emerge that will thrust into political leadership a president with a platform committed to the kinds of fundamental restructuring that have followed our previous awakenings — in 1776, in 1830, and in 1932. Prior to this institutional restructuring must come an ideological reorientation. Such a reorientation will most likely include a new sense of the mystical unity of all mankind and of the vital power of harmony between man and nature. . . . The nourishing spirit of mother earth, not the wrath of an angry father above, will dominate religious thought. . . . Sacrifice of self will replace self-aggrandizement as a definition of virtue; helping others will replace competitiveness as a value.

What we see happening now is the "ideological reorientation," and this is especially manifest in the increasingly broad social acceptance of the need for environmental protection and in the gradual shift toward a new environmental paradigm.

As the environmental movement matured during the 1970s, its protests against pollution deepened and evolved into a broad and fundamental critique of industrial society. Arguments for the reform of industrial modes of production evolved into arguments against industrialism. The core values of industrialism derive from its emphasis on creating material wealth and include the notions that humans should dominate nature, that the natural environment is a resource for industrial productivity, and that progress is measured by economic growth. Social scientists who have done empirical studies of environmental attitudes have found that the values of industrialism are gradually losing out to a new set of environmental attitudes.

In his recent book *Environmentalists: Vanguard for a New Society* (1984), Lester Milbrath reports that surveys of environmental attitudes show that people value environmental protection over economic growth by a ratio of 3 to 1. And similar results were obtained from public surveys during the early 1980s in Germany and in England. Attitudes on related topics were consistent with this emphasis on environmental over industrial values. This represents a shift to a new environmental paradigm which includes the beliefs that the natural environment has intrinsic value (apart from being a "natural resource") and that humans can live in harmony with nature rather than dominating her. Above all, non-material values tend to replace the emphasis on material wealth in the older industrial paradigm. This may be a decisive issue for "Yuppies" who profess Green values along with the acquisition of material wealth. And, as Nora Gallagher acknowledged in the June-July ('85) *Utne Reader*, the result of such a conflict is "cognitive dissonance."

It is especially important to notice that these studies by environmental sociologists emphasize the disjunctions we discussed earlier as the underlying causes of revitalization movements. Milbrath concludes his study of the growth of environmentalism by commenting on the incongruity between the power of modern society to dominate and destroy nature, on the one hand, and a normative and ethical system based on a 2,000-year-old religion, on the other. He asserts that "the lack of congruence between these two systems threatens the continued existence of our civilization. . . . The normative prescriptions from inherited religion do not address the power and exuberance of modern human activities."

In fact, the main influence of the Judeo-Christian tradition, as the "established" religion of the West, has been to reinforce this power and exuberance, with its divine imperative to "be fruitful and multiply, and fill the earth and subdue it, and have dominion" over the creation. And as the resulting dissonance between this ethical and ecological disruption is consciously felt and acknowledged, it can lead to a paradigm shift. Stephen Cotgrove, Milbrath's British counterpart, also comments, in his *Catastrophe or Cornucopia*, on the fact that "all the signs point to the disjunction between culture and society as a persisting feature of industrial societies." These comments emerge out of empirical studies of changing environmental attitudes, and they reinforce McLoughlin's thesis that American society is suffering the cognitive dissonance which accompanies a revitalization movement.

The movement toward Green politics is both deeper and stronger than the activists who promote it seem to recognize. It is deeper because it is part of a sea-change on a level of religious depth, and such a change includes not only the concerns over ecology, nonviolence, world peace and feminism, but also many aspects of contemporary life not directly relevant to Green Politics, such as the resurgence of premillennialist Christianity or the rise of New Age spirituality. This movement is stronger because it is part of the subtle and little-understood shift on an economic level away from total dependence on commodities.

Although Green activists are highly critical of industrialism, they have not yet evolved a clear vision of an ecological post-industrial society. But if cultural transformation on a deep level includes a general reaction against the industrial paradigm, the dependence of urban-industrial society on the market economy is called into question. This is suggested by the title of Robert Heilbroner's book *Business Civilization in Decline.*

Despite the favorable attention it is receiving during the Reagan administration, the growth-oriented, resource-consuming and profit-maximizing market economy is increasingly regarded as the outmoded relic of industrial civilization. The values of the new environmental paradigm cannot be realized within the confines of urban-industrial society. The shift to a post-industrial society is thus prompted by these new values and reinforced by economic pressures.

Economic pressures are manifest in rising costs for industrial products — goods and services. Costs rise as resources become scarce, as military force is needed to insure access to them and as unpaid externalized costs come due. Costs also rise because environmental reformists demand less polluting modes of production. This requires not only pollution-reduction technology but also battalions of bureaucrats, lawyers, economists and engineers who figure out cost-benefit ratios in determining which industries should be regulated and how much. The industries, in turn, cut costs by automation. Thus, unemployment rises, along with costs of welfare and of the social-service bureaucracy. All these costs are passed on to the consumer or taxpayer.

No wonder, therefore, that increasing numbers of people opt out of being consumers or producers whose earnings are taxed. These people bridge the split between production and consumption which has characterized industrial society as they become what Alvin Toffler has called the "prosumer." As such they constitute the "Third Wave" which, says Toffler, is to succeed industrial civilization — "indust-reality." Production for sale in the market economy is reduced, while more production is for use in the household economy.

A significant part of this do-it-yourself activity is backyard gardening. Not only did we see an unprecedented "migration reversal" during the 1970s, with more people moving to rural than urban areas, but a rapid increase in backyard food production. By 1983, 53 percent of all U.S. households were growing some of their own food, amounting to a retail value of about 19 billion dollars — roughly equal to the value of the corn crop in 1983. This is a sizable part of the total food production. Many growers rationalize their efforts as an attempt to save money, but surely they are prompted also by the quest for a simpler life, in harmony with nature and less dependent on technology and the market economy.

It is easy to ignore these mundane activities, but they are practical responses to the same set of problems which Green Politics addresses on a theoretical or ideological level. And, as practical responses, they illustrate a possibility in the transition to a post-industrial society, as local production for household use displaces production for a centralized market economy. It is a possibility which is easily overlooked from the conventional urban-industrial perspective but which needs to be recognized if Green Politics is to develop a coherent vision of an eco-logical, resource-conserving and nonviolent future.

Anvil gathering, mid 1970s.

Learning the Names

I have come to a place
where the White Birch and Aspen grow
right down to the water.
My canoe slips in, a silver fin,

spreading the lips of the Ottertail River.
Heron drum in the reeds.
And where I drift I am close to the nests
of the red-winged blackbirds.

These names become the guide I look for.
They mean a place between, a passage,
and they cry across the water, defining the close
and heavy forest I have come from.

Now there are loons walking on the river.
They dive and come together.
And making love they beat each other
with dark and tensile wings.

—Cary Waterman
(Anvil #6)

Lying in Bed, Listening to Snowmobiles on Cottonwood Lake

I

The whine of the snowmobiles grinds higher and higher.
The snowmobiles are mating!
One snowmobile fights with another
for the right to a snowmobile cow,

while inside their bellies men crouch,
fingering the rutting
mechanical dark,
who once knew their daughters' touch.

II

When the snowmobiles grow quiet
and leave the lake to the lake,

something at the bottom stirs,
a darkness vast and brooding
like a great face,
a face that would slowly rise
and open itself to the surface,
an enormous, wet flower,
a mother.

—Philip Dacey
(Anvil #9)

This Wet Spring

This wet spring
I bent above a sacred space
under leaves outdoors,
where mice give birth
to pink blind young,
where owls hide to whoo;
and all the air of their world
grew hazy green
into my human face.
This mist twisted into my brain
through ear and eye;
it made me sigh to think
when I might have time in life
to do a thing that matters.

Someone should watch the moon every night each month,
noting color and cloud,
drawing moon-spirit into arteries and veins.
Someone should follow
the violets across the earth,
trek from grove to grove
as they bud and purple and die.
No one has kept track
of the snail I met when I was eight,
dripping down the lane
on a path of silver saliva.
He might be in the next state by now,
or trundling the river caves.
For heaven's sake, and for my own,
I should have kept an eye upon
that stream below the hill;
it has taken such great strides without our knowing;

it's uprooted the slim willow;
for some reason the watercress stopped growing.
You know the rabbit skull
that lay in the gully by the road?
It's mold and black by now;
someone should have sat there to see
what happens to things beautiful and bone.
Worst of all, I think of the horse I sold
to a soul-less man;
the hairs of her winter coat tangled as we rode.
What new jumps does she know?

Let me assign you to the iris by the barn.
I will take the rusty hollow of the pool
now deserted by the stream.
We will watch and smell
and use the days well,
as a part of the sacred green haze.

—Freya Manfred
(Anvil #11)

Sitting Beside Bear Creek

(Alabama, June '73)

My daughter has thrown a stone for the first time in her two years and laughs at the confusion she makes in the water running so fast and clear. She doesn't understand the future and the plans of engineers. But this is home and I am pleased with the ancient beauty of our bare feet. In the sand I see in one circle a black ant, a red spider, and a tiny fly fanning its green wings. I look at my wife, as if to ask: What is the meaning of this? She picks up a pebble and throws it. I watch it sink to a dark bottomless sea, counting the bubbles that rise to the light, one by one, and disappear.

—John Mitchell
(Anvil #12)

from It Might Be Spring

It might be spring in Minnesota. March 30th.
The air stirs cool like a wind inside a music box;
a hint of melody moves the boxelder branches.
The snow melts from the hills,
a glacial melt, like every year.

Not a single tree has fleshed into green
by the "fifth largest river in the world,"
not a single blackbird with red bars on its wings
has shrieked through the river willows,
though last night the college students sang drunkenly
returning from the bars like drunk college students.

I am lucky. Born in El Salvador,
I would have been killed fighting the Capitalists.
Born in Poland, the Communists would have killed me.
Here, I battle only the wolves of my own heart,
and during election years, the Republicans.

The cumulus pass overhead like waved handkerchiefs.
And the trees listen intently — maybe conspiracy.
Wind, you can tell me, what are you up to now?
What are your plans for the invisible subversion?
What are the plans for this earth? Revolution!
It might be spring in Minnesota.

—Paul Wadden
(Anvil #49)

Photos by Wade Britzius

"Hammering it Out"—The Closing Years

In 1983 Jack Miller once more took up editorship of the magazine after an absence of three years. He also resumed "Hammering It Out," and his soul-searching continued. During the last six years (1983-1989) his essays reflected the gradual loss of hope for voluntary change in American society and his own shift toward a more religious base.

Spring, 1983—

The most perceptive thinkers among us have known for some time that we are at the end of one era and the beginning of another. The era that is ending is what we can loosely call the industrial way of life. The era that is beginning has as yet no name, and its shape is uncertain. What we do know is that the party is over; the brief, mad pursuit of material wealth and power during the last forty years or so is coming to an end. It simply cannot be sustained. Whether we are headed toward a full-scale collapse or a period of painful readjustment, no one knows. . . . As the crisis develops and deepens, however, we are reinforced continuously in the hope that — if we don't lose heart — we can continue down the same megatechnic path to a land full of all the goodies we have come to expect — and more.

One of the false promises held before us is that high technology — whose symbol and central artifact is the computer — will carry us onward, past the devastation and unemployment of a collapsing way of life to a new and even more wondrous world of efficiency, productivity, profit and leisure. . . . We are dealing with dangerous fantasy. . . . Our love affair with the machine has not been a flight into the higher regions of life but a descent into the lower.

Some among us have long since realized that if we are to reclaim the world for sanity, indeed, if we are to survive, we are going to have to stop worshipping the Goddess of Technology. We should have learned the disastrous consequences of this cult-worship back in 1945 when the first atomic bomb was exploded. We should have learned that we cannot go on in reckless pursuit of power and prosperity through technology — unless we are prepared to sacrifice our very lives, our very earth, our very children, and our very future. Unless we stop, take stock, and look at where we are going, we will continue our blind rush to the brink, and beyond.

❖ ❖ ❖

Fall, 1983—

Scott Nearing died recently at the age of one hundred, and in reflecting anew on his life and on that of his wife, Helen, I am struck by the depth of the insight they have given us.

Scott was first of all a socialist. Before he and Helen headed for a homestead in Vermont in the mid-1930s, Scott had been a member of the Communist Party, until he was expelled. . . . It is clear from the life that he and Helen lived and from the books he and they wrote, that he understood profoundly what *real* socialism is about. Real socialism is about *Living the Good Life*, which is the title of the Nearings' most famous book.

Though the good life can be lived in cities as well as in the country, the Nearings found the small, rural homestead suited to their needs. On it they were able to support themselves by systematically working half-time at "bread labor" and half-time at other pursuits. They did this with a minimum of machinery and a maximum of intelligence and regular manual labor.

I am well aware, from my own failures, how difficult it is to do this. . . . For the good life is not the attempt to get all we can for ourselves. It is living so that others can live. It is a life of renunciation that can only emerge from a powerful affirmation. The good life is a hard life, a life of hard work and hard choices. There are no guarantees of "success." It is also the only truly satisfying, the only satisfactory, way to live.

❖ ❖ ❖

Spring, 1986—

Ten years ago I was a nearly middle-aged, mechanically incompetent ex-reporter trying to teach myself how to run a printing press. It was a slow and painful business. I usually worked from morning until well into the night in a crudely converted part of my grandfather's old in-town barn. One of my pleasures in those days was to walk over-town to visit my friend George, a hard-core old country character who had agreed to live in town for a few years to help his wife run the local cafe. By ten o'clock or so George was usually ready to leave off his day's work, and he'd grin at me behind his bushy white beard.

"Hello, Jack! How's it coming?"

"If the impossible can be done, I guess I'm doing it."

He'd pull me up a chair in the midst of potato sacks and big cans of peaches at the back of the cafe and say, "Jack, let's sit down here and talk a few things out."

And sometimes, in moments of ensuing grace, we would move beyond ordinary good conversation between friends and find ourselves in that magical realm of real understanding. It was as if we had entered a luminous meadow, a place that was neither my turf nor his, but a new space between us. Here we left behind our normal self-consciousness and the conversation moved forward not as first-one-and-then-the-other but as each together. And when it was right, we had the ecstatic sense that we could answer any question, solve any problem.

I believe that this kind of coming together, which many of us have experienced at some moments in our lives, is what the great Jewish philosopher Martin Buber means by the I-Thou relationship. He means the discovery of another person not as an "It" but as "Thou."

I tell of this experience with my friend George because I think it shows, by contrast, something about the human condition at this point in history. . . . We are unable to communicate with each other in genuine depth. We tend to treat each other not as we really are — unique and unrepeatable expressions of the Creator — but as things, as objects, to be used for our own purposes. We do this because we lack a strong sense of self, which is a prerequisite for true relationship. In our isolation and need, we feel the necessity of using every other person and situation to prop up what fragile selfhood we have. Hence, "the games people play," the one-upmanship we know so depressingly well.

Spring, 1987—

Ellery Foster, one of the earliest and most faithful of the *Anvil's* helpers during the past 15 years, is dead at the age of 81. With his passing we have lost a great spirit and an unforgettable personality. From the time Ellery retired from government service in Washington, D.C., in the mid-1960s and returned to his home territory in southeastern Minnesota, he crusaded tirelessly for a peaceful, cooperative society. And he fearlessly attacked capitalism, communism and organized religion alike. He also advocated celibacy and the replacement of money with exchange certificates. He was an idealist, a prophet, a gadfly, a rebel, and a crank. I loved him.

My fondest memory of Ellery is trimming up some of the thousands of *Anvils* we used to have printed in Red Wing in the early years. As we labored together at a big, old, hand-operated cutter, after all the other volunteer workers had left, we talked and laughed together, every now and again regaling each other by playing the part of the imaginary boss: "All right, let's see some production back here. If you guys don't like the pay or the working conditions, you know there are a lot more like you out there who are willing to work."

Some people have a soul you can't feel. Ellery's you could. A bond formed between us that outlasted the many arguments we had over the years. And arguments we had. I continually despaired at his way of walking across whole fields of common ground and taking up an entrenched position at some far corner of contention.

In Millville he is still remembered as a curiosity — a tall, skinny-legged old man with a bushy beard and long hair who strode along main street in shorts and thongs. People used to ask garage-man Francis Appel, who liked Ellery: "Who is that — some kook Miller brought in?". . . Some people ridiculed him. But he managed over the years to touch many lives and to make a significant contribution to many alternative ventures. . . . His physical presence is gone from us now, and it is time to bid that person farewell. The spiritual Ellery lives on, in and among those of us who knew him, and, we hope, united now with what he called the Divine Central Intelligence ("the D-C-I," he often said with a wink).

Summer, 1987—

To a greater or lesser extent, we modern folk are all placeless. . . . We want to be at home, rooted in a place where we belong. We dream of such a place. And we do what we can to create the character of such place in our lives, buying land and building homes, surrounding ourselves with objects of special meaning, such as photographs, family heirlooms and memorabilia. But we remain a people uprooted, alienated from the locality and region in which we live, alienated from a coherent community, alienated from family, and alienated, finally from ourselves.

The reason for our alienation from place is the nature of the modern urban-industrial world. In the modern way of life, place has no particular importance. Modernity has uprooted us and our traditions, cutting our ties to community and to the past. What we have lost is the framework that has given the human race, through most of its history, a sense of who we are, how we are to live, and where we belong.

Most of us have been willing co-conspirators with the forces of modernity. For example, when my friends and I were growing up in small towns in Minnesota, we were expected to leave after high school and go elsewhere to become successful. Most of my boyhood friends did just that, becoming doctors, lawyers, ministers, businessmen. . . but not in our home town. Meanwhile, other professionals and business people left their towns and cities and came to ours. There they have raised children who also have left. And it is precisely uprooted people such as these who, wherever they are, come into positions of leadership and set much of the tone and character of life in our culture.

Being in a place, being truly *of* it, is more than a superficial sentiment. It demands commitment over time. It demands that we take responsibility. In a place, we endure the sufferings and we celebrate the good times. In a place we feel the ache of despair and aloneness as well as the joy and peace of belonging. A place is a space we become part of, and which becomes part of us.

To live authentically in a place, we need to know it — to know its soils and rivers and lakes and rock formations, to know its trees and flowers and grasses, to know its birds and animals, to know its seasons and the nuances of its weather, to know its air currents and its water supplies. We may never match the intimacy of Henry Thoreau's relationship with the environs of Concord, Massachusetts, but we can and should know our turf. We need, too, to know the people of our place, their past as well as their present. Only as we know our land and its people do we experience a place as more than our own piece of ground, our address, our dwelling unit, our subdivision, and begin to cherish and love the particular part of the earth we call home.

❖ ❖ ❖

Spring, 1988—

The governor of Minnesota, Rudy Perpich, believes that the future of our state depends on how successfully we can become world leaders in what is loosely called "high technology." He urges us, and our children, to devote ourselves to the ways and means of the Information Age. This, he says, is the future. Those who pursue this path successfully will prosper; the others will be left behind.

I believe that this analysis is drastically, and perhaps disastrously wrong. Let us take a look at a plant whose operation is often singled out as a model, or prototype, of the kind of high-technology facility toward which the governor would like to steer our state. This model is the IBM plant in Rochester.

Sometimes known as the "Blue Zoo," it is a huge (3.5 million square foot) layout dominated by the big blue building housing "the largest IBM plant in the world under one continuous roof." Here work 6,600 people, a third in direct manufacturing, a third in laboratory development efforts, a third in support.

IBM-Rochester is known for its good pay, exceptional working conditions, job security, opportunities for career advancement, and so on. In other words, a workers' paradise. No wonder such plants bedazzle and beckon not only our political and community leaders but most of the rest of us. We would be led from the face of things to conclude that this "work of the future" has released the workers from the worst aspects of old-style industrial labor: heat, cold, dust, dirt, the dangers of hot and heavy raw materials and machines and — most of all — the deadening drudgery of the assembly line. But what are the dangers of working in a pleasant but utterly artificial environment?

IBM Rochester binds its employees to secrecy about what they do at the plant. What are the dangers of secrecy — of being forbidden the pleasure and the learning capacity that comes from being able to talk about our work with friends and spouses and children and colleagues? And what are the dangers of not knowing the uses to which work ultimately is put? The secrecy of IBM-Rochester is no different essentially from that of the Central Intelligence Agency or of many military operations. In each case it has the ominous effect of conditioning the worker (agent, soldier) to authoritarianism: you are responsible only for what you are told, you have only a vague understanding of the ultimate effects of your work and therefore you have no right (much less duty) to make judgments about your work as part of the over-all undertaking. Can we expect people to spend their working days under such constraints and yet be able, as soon as they "code out" of the authoritarian workplace, to become miraculously fit for responsible decision-making as members of a democratic society?

The detachment of IBM-Rochester is that of an impersonal, international corporation whose effect on its workers and locality is to encourage rootlessness. IBM's place in the world is everywhere, and nowhere. By its nature (not by the malice of its managers) it is an alien institution that functions as well in Rotterdam as Rochester. . . . Here is the heart of a system that determines to a large extent the kind of world we must live in and even who we are and are becoming. If we choose to encourage this kind of high technology, we are opting for *more* — more complexity, more abstraction, more destruction of an already groaning environment, more exploitation of people, more speed, more pressure.

❖ ❖ ❖

Fall, 1988—

When we put out the first issue of the *Anvil* in 1972, our country was involved in an unpopular war in Vietnam. As has often happened during such wars through history, the discontent led people to question all sorts of things about the society. This became, in the late 1960s and early 1970s, a small-scale social revolution in which hippies, socialists, populists, and many other groups were searching for a new politics and a new way of life.

It was a messy period in which people did all sorts of bizarre things; but it was extraordinarily creative. In a short time, individuals and groups managed to accomplish all sorts of things that hardly anyone would think of trying now. They came together in thousands of communes, organized a nationwide network of food co-ops, and started alternative projects of every conceivable kind, from publications to new religious groups, to collective farms and shops—the list goes on.

For new publications like ours it was a fertile time. Readers were hungry for new approaches, and lots of people were eager to write or otherwise tell about their new experiences and visions. Idealism, hope, and excitement fairly crackled in this North Country air, as they did elsewhere.

As the "movement" faded (it has not disappeared, but distilled into a quieter and deeper stream), we at the *Anvil* became more reflective. We began to look at various social movements of the past and present. One of these was anarchism, a revolutionary working-people's movement that emerged parallel to state socialism in the 19th century. . . . Though we remain anarchists of a kind, we have focused our attention in recent years more closely on other concerns, such as the plight of farmers and the land and the problems of pollution. We have also advocated the rebuilding of community, including the formation of intentional communities. We have continued to promote home-schooling, home birth, and the rebuilding of society from the ground up. We have been supportive of anti-nuclear and other peace efforts, including the use of civil disobedience.

Yet we have come personally to some new ways of seeing the world, especially through the renewal of our Christian faith. Pauline and I have recently become members of a local Lutheran Church, and Bob Stuber, our partner for the last two years, has strengthened our connections with the Catholic Worker movement. This new stage of our pilgrimage has put us "out of synch" in certain ways with the path the *Anvil* has followed over the years.

Let me give one example of the conflict this has produced in our thinking. A central element in the "movement" faith has been the desire for *liberation*. We want to liberate ourselves and our children from all those oppressive structures (especially, for many of us, the church and what it seems to have become). This desire has motivated our search for sexual liberation, for workers' rights, for a new kind of spirituality and a new socialism. It has been a significant element in the major movements of our time for civil rights and for new opportunities for women.

By no means has this "liberation movement" entirely lacked restraint, respect for others, or the willingness to take personal and social responsibility. At its best, it has raised the level of idealism and made us less self-centered and gentler toward other people and the earth. And yet it lacks a fundamental ethic, which is self-denial, or self-sacrifice. Its central ethic is, in fact, the very opposite: the freedom to pursue our desires.

This hard reality is pitilessly exposed in Philip Rieff's 1966 book *The Therapeutic Society: Uses of Faith After Freud.* Rieff argues that in this century we have been on an unholy crusade to wipe out the last trace of belief in anything sacred — anything, that is, except the self. He says we have become unable to conceive of any activity (even apparently selfless acts of sacrifice) that is not, actually, self-serving. We think, in other words, that "everybody is out to get whatever they can for themselves, just as I am." As a young local agribusinessman once expressed it to me, "Look, we've all got our own hustle."

Such destructive cynicism has grown up to replace the traditional teachings which, as thoroughly modern folks, we have put behind us. . . . Without a belief in self-sacrifice — even in small, daily things — is it any wonder that we find the ethic of simple living (much less "voluntary poverty") so difficult; or that, for example, we are so ready to take a job rather than stay home with our small children?

This fresh critique of the "struggle for liberation" is but one element of our present re-evaluation. But perhaps it will give you an idea of why we sometimes feel "out of synch" with where we have been.

❖ ❖ ❖

Summer, 1989—

At the close of an *Anvil* Gathering, as we were holding hands in a circle of silence, one of our brothers said quietly, "Let us care for one another."

These words express the essence of what the *Anvil* stands for. They summarize our analysis, our agenda, our program, our strategy. As various ideas and activities seize our attention, we drift from the center. Then something happens that draws us back and reminds us what we are about. This I have experienced lately as we have shared the suffering of friends, especially that of our friend and colleague Jim Mullen and his family.

In the midst of shock and grief and confusion, I have felt forced to look at my life, at what I have stood for and worked for, both individually and with others. I have been shaken, and my feet are not yet entirely steady.

As we grieve from fresh loss, as we work through confusion, we return to the center of our existence. We remember what we are about. We care for one another.

NORTH COUNTRY
ANVIL
No. 57 $3.00

John Kinsman, Activist Farmer

How We and the World Have Changed • Tragic, Sacred Ground

NORTH COUNTRY
ANVIL
No. 58 $3.00

Cover Story: Juanita and Wally Nelson—Resistance and Right Livelihood
Also: Larry Long Honors Woody Guthrie
        A Visit With Ann Kanten
        Building Earthward
        Holland, Minnesota: My Town, Then and Now

About the Editor

RHODA R. GILMAN was born in Seattle, graduated from the University of Washington with a B.A. in labor economics, and received an M.A. from Bryn Mawr College. In 1950-51 she worked for the American Friends Service Committee in Philadelphia as a secretary for the American Indian program, then spent nine months as director, with her husband, of a Quaker work camp in Xochimilco, Mexico. She moved to St. Paul in 1952 and in 1958 began a 34-year career with the Minnesota Historical Society as an editor, writer, and administrator. She retired with the title of senior research fellow in 1992. Among her many books and articles about Midwestern history is *The Story of Minnesota's Past*, which was written as part of a curriculum of the state's history, for students living in a multicultural society. She was a regular contributor to the *North Country Anvil* from 1975 to 1989.

About the Contributors

ROBERT BLY'S most recent books are *Meditations on the Insatiable Soul, The Darkness Around Us is Deep: Selected Poems of William Stafford*, and *The Rag and Bone Shop of the Heart*, edited with James Hillman and Michael Meade (all from HarperCollins). His home is in Minneapolis.

WALT BRESETTE is a Lake Superior Chippewa from the Red Cliff Reservation. He co-authored *Walleye Warriors* which won the 1994 Nonfiction Award of the Wisconsin Writers Council. He's currently working on a national radio series entitled "All My Relations." He lives in Bayfield, Wisconsin.

RICHARD BRODERICK is the author of *Night Sale*, a collection of short stories from New Rivers Press and is currently poetry editor of *Minnesota Monthly Magazine*.

J.V. BRUMMELS has been writing and publishing poems for twenty years. He has been awarded an NEA Fellowship and the Elkhorn Poetry Prize. His most recent collection is *Sunday's Child* (Basfal, 1994). He teaches at Wayne State College and lives with his family in western Wayne County, Nebraska, where they run a jackpot cattle company.

FLORENCE DACEY, a 25-year resident of Cottonwood, Minnesota, has been a teacher and organizer in community arts programs for over a decade. "Mammogram" was included in her collection *The Necklace* (Midwest Villages & Voices).

PHILIP DACEY is the author of six books of poetry including *The Deathbed Playboy* forthcoming from Eastern Washington University Press. He lives in Lynd, Minnesota.

EMILIO DE GRAZIA'S first published story ("The Enemy") appeared in the *North Country Anvil*. He has published three books including *Enemy Country* (1984), *Billy Brazil* (1992), and *Seventeen Grams of Soul*, a 1995 Minnesota Book Award winner. He lives in Winona, Minnesota.

MARJORIE DORNER'S four mystery/suspense novels are: *Nightmare* (1987), *Family Closets* (1990), *Freeze Frame* (1990), and *Blood Kin* (1992). Her short story collection from Milkweed Editions, *Winter Roads, Summer Fields* (1992) won the 1993 Minnesota Book Award for Fiction.

SHIRLEY DUKE (aka Sun-Fire) has lived on the North Shore since 1975. She is an energy auditor and coordinator in a nonprofit agency serving low-income people. She is also on the board of a transitional housing coalition for homeless women and their children and is the program chair for the Northcountry Women's Coffeehouse.

MICHAEL W. ELISEUSON lives (!) in Grand Rapids, Minnesota.

KEVIN FITZPATRICK lives in Minneapolis and works as a civil servant. His book of poems, *Down on the Corner*, was published by Midwest Villages & Voices. A founder of the *Lake Street Review*, he was its editor from 1977 to 1991.

SYD FOSSUM, whose satirical painting "Ladies and Gentleman" illuminated the cover of the *Anvil's* first issue, was born in South Dakota in 1909 and died in California in 1978. He studied at the Minneapolis School of Art and the Universidad Michoacana in Mexico. Like the radical Mexican muralists of the 1930s, he used art as a means "to say something, to comment, to sound off."

PAULA GIESE taught at the University of Minnesota and wrote many articles for the *Anvil* in the 1970s, including several on Dakota Indian affairs in the aftermath of Wounded Knee. She lives in Minneapolis.

PAUL GILK was born in Lincoln County, northern Wisconsin. He was raised on a small dairy farm and has worked as a cowboy, surveyor, and alternative school janitor. He has three children, works as a stone mason and occasional writer, and lives a "more or less" subsistence life in northern Wisconsin.

LOWELL GOMSRUD was a U.S. Army lieutenant in Viet Nam in 1967 when he fell in love with Nguyen Thi Ngoc-Mai, who was killed five months later in the Tet offensive of 1968. Combat prevented him from finding her grave then and also in 1972 when he returned to Viet Nam to work as a civilian volunteer in a Saigon orphanage. In 1973, after a third trip to Viet Nam he wrote "In Viet Nam Mai is the Name of a Flower." In April 1975 he returned to Saigon a fourth time to participate in the airlift of Vietnamese and Vietnamese-American orphans to the U.S. in the midst of the collapse of the South Vietnamese government. In 1991 a collection of his poetry, *Remembering the Women of the Viet Nam War*, was published by Tessera Publishing, Inc., Edina, Minnesota.

DON GORDON'S six books of poetry include *The Sea of Tranquility* (Curbstone Press, 1989). Thomas McGrath described Don Gordon as "one of our great lost poets. Blacklisted in the fifties, he continued to write all through the bad times while the semi-official academic poets hunted for symbols, too removed or too cowardly to notice war and repression just outside the window." Born in 1902, he lived in Los Angeles until his death in 1990.

PAUL GRUCHOW'S newest collection of essays is *Grass Roots: The Universe of Home* (Milkweed Editions, 1995). He lives in Northfield, Minnesota.

LINDA HASSELSTROM has ranched on the Great Plains for forty years, writing of the landscape and people, with particular concern for how they affect one another.

CURT JOHNSON has published over sixty short stories, six novels, and assorted nonfiction, among which is *Wicked City Chicago: From Kenna to Capone*, (1994). He is the editor of December Press in Highland Park, Illinois.

MAYNARD KAUFMAN retired early from teaching courses in religion and environmental Studies at Western Michigan University in order to work on Green Politics and other community organizations. In 1992 he organized the Michigan Organic Food and Farm

Alliance, a statewide group working to promote local food systems. He lives in Bangor, Michigan.

WENDY JOAN KNOX published many poems in the 1970s and early 1980s including her collections *Message for the Recluse, Roaring Mouth,* and *Warring & Whoring.* Since then she has been teaching, parenting four children, reading religious studies and working at Liberty Books in Montevideo, Minnesota.

REBECCA ("BECKY") LAMOTHE lives with her mother, Neola, and her five-year-old son, Charlie, in the peaceful, green environs of Eugene, Oregon.

SANDRA LINDOW has two published chapbooks: *Rooted in the Earth* (1989) and *Heroic Housewife* (1990). Her third chapbook, *A Celebration of Bones,* will be published in 1995. She is a reading specialist in Eau Claire, Wisconsin.

BOB MALLES worked in the Twin Cities food co-ops from 1970 to 1976. He was fired from the People's Bakery in May, 1975 during the heat of the co-op struggle. He currently works in a European-style bakery.

FREYA MANFRED writes poetry and fiction and has recently completed her first screenplay. In 1985, Overlook/Viking published her book of poetry, *American Roads* and, in 1994, KTCA-TV produced her documentary poem, "The Madwoman and The Mask." She lives in Shorewood, Minnesota, with her husband Tom Pope (a screenwriter) and two sons.

JOHN MARKS, with Katie McMahon, operated a store near Hegg, Wisconsin (Trempealeau County). His article, "Reviving a Country Store," was published in 1976.

THOMAS MCGRATH, a native of North Dakota, graduated from the University there in 1939. As a writer and teacher of English his radical politics and outspoken opposition to capitalism and industrial technology kept him on the move. His longest tenure was at Moorhead State University from 1969 to 1981. He wrote poetry, criticism, and a number of filmscripts. His major work, *Letters to an Imaginary Friend,* was completed in 1985. He died in Minneapolis in 1990.

FLORENCE MEAD lived in Lake of the Woods, Minnesota when her poem "The Drowning" was published in 1975.

MADGE MICHEELS-CYRUS has worked in civil rights, social justice and peace work since the 1960s. In Minneapolis she was employed by the American Friends Service Committee and by Friends for a Nonviolent World. She co-edited a book, *Seeds of Peace,* that contains 1,700 quotations on war and peace. She and her husband Jack live in Birchwood, Wisconsin.

JOHN MITCHELL teaches film and literature in the English Department at Augsburg College in Minneapolis. A fifth generation Alabamian, he has lived in Minnesota since 1968. His poems have been published mainly in the *North Stone Review,* and a short story appears in *25 Minnesota Writers.*

TOM O'CONNELL teaches political science at Metropolitan State University. He is a student of the progressive/populist tradition in Minnesota—both past and present.

JOE PADDOCK is a freelance writer who frequently does statewide residency work for COMPAS of Saint Paul. He is the principal author of the environmental book *Soil and Survival* and his three books of poetry are *Handful of Thunder, Earth Tongues,* and *Boars' Dance.* He lives with his writer wife Nancy in Litchfield, Minnesota.

SANDRA PRICE (the former Sandra Gue) lives on Haida Gwaii/the Queen Charlotte Islands off British Columbia. During the twenty years she lived in LaCrosse, Wisconsin and Saint Paul she wrote feature articles about environmental issues and visual artists. A marine biologist by training, she lives with her husband in a float-house. She is a frequent contributor to *Fiberarts* magazine and is writing a book about Haida button blankets.

EVELYN ROEHL typeset the *Anvil* and contributed articles and hundreds of production hours from 1976 to 1982. She currently operates Kin Hunters, a historical research service, and lives in Seattle, Washington.

PAUL SCHAEFFER works and lives as a family teacher, researcher, and community organizer in Hager City, Wisconsin.

NEALA SCHLEUNING continues her advocacy of women as director of the Women's Center at Mankato State University. She holds a Ph.D. in American Studies and has published three books: *America—Song We Sang Without Knowing: The Life and Ideas of Meridel Le Sueur, Idle Hands and Empty Hearts: Work and Freedom in the United States,* and *Women, Community, and the Hormel Strike of 1985-86.* She has in progress a book on the meaning of ownership and property in the United States and another volume on women and family economics in Russia in the transition to a market economy.

RANDALL W. SCHOLES was Art Director of Milkweed Editions for many years. As a partner of Swineherd Studios, his graphic work appeared in numerous journals and book publications. He lives in Minneapolis, Minnesota.

STEVEN SCHWEN grew up in Blue Earth, Minnesota and began college at Northwestern University in 1968. He became somewhat "radicalized" by events related to the Democratic Convention, the Conspiracy-8 Trials, and the anti-war movement. He left Mayo Medical School after two years in 1974 and went into "world saving." He currently farms organically, using draft horses, wind and solar power, and burns wood for heat. He lives in Lake City, Minnesota.

JAMES SHIELDS was forced to leave his job as a teacher and school administrator in North Carolina after publishing a radical novel. In 1936 his love of the outdoors brought him to Minnesota, where he worked with the State Department of Education and later served on the National Labor Relations Board. He was the author of *Mr. Progressive,* a biography of Minnesota Governor Elmer A. Benson. He died in 1979.

MORDECAI SPECKTOR writes about political and environmental issues. He is a regular contributor to *The Circle,* the Minneapolis American Indian newspaper. He is currently employed by the Minnesota House of Representatives as a writer for the Public Information Office. He is married to Maj-Britt Syse and has three children.

ERIC H. STEINMETZ returned to Mankato, Minnesota after living in Millville and currently drives a taxi and continues to be meddlesome.

JOAN STRADINGER is a school psychologist in southeastern Wisconsin. She and her husband live in Whitewater, Wisconsin. She continues to draw and spends way too much time in the garden.

MYRA L. SULLIVAN is a Master Tutor in association with the Dyslexia Institute of Minnesota and works with students in the public and private schools and at Carleton College in Northfield, Minnesota. She was a columnist for the *Wanamingo Progessive* and wrote articles about farm life and small towns. Her book of fiction, *Emma's Journal,* was published in 1994.

BARTON SUTTER was a member of the *Anvil* staff in 1975 and a contributing editor thereafter. He is the author of *My Father's War and Other Stories* and *The Book of Names: New and Selected Poems*, both of which won Minnesota Book Awards. He is married with two step-daughters and lives in Duluth.

JANIS THESING lives with her husband Chuck and son Luke on Pineyhill Farm near Lewiston, Minnesota. They grow organic produce and sell it directly through farmer's markets and their community-supported agricultural program.

KENNETH TILSEN is an attorney who practiced law from 1950 to 1993 when he left the practice to teach public interest litigation at the Hamline School of Law. He is best known for serving as legal coordinator of the Wounded Knee Defense Committee, and for representing Black students at the University of Minnesota "Morrill Hall takeover," the "Minnesota 8," Honeywell peace activists, power line opponents, Hormel workers, farm foreclosure protestors and other political activists.

ALICE TRIPP wrote her article when the farmers were involved in a struggle to keep huge power lines off their farms. The struggle was her "awakening" and she became involved in politics, ran for governor, and spoke at the 1966 National Democratic Convention. Now she leads a quiet life in Glenwood, Minnesota.

MARK VINZ is the author of several collections of poems, most recently *Late Night Calls* (New Rivers Press) and *Minnesota Gothic*—a collaboration with Wayne Gudmundson photographs (Milkweed Editions). He is also the co-editor, with Thom Tammaro, of a collection of Upper Midwest essays, *Imagining Home*, published in 1995 by the University of Minnesota Press. He lives in Moorhead, Minnesota and teaches at Moorhead State University.

GERALD VIZENOR is professor of Native American Indian literatures at the University of California, Berkeley. He is the author of *The People Named the Chippewa*, narrative histories; *Interior Landscapes*, an autobiography, and five novels. *Griever: An American Monkey King in China*, his second novel, won the American Book Award.

PAUL WADDEN is a Minnesota-born poet and essayist who for the last ten years has lived in Japan. He is the author of *Labor for the Wind*, a book of poems. His articles have appeared in the *New York Times*, the *Washington Post*, and many other newspapers and magazines.

JAY WALLJASPER is editor-at-large of *Utne Reader*. For more than ten years he was editor of *Utne Reader*, and before that, editor at *In These Times*. He lives in Minneapolis and consults for a number of publications.

CARY WATERMAN'S most recent book, *When I Looked Back You Were Gone*, was published by Holy Cow! Press in 1992. She lives in Saint Paul and works at Normandale Community College. She is currently writing a memoir.

BRUCE M. WHITE is a historical anthropologist and lives in Saint Paul, Minnesota. His guide to manuscript sources, *The Fur Trade in Minnesota*, was published by the Minnesota Historical Society.

J. YARROW lives and works in Seattle, Washington as a writer and editor. She has published work in *Poetry Seattle, New Mexico Humanities Journal, Edge*, and *Duckabush Journal* among others.